Germany, 1871 _. __

A Concise History

Raffael Scheck

BERG

Oxford • New York

First published in 2008 by
Berg
Editorial offices:
1st Floor, Angel Court, 81 St Clements Street, Oxford, OX4 1AW, UK
175 Fifth Avenue, New York, NY 10010, USA

Berg is the imprint of Oxford International Publishers Ltd.

Library of Congress Cataloguing-in-Publication Data

Scheck, Raffael, 1960–
    Germany, 1871–1945 : a concise history / Raffael Scheck.—1st ed.
    p. cm.
    Includes bibliographical references and index.
    ISBN-13: 978-1-84520-815-8 (cloth)
    ISBN-10: 1-84520-815-3 (cloth)
    ISBN-13: 978-1-84520-817-2 (pbk.)
    ISBN-10: 1-84520-817-X (pbk.)
    1. Germany—History—1871–1918. 2. Germany—History—1918–
1933. 3. Germany—History—1933–1945. I. Title.

    DD220.S25 2008
    943.08—dc22

                                                        2008025859

British Library Cataloguing-in-Publication Data

A catalogue record for this book is available from the British Library.

ISBN 978 1 84520 815 8 (Cloth)
ISBN 978 1 84520 817 2 (Paper)

Typeset by JS Typesetting Ltd, Porthcawl, Mid Glamorgan
Printed in the United Kingdom by Biddles Ltd, King's Lynn

www.bergpublishers.com

To Lori with love

Contents

Illustrations

Maps

Preface

This book aims to offer undergraduate students and other interested learners an introduction to the history of the first modern united Germany, which lasted from 1871 to 1945 and left a mixed and still controversial legacy of industrial and technological achievement and utter devastation. The book evolved out of the lecture notes that I developed for my course on Germany from 1871 to 1945 at the start of my teaching career at Bowdoin College in 1993. As a nervous young professor, I prepared a refined manuscript for every single lecture. Toward the end of the semester, however, I forgot my lecture notes on my breakfast table – between the coffee cup and the honey pot. I noticed this too late to run home and fetch the notes, and therefore I spoke freely in class, following a rough outline on the board. After class, a student tapped me on the shoulders and said: "Hey professor, that was the best class you ever gave. Maybe you should forget your lecture notes more often." I did indeed leave my lecture notes out of the classroom from then on, but I had all those detailed notes for most of the semester. When I taught the course again in my present position at Colby College a year later I printed out my completed set of lecture notes and distributed them to the students. In 1996, when I taught the class for the third time, I put the entire text onto my personal home page on the Colby website. I soon found out that this freely accessible website was widely used outside of Colby. I have received hundreds of emails from all over the world commenting on this website. A South Korean student studying for a dreaded exam asked me some desperate questions about the text. An American filmmaker interested in the Weimar Republic thanked me for providing important context for her project on a Weimar artist. A Romanian student writing a paper on the causation of World War I debated with me about war guilt. A Scottish media team distributed the contents of my website to teachers as an example of how to use the web for teaching purposes, and professors in many countries have assigned parts on my online German history textbook to their classes. The website also attracted some more disturbing comments, as when some North American Holocaust deniers tried to convince me that I was on insecure ground when talking about this subject. But overall, the website drew countless expressions of appreciation, particularly in the days before Wikipedia.

To be converted into a textbook, the online text needed massive expansion and revision. I hope that the readability and clarity have not suffered. As an experienced teacher, I am aware of the frustration students undergo with most textbooks. Student evaluations often comment on the textbook being dry and boring, but whenever I try to do without one students criticize the *lack* of a textbook. I have tried to focus on the big and intriguing questions and I have tried to keep the text alive by largely following my own interests. This means, of course, that the text is not a complete history. But there is nothing wrong with that. A complete history would be nothing but a vastly oversized encyclopedia article. Given that this book deals with the history of a state, its primary focus is on political history. But every meaningful political history is inseparable from other aspects such as developments in society, the economy, culture, and the international stage. I have tried to consider all of these aspects in my narrative. A professor using this book as a textbook will fill in more information where he or she deems it advisable, as I do myself, and other book assignments will open different perspectives and provide new insights. This book is meant to offer a system of connecting points that provide context for further learning experiences and allow them to "stick" to something.

Many scholars have greatly influenced my perception of German history, and I am naming just a few of them. My graduate school teachers at Brandeis, particularly Rudolph Binion and Stephen Schuker, were generous and influential, as have been colleagues such as Shelley Baranowski, Doris Bergen, Richard Bessel, Christopher Browning, Roger Chickering, Thomas Childers, Geoff Eley, Gerald Feldman, Peter Fritzsche, Peter Hayes, Kirsten Heinsohn, Rainer Hering, Eberhard Jäckel, Larry E. Jones, Katharine Lerman, Hans Mommsen, James Retallack, Dennis Showalter, Jonathan Steinberg, Jill Stephenson, Hans-Ulrich Wehler, and Gerhard Weinberg. My colleagues at Colby College have provided a supportive environment for teaching and scholarship, and my students have enriched my perspective. Sommer Engels and Michael Hempel worked as my research assistants and did much appreciated work. Michael Hempel drew the maps for this book. I am grateful for my children's interest in German history; my son Anselm (13) asks probing questions about it, my daughter Adelia (11) shares my sadness about many events, and my daughter Sophia Isabella (2) loves to empty the lowest German history bookshelves – and occasionally puts some of the books back. This book is dedicated to my wife, Lori Scheck, in appreciation for all she means to me.

–1–

Introduction: A Plea for Understanding History in its Openness

"There are, it appears, some creations of the human hand, the establishment of states among them, upon which a curse weighs from the very beginning. The gods turn away and relinquish their place to the lesser demons. The Reich of 1871, the German national state, belonged to these creations ... [It] was too big and too mighty in achievement to fit reliably into the European balance of power and too limited to be a real world power. That was one part of the curse. And the attempt to base self-confidence of a nation on domination and hierarchy instead of freedom and equality, an experiment that contradicted European civilization, that was the second part."

> Christian Graf von Krockow, quoted according to Gordon Craig,
> *The Germans*. New York: Meridian, 1983, p. 343.

This book is a history of a nation state founded in war and destroyed in war. The first modern and unified German state played a critical role in the start of one world war and definitely caused a second world war, during which it organized the worst mass murder of known history. In the light of these depressing facts some perceptive observers have argued that this state should not have been created in the first place. Unlike Italy, which was united only a few years before, the new Germany carried too much economic and military weight to leave the European balance of power unchanged. The problems of integrating this new giant into a stable European security system helped put Europe onto the road to the First World War. Not unrelated, the authoritarian domestic structure of the new Germany may have bolstered an aggressive foreign policy and left a legacy of repression and unquestioned state authority that later helped the Nazis take and wield power. The ignominious end of the first united Germany in the midst of war, destruction, and unprecedented crimes in 1945 appeared as the logical end of a state that was founded through violence and against democracy.

There is much wrong with this view, however. Short of denying the destructive and undemocratic aspects of the first German nation state, I want to argue for a much more open view of German history in this period. History is not predetermined. The state created in 1871 should not be interpreted only in the light of its end in 1945. Although there are disturbing lines of continuity from 1871 to 1945, which many sophisticated historians have outlined, Germany also had other traditions than the aggressive and repressive aspects that seem to dominate its history from Bismarck to Hitler. At several junctions in the history of the first German nation state these traditions came to the forefront. Under different circumstances they might have prevailed. Arguments about an aggressive and submissive German national character are, like all national stereotypes, misleading generalizations – and often wrong. That Germany was too powerful to be easily absorbed into the European state system was hardly its own fault, and German statesmen, their documented aggressive outbursts notwithstanding, often felt just as threatened themselves as they appeared threatening to the outside world. The causation of the First World War was a European drama, not simply a German one, although there is no doubt that German leaders played a crucial role in it. Moreover, those who argue that Germany's authoritarianism was a deviation from "European civilization" need to consider that democracy and freedom were by no means the European norm in 1871. By the standards of the European great powers in 1871, Germany was not at the forefront of democracy and freedom, but it was not a backward authoritarian state either. It had universal manhood suffrage at the national level, although not in the single states, and it had a constitution and a fairly well developed legal system. France had introduced universal suffrage for men in 1848, but it became a democracy only in 1870, largely in reaction to defeat in its war against the German states, and it took French democracy a long time to consolidate. Britain, although adorned with a powerful parliament since the seventeenth century, introduced nearly universal suffrage for men only in 1884. The ability of the aristocratic House of Lords to put brakes on the democratically elected Lower House remained significant until 1911, however. The two other European great powers were much farther removed from democracy than Germany: Austria-Hungary introduced universal suffrage for the Austrian half of the empire only in 1907, but the democratically elected parliament remained powerless and was quickly paralyzed by tensions among the many national groups of this multinational state. The Hungarian half of the Empire remained authoritarian and repressive until the dissolution of the Empire in 1918. Russia was administered in similar ways as many German states before the revolutions of 1848. It had no national parliament until 1905, its peasantry had only recently been released from serfdom (1861), which was a system of forced labor comparable to slavery, and most Russian peasants in 1917 still carried much of the debt that their ancestors had been forced to take on with emancipation in 1861. The Russian legal system was slow to constitute itself, and the Tsarist police was a repressive, although not usually efficient, force largely outside the law. In terms of human rights and democratic participation, Germans in 1871 had a long way to go, but they were much better off than Eastern Europeans. Within Germany, more liberal state traditions in the South and West co-existed with more authoritarian political and social structures in the East, which was dominated by large land holdings mostly in the hands of aristocrats. Moreover, although industrialization and expanding educational opportunities favored a growing involvement of the masses in the political process, it was by no means assured that parliamentary democracy would be the universally accepted and most useful model for that involvement. Democracy seemed to work well in the smaller states of Europe, particularly in Scandinavia, the Netherlands, and Switzerland, but the trials and tribulations of French democracy after 1870 did little to recommend it to larger states. Britain and the United States, with their insular position and hence a much less urgent need to keep up a large army, may not have offered an easily adaptable model for continental Europe. Finally, those historians who stress the autocratic and authoritarian continuities in German history have to recognize that Germany by 1919 had transformed itself into one of the freest and most democratic states of the world, with a constitution modeled after elements in the American, French, and British political systems. Germany granted universal women's suffrage before Britain and long before France. Granted, the German democracy of 1919 followed in the wake of defeat (but so did French democracy), and it was weak (but so was French democracy – at least for several decades), but it would be wrong to deny its genuine German roots and to call it a foreign transplant, which would echo precisely the arguments of German democracy's right-wing opponents, including the Nazis.

Was there an alternative to uniting Germany in 1871? Probably not. The small states, based on fiefdoms of a disintegrated huge medieval and early modern kingdom, had modernized themselves in different and sometimes impressive ways, but they were increasingly seen as an anachronism in a world of heavy industry, railroads, and increasingly global trade patterns. Germans had, and to some extent still have, strong regional identities, but there definitely was a sense of German speakers belonging together in one state by 1871, even if Bismarck's Germany of 1871 left out millions of ethnic Germans – mostly in Austria-Hungary. Not least, the unification of Germany was an idea with democratic overtones. Whereas the existing kingdoms had emerged from dynastic holdings of powerful aristocrats, a unified German nation carried the promise to be a state for all Germans, not only the aristocrats. Sadly, the democratic and liberal aspirations of German nationalism were shaken by the brutal monarchic and aristocratic reaction that followed the initially successful revolutions of 1848, but they remained a powerful force in the continuing push for national unification – a force that greatly worried conservatives, aristocrats, and monarchs alike even after Germany was united. Why did no democratic, united, and peaceful Germany emerge? Historians have tried to explain this by focusing either on geography, previous history, or socio-political structures.

The geographic argument stipulates that the German states occupied a middle position in European power politics at least since the seventeenth century. This made the Holy Roman Empire of the German Nation the battleground of the Thirty Years War (1618–48) and led to the exploitation and domination of many smaller German states by more powerful neighbors, above all by France. The Austrian Empire, a collection of vast German and non-German lands, also exploited the weakness of the German states after its own attempt to unite them had failed because of

Danish, Swedish, and French interventions during the Thirty Years War (1618–48). Partly in reaction to the disorders of the Thirty Years War, a military monarchy developed in Prussia that tried to make society subservient to a strong military (an exemplary case of militarism). Giving up its initially defensive mindset, Prussia expanded in the eighteenth century and won the contest for domination over the German states against Austria in the war of 1866, thereafter excluding Austria from a Germany under Prussian predominance. But united Germany in 1871 inherited the exposed position in the center of a system of great powers, with large border strips unprotected by natural barriers. In the light of this strategic position, the geographic argument goes, a democratic system could not easily take root in Germany, which tended to preserve Prussia's militaristic tradition after 1871. Geography, however, always leaves several political options to a state. Perhaps the position in the center of European powers was a drawback and security risk, but it also offered opportunities for expansion. Germany, moreover, was not alone in the middle of Europe. Poland, the largest European state at the end of the middle ages, disintegrated in the course of the eighteenth century, partly to the benefit of Prussia and Austria. To some extent, Austria could also be seen as a middle power, fighting advances by the Ottoman Empire in the Balkans over several centuries while also being a major rival of France in Italy and southern Germany. Italy itself also has a long history of being a contested ground between rival forces in North and South, East and West. None of these countries could claim a particularly strong democratic tradition by 1870, but not all of them developed the strong militarism of the German Empire after 1871. Although I do believe that occupying a central position in the European great powers system after 1871 was a problem for Germany, geography alone cannot explain the path to the ultimate catastrophe of 1945.

Other historians have argued that national unification came too late to allow Germans to develop a secure national consciousness (I propose to call this the "delayed unification" argument). Whereas the French monarchy had started subduing local lords already in the middle ages and built up a unified nation state in the Early Modern period (roughly 1500–1800), the once magnificent and powerful Holy Roman Empire of the German Nation had disintegrated in the Middle Ages and lost all but folkloristic meaning after 1648, leaving its countless local rulers with nearly full autonomy. England, despite the failure of monarchic centralism, had also constituted itself as a nation state long before German unification. Germany, when it was finally unified, seemed to fit poorly into a Europe that had for centuries counted on a fragmented center. The delayed unification argument, like the geographic argument, contains some truths, but it is difficult to establish a causal link between Germany's late unification and the course of German history 1871–1945. Let us compare Germany with other states that were united comparatively late, such as Italy (united in 1859–61) and Yugoslavia (united only in 1918). Both states did not develop a stable democracy; Italy's liberal constitutional monarchy, never stable and never truly democratic, was transformed into a fascist dictatorship by Mussolini after 1922. Yugoslav democracy, handicapped by centrifugal separate[?] from the beginning, mutated into a royal dictatorship in 1929 and, after [?] invasion and horrific ethnic strife, into a communist dictatorship in 1945, only to fall apart in the midst of more bloodshed after the dismantling of communism. On the other hand, Germans may not have been much later in developing a strong national consciousness than the British and the French. Some evidence suggests, for example, that only railroad building, compulsory schooling, and the draft helped to establish a secure French national consciousness, and this largely happened *after* 1870![1]

A more sophisticated argument for explaining Germany's disastrous history of 1871–45 was developed by German social historians, foremost by Hans-Ulrich Wehler, in the early 1970s (I call this the social-political argument). Wehler, who takes great pains to place German history in the context of Western Europe and the United States, sees the initial drama of German history in a missing bourgeois and democratic revolution and hence in the continuing power of a pre-industrial aristocratic elite in Prussia and later unified Germany. In France, the bourgeoisie (the middle classes - businessmen, shopkeepers, small producers, employees, wealthier farmers) managed to abolish the economic and political privileges of the landed aristocracy already during the Revolution of 1789. The French middle classes continued to challenge the monarchy so successfully that it was abolished for good in 1870. At the same time, a democratic movement of lower middle-class and working people challenged the power of the upper bourgeoisie (rich industrialists, bankers, and landowners), winning a victory of sorts with the establishment of the democratic Third Republic in 1870. The same process happened less dramatically in Britain, where Parliament had curtailed the monarchy's powers since the revolutionary seventeenth century. Through gradual reform, the suffrage was extended to all men, and the privileges of the House of Lords were gradually cut back between 1832 and 1911. The United States, of course, started out with a democratic revolution. Elimination of the power of the nobility was closely linked to winning independence. In Germany, however, the bourgeois, liberal revolution of 1848, which had tried to unite Germany under a liberal-democratic framework, had failed. This, Wehler argues, happened because the German liberals did not carry out "their" revolution to full success. After initial breakthroughs they were afraid that the restive lower classes would turn against them and get out of control, transforming the political revolution into a social one that might forfeit the economic and political advantage the liberals hoped to gain. (That the poor masses had gotten out of control during the French revolutions of 1789–94 and 1848 served the German liberals as a warning.) The German princes soon recognized the divisions among the revolutionaries and the liberals' reluctance to arm the lower classes. Facing only words and declarations but no armed revolutionary masses, the Prussian landed aristocracy and – with its military help – many other German princes were able to crush the revolution and defend their privileges against the liberal bourgeoisie. Meanwhile, the Austrian dynasty

...ing advantage of the rivalry of the national groups
... noble landlords, the Junkers, preserved their influence
...ary after 1848, while rapid industrialization increased the
the tamed bourgeoisie. Later, it was the conservative Junker
Prussian military who achieved German unification, not the liberal
geoisie. After 1871 the financial and industrial bourgeoisie received
...s from the landed aristocracy, which made possible the famous "alliance of
...d rye" (heavy industry and large landowners), but the Junkers, a preindustrial
elite, continued to exert a predominant influence even in the industrialized society
of the late nineteenth and early twentieth centuries. The alliance of iron and rye,
Wehler argues, dominated German politics from 1871 to the Third Reich. Only
during the years of the democratic Weimar Republic (1918/19–33) did it suffer
some loss of influence. This experience, however, made it all the more determined
to destroy democracy and organized labor by relying on the help of Adolf Hitler's
propagandistic skills.[2]

The critique of Wehler's approach was articulated by a group of British historians,
among them Geoff Eley and David Blackbourn. Eley and Blackbourn claim that the
liberal bourgeoisie in Germany did not need a successful revolution. The foundation
of a united German state was itself a liberal idea and benefited liberal bourgeois
interest: it enhanced freedom of enterprise and removed many barriers to trade
within Germany. Eley and Blackbourn argue that Wehler, by blaming the German
liberals for having betrayed their principles, applies twentieth-century standards of
liberalism to people who were concerned primarily with other things than democracy
and civil rights. National unification, the British historians admit, did not fulfill all
liberal dreams of the period, but it created a welcome basis for further improvement.
Other historians have expanded this argument by showing that the German Empire
after 1871 was much less authoritarian than it seemed and that a strong popular
groundswell and an increasingly outspoken parliament had made Germany's political
system almost democratic by 1914.[3]

In my own opinion, Eley and Blackbourn correctly criticize Wehler for setting
German history too much into a purely Western context. Although the German
social structure west of the Elbe River resembled the French, the eastern regions of
Germany, mainly Prussia east of the Elbe River, remained predominantly agricultural
and dominated by aristocratic landlords; the eastern regions resembled Poland and
Russia more than France or Britain (with some important exceptions such as the
Berlin area and parts of Silesia). Wehler is not wrong in pointing out the astonishing
tenacity with which the Prussian Junkers held fast to their privileges up to the 1930s.
But historian Arno Mayer has shown that the old aristocratic elites in all European
countries managed to keep significant social and political influence at least until
1914. This was true even in France and Britain where the old aristocracy had lost its
most powerful institutions and legal privileges.[4] Setting Germany into the European
context in my opinion requires a broader framework of reference than the liberal

and democratic "Atlantic" tradition. It is understandable (and laudable) that Wehler and many German historians after 1945 wanted Germany to be firmly rooted in the Western world and its democratic traditions, but the history of Britain, the United States, and France (often in idealized form) cannot serve as the pattern against which we measure every other country's history. Russia, Italy, and the Balkans belonged just as much to the European context in which the German nation state evolved, and democratic-liberal traditions were even weaker in those parts of Europe than in Germany. Russia, in particular, had been linked to Germany through dynastic and cultural ties since the eighteenth century. Set between England and Russia, the Germany of 1871 truly appears as a middle state that cannot be compared to either of them alone. By English standards, Germany industrialized late, but Russia industrialized even later. Compared to England, Germany's industrialization was fast, but Russia's was even faster. Industrialization created severe tensions in English society; so it did in Germany, and so it did, perhaps worst of all, in Russia after 1900. Finally, seeing Germany only through its seemingly dominant militaristic culture does not do justice to the many diverse traditions within its culture. The attitude of the rulers is only partly representative for the attitudes of the people, and much of the repressive tone of Germany's elites came from the fact that they at times faced strong opposition from within.

We need to consider the question of Germany's relationship to the rest of Europe and the issue of German peculiarities and continuities with a fresh eye. There was nothing inevitable about the path from the authoritarian unification in 1871 to the orgy of violence in 1914–18 and the ultimate catastrophe of 1939–1945. It is true that Bismarck united Germany through war, but after 1871 he pursued a policy of peace and stability based on strength. The German political framework created in 1871 was a compromise between authoritarian and (weak) democratic elements, but it was reformable, and political culture became more democratic after Bismarck's resignation in 1890. True, the German elites fiercely resisted democratization, but Germany also had the largest socialist movement in the world, one that was strongly committed to democracy and freedom; in the long run, it seemed impossible to exclude the supporters of this party from the political process. Industry depended on them, and so did the army. As historian Friedrich Meinecke wrote just after the First World War:

> He [Bismarck] had to admit to himself that the modern war all but automatically pressed toward democracy, because one cannot conduct a war over the long run with masses – both those who fight and those who work for the war in the factories – unless one also includes them, over the long run, in politics.[5]

It was not a democracy deficit in Germany or a Prusso-German tradition of militarism and aggressiveness that caused the First World War; poor political choices of governments and military leaders in several countries caused its outbreak. The

German government played a key role in this, but it faced a complex situation and expected a war that would have been very different from the one that actually developed. Although Germany and its allies fought against a superior coalition, it was conceivable that they would win, and this would have drastically altered the postwar period. The Weimar Republic was no doubt a weak democracy, but it might have survived in less harsh economic circumstances. With democracy compromised, it was by no means a foregone conclusion that Germany would become a Nazi dictatorship rather than, like so many other states with recently established democracies in the period, a conservative, authoritarian state based on the military. Such a state would have pressed for a revision of the outcome of the First World War, perhaps even at the risk of war, but it would have pursued a very different course from the one Nazi Germany adopted in the late 1930s and pursued with fanatical devotion to the apocalyptic end. If this book sharpens the reader's sense for the openness of historical developments and the specific responsibility of each successive generation in shaping it, it will have achieved its most noble aim.

–2–

German Unification

Why was Germany united so late? Or, as one might also pose the question: why was unification finally successful in 1871? As is clear from the European context, Germany was not alone in unifying rather late, given that the states on the Italian peninsula formed a united nation state only a few years earlier and that Yugoslavia followed suit only in 1918 by amalgamating a group of territories formerly under Ottoman and Austro-Hungarian control. But the lateness of German unification still poses a problem in comparison to France, Britain, and Russia because there appeared to have been a German kingdom as there was a French, English, and Russian state in the Middle Ages – a kingdom that could perhaps have provided the foundation for a united nation state in the nineteenth century.

The modern German nation state has looked back to the Frankish Empire of Charlemagne (who ruled from 768 to 814) as its first predecessor. But this empire included almost all of today's France, West Germany, Belgium, the Netherlands, northern Italy, northern Spain, and Switzerland. Its core was an area comprising the northeast of France, the south of Belgium, and the west of Germany. In 843 this too-large empire was partitioned among the three grandsons of Charlemagne into a western unit, a central unit, and an eastern unit. The middle empire, from the Netherlands through Lorraine, Burgundy, Savoy, and Northern Italy, was slowly absorbed by the eastern empire, which also expanded eastward and became a bulwark against invasions of Hungarians and Mongolians. The eastern empire called itself the Holy Roman Empire (later adding: "of the German Nation"). It claimed successorship to the glorious Roman Empire and supported the idea of spiritual and secular power in one empire, not least because it at one time included Rome, the seat of the Pope. To be sure, no national conception existed yet in the Middle Ages in the German-speaking lands. The word "deutsch" (German) only slowly came into usage for a group of Germanic languages. Still, in the tenth and eleventh centuries, the Holy Roman Empire was the strongest power in Europe. It was overextended, however, and its claim to unite secular and spiritual leadership of Western Christianity proved too ambitious. Hence, a consolidation of power and effective unification never succeeded in the Holy Roman Empire. Most Holy Roman emperors in the middle ages were wandering rulers with a small bureaucracy and little power. They constantly tried to stay on top of rivaling centers and dynasties and sought to mediate in numerous conflicts between cities and territorial states within their realm. Particularly detrimental was the medieval emperors' struggle with a revived and assertive papacy. The popes fostered effective alliances with all the forces opposed to centralization and stronger control of the emperor, such as the cities in northern Italy and the territorial lords in Germany. As a consequence, a hereditary monarchy never took hold and the selection of the emperor by the electors (for a long time seven, later ten) became dependent upon the size of a contender's armies and on foreign bribes. While France and England built states around a powerful and wealthy center, the Holy Roman Empire did not have such a center and fell increasingly under the control of a dynasty at its periphery, the Austrian Habsburgs. The Habsburgs were powerful enough to dominate, but not to consolidate, the still huge but incoherent Holy Roman Empire.

The Reformation, started in central Germany, added a religious element to these divisions and triggered over a century of internal and external warfare. This destructive rearrangement of German politics and society along confessional lines arrived at a time when the main European trade routes moved west of the Rhine to the Atlantic coast (Spain, Portugal, Flanders, the Netherlands, France, England). The German regions were already in economic decline, worsened by the notorious rivalry of the small princes. When it seemed possible during the Thirty Years War (1618–48) that Catholic Austria might crush the Reformation and conquer the whole of the empire, Denmark, Sweden, and France intervened. The result was a catastrophe that left the empire devastated and weak. Overall, the German regions suffered a population loss of 35 percent. Many provinces were destroyed and largely depopulated. The economic and cultural impacts of the war are hard to overrate. When historian Robert Darnton observes that the German version of fairy tales is almost always more brutal than the French version of the same tale, he seems to give ammunition to the stereotype of a brutish German national character.[1] However, it must be considered that many of these fairy tales took shape around the time of the Thirty Years War. It appears perfectly understandable that the massive brutalization that occurred in the German lands over more than a generation would have left deep scars on folk culture. France suffered vicious religious conflicts in the second half of the sixteenth century and England experienced violent religious war in the 1640s, but none was as devastating as was the Thirty Years War to most of the German lands.

The peace settlement of 1648 brought even more power to the territorial lords at the expense of the central authority. Recovery after 1648 took a long time. It was made more difficult because the Holy Roman Empire lost almost all coastal lands and many of the less damaged provinces. The Netherlands seceded, Denmark and Sweden took the north German coast, and France acquired some wealthy provinces in the western parts of the empire. Two territorial states recovered most successfully from the bloody drama, however: Austria and Brandenburg-Prussia. Austria, which ruled over some of the less damaged areas, profited from a weakening of the Ottoman Empire, which had conquered most of the Balkan peninsula since the fifteenth century, and Brandenburg-Prussia (after 1701 called just Prussia), though a poor state, emerged as one of the smaller "great" powers in the eighteenth century through a thrifty state policy and the buildup of a well trained and disciplined army. As the French philosopher Voltaire explained after having been the official guest of Prussian King Frederick II the Great, "In most places, the state has an army. In Prussia, the army has a state." Under the dynamic leadership of Frederick II, who aimed to apply enlightenment rationalism to his statecraft, Prussia seized Silesia, a wealthy province, from Austria in 1740 and defended itself against large European coalitions over the following twenty-three years. Frederick later became one of the heroes in the pantheon of German nationalists, more because of his military exploits against superior enemies than because of his considerable cultural contributions – he was a promoter of the arts and a philosopher and composer in his own right. That he was a Francophile and expressed contempt for the German language was conveniently overlooked. In the light of later history, it is noteworthy that both of the two leading "German" powers, Prussia and Austria, in this period expanded into regions inhabited mostly by non-Germans: Prussia annexed Polish territory, and Austria expanded into the Balkans and also seized a part of Poland. These conquests came to play a problematical role in the unification of a German state in the nineteenth century.

While the declining and weak Holy Roman Empire was unable to serve as the foundation of German statehood, particularly after 1648, a cultural notion of "Germanness" existed already centuries before the foundation of a German nation state. Much as the Reformation divided Germany along religious lines, Martin Luther, a genius of language, helped the consolidation and codification of a supraregional German language through his translation of the Bible. In the eighteenth century the German speech area started building a rich culture, largely on the foundations of this language, which compares well with the best phases of the older Italian, French, and English cultures. Germany became a center of music after 1720 (J. S. Bach and his sons, Händel, who was later hired by the English court; Haydn, Mozart, Beethoven, Schubert) and developed a powerful and poetic literature after 1770 (Goethe, Schiller, Kleist, Hölderlin, and many others). Together with music and literature, philosophy (Kant, Hegel, Schopenhauer) made the German speech area a foremost center of European culture. Even in the absence of unified statehood, one could call Germany around 1800 "the country of poets and thinkers" ("*das Land der Dichter und Denker*"). At least for the educated elites, this culture represented a powerful connection across the narrow boundaries of the small and miniscule states.

In light of the later Franco-German hostility, it is ironic that the French triggered the first wave of German nationalism. From 1794 to 1814 French troops, serving first the revolutionary governments and then Napoleon I, successively conquered and occupied the area that later constituted the German Empire. French domination helped to modernize and consolidate Germany and – toward the end – sparked the first upsurge of German nationalism. In different ways, and definitely against his intentions, Napoleon I helped German unification. It was important that he encouraged many of the middle-sized German states to absorb huge numbers of small independent territories, mostly bishoprics, church lands, and local principalities. The more powerful German princes eagerly seized this chance to aggrandize their lands; not surprisingly, they refused to restore the annexed units to independence after Napoleon's defeat. The number of independent and semi-independent German states had been around one thousand in 1792 (of which 300 to 400 units could claim full independence). Twenty-five years later only thirty-nine remained. This consolidation process, called mediation, coincided with the final dissolution of the Holy Roman Empire in 1806. The French occupation also brought the same French legal codes, measurements, and weights to most German-speaking areas, thus helping to modernize them. In 1806 Napoleon defeated the last independent and defiant German state, Prussia. The defeat induced the Prussian royal administration to undertake a thorough reform and modernization of the state and army. Reformed Prussia became the hope of many other Germans who started to suffer increasingly under French occupation. Although the French had come as liberators of the people by establishing democratic "sister republics" in the 1790s and later by introducing the French law code (Code Napoléon) in the various German regions they annexed or dominated, by 1810 their occupation had turned sour for many Germans. The French boycott of British goods, called the Continental System, hurt many German regions economically and encouraged smuggling, which was punished in a draconian way by the French. Moreover, Napoleon's unending wars claimed ever more non-French soldiers. When Napoleon invaded Russia in 1812, his *grande armée* consisted largely of foreigners, predominantly Germans, and these soldiers, together with their families, resented this coerced service for a foreign ruler.[2] Anti-French sentiment erupted when the Russian armies, pursuing Napoleon's defeated invasion force, approached Germany at the end of 1812, and a popular uprising as well as the defection of Prussia and Austria from Napoleon helped to drive the French out of Germany. This common fight of people from different German states against a common enemy gave strong impulses to German nationalism. A few intellectuals consequently demanded the unification of all German-speaking lands, but they still represented a minority and their aspiration seemed impossible to realize given the revived power of the German princes after 1815.

The Congress of Vienna, meeting in 1814–15 to rebuild the European state system after the upheavals of the revolutionary and Napoleonic wars, created the German Confederation under Austrian and Prussian hegemony, including most of later Germany, Luxembourg, the German-speaking regions of Austria, as well as Bohemia and Moravia (today's Czech Republic). But this unit disappointed German nationalists. The German Confederation had hardly more central authority than the defunct Holy Roman Empire, and the rivalry of Austria and Prussia often paralyzed it in a way comparable to the effects of Soviet-American dualism on the United Nations during the Cold War. Almost everywhere, moreover, the princes repressed the nationalist movement, which was dominated by students and professors, after

1815. National unification seemed impossible without a reform or even destruction of the traditional monarchic states. In a united Germany the princes would have to cede some rights to a central authority. That the nationalists often voiced liberal demands such as the granting of constitutions and parliaments further alarmed the princes and their aristocratic supporters, who were also unwilling to share power with broader circles of society.

After several decades of repression a strong desire for reform and freedom had developed mostly among the educated and wealthy town dwellers in the German Confederation. Most of these people considered themselves liberals, which meant that they above all wanted the monarchs to grant human rights and basic freedoms, a constitution, and a parliament. Not all liberals were committed to universal suffrage and democracy, but the vast majority of them desired some form of German unification. Moreover, unemployment among small artisans made this traditionally urban group ready to join a revolutionary cause in hopes of secure jobs. Some liberal claims, above all the demand for individual freedom, also resonated with the peasants. Feudalism, which had been abolished in France at the beginning of the Revolution of 1789, was still part of daily reality in many German-speaking lands. This meant that the peasants in these lands continued to perform a certain amount of unpaid service to a local lord and to pay him a share of their products. Inspired by a successful revolution in France, German town-dwellers and peasants began to agitate for radical reforms in March 1848. The princes, frightened and poorly prepared for revolution, granted constitutions and parliamentary assemblies and appointed liberal ministries all over the German Confederation. They also pacified the peasants by canceling the remaining feudal dues. German nationalists called a National Assembly in Frankfurt am Main to prepare the unification of Germany.

A National Assembly elected by voters from most German lands did indeed meet in Frankfurt and began drafting blueprints for a united and liberal Germany. However, the lawyers and professors, who constituted the largest group in the Assembly, found it hard to determine what should become part of united Germany. The multi-ethnic Austrian empire (including the German-speaking Austrian provinces and German parts of later Czechoslovakia) posed the most serious problem. What should happen with the Austrian Empire's vast non-German lands if its German provinces were integrated into a German national state? Not seeing a solution to this issue, a minority in the Assembly advocated the exclusion of Austria from the German nation state and the foundation of a smaller (*kleindeutsch*) state under Prussian leadership (*kleindeutsch* meaning "smaller German," as opposed to *großdeutsch*, a state including the German-speaking lands of Austria). The deliberations of the National Assembly, however, soon became irrelevant because it lacked the power to enforce its vision. The position of the National Assembly became precarious when the princes, aware of the power of their still intact armies under the command of loyal aristocrats, started recalling their concessions to the liberals in the winter of 1848–9. The monarchs gathered troops for bloody repression of the liberals, and

Prussian armies helped crush democrats in central and southern Germany. In an act of desperation, the National Assembly tried to save at least the project of national unity by offering a German imperial crown to the Prussian king Friedrich Wilhelm IV. The king, however, refused to accept a crown from revolutionaries, and the Assembly, having fled to Stuttgart in May, was disbanded by local troops in June 1849.

Still, the revolutionaries of 1848 did not loose completely. Most monarchs agreed to keep a constitution and a parliament. They did rewrite their constitutions with a more authoritarian pen and made sure that the suffrage would benefit mostly the rich, but this meant that substantial circles of liberals such as businessmen, lawyers, and professors retained a strong political voice after the crackdown of 1849 (in fact, the liberals gained majorities in the Prussian parliament and in other states by the late 1850s). These groups, who had become alarmed at the democratic and socialist radicalism of some of their lower middle-class supporters in 1848, were perhaps not too unhappy about the royal armies taking control and preventing a radicalization of the revolution, which had happened so dramatically in France in 1789–94. The peasants were satisfied that feudalism remained consigned to the past and became a conservative group. In political terms the losers were the more radical liberals and the democrats, particularly the artisans. Most of them were not wealthy enough to qualify for the suffrage and many of them greatly resented the reimposition of censorship and other repressive measures. Quite a few emigrated to the democratic United States, foremost among them Carl Schurz, who became a Union general, a notable statesman and reformer, and a prominent Independent in his new home country. In economic terms, however, even these groups did not loose completely. After 1848, the royal governments became more aware of social issues and attempted to initiate some measure of social security. The large-scale politicization of Germans in 1848 also was difficult to erase. Many later German parties traced their lineage to organizations formed during the revolution of 1848. The German women's movement, too, looked back to powerful precedents from 1848 when it reconstituted itself in the 1890s. The national idea, finally, remained very much alive. In 1850, the Prussian king even tried to harness it by attempting to build a closer union of the smaller German states with Prussia – this time on his own terms, not on the terms of an assembly. This attempt, however, was a fiasco. It brought Prussia to the brink of war with Austria, which was unwilling to let its German rival increase its power through domination of Germany, and it almost triggered a foreign intervention by Russia and France, possibly even Britain. Prussia quickly backed down. Obviously, German unification was not only a challenge for the German states but also for the European powers. The bloody failure of the revolution and the international complications raised by Prussia's attempted unification from above made many liberals conclude that Germany could only be united by military power.

The demand for national unification was powerfully revived in the late 1850s as a consequence of industrial and economic development. After 1850 the industrial revolution in some German lands entered its takeoff phase. New factories were built at a breath-taking rate, the production of textiles and iron soared, railroads started to connect many distant regions, and coal production and export reached record levels every year. These advances profited from a high level of education, the result of an advanced school and university system, particularly in Prussia, which had the highest literacy rate and exemplary schools as a result of the reforms undertaken in the wake of the defeat against Napoleon. Industrialization was accompanied by rapid population growth, urbanization, and the expansion of the middle classes and of the industrial working class, the proletariat. After having lagged economically behind western Europe for three centuries, the German lands caught up within a few decades. Economic progress was most powerful in Prussia but less impressive in Austria. At the Congress of Vienna, Prussia had received areas that turned out to be enormously beneficial for industrialization, namely the Ruhr district, the Rhineland, and parts of Saxony – all with rich coal deposits. Ironically, the Prussian king, still focused on eastward expansion into Polish territories, had not initially wanted these territories, whose economic value nobody in Vienna seems to have appreciated. The Congress of Vienna, with just as little awareness, also set up Prussia as a future champion of German unification through another territorial stipulation: it divided Prussia into one large eastern part and a smaller western part, the latter containing the Rhineland and the Ruhr, the area with the highest concentration of industry by the 1850s. At a time of dynastic politics, which the Congress of Vienna meant to restore, such disparate territories were not considered a problem – much in the way of a large multinational company today owning factories in different countries and in different fields of economic specialization. At a time of industrialization, expanding trade, and railroads, however, such a territorial division was highly inconvenient. Small wonder that the Prussians since the 1820s began to negotiate customs agreements with some of the small German states, particularly the ones that lay in between Prussia's two territories. From the 1830s to the 1860s, Prussia masterminded the buildup of a customs union (*Zollverein*) with an increasing number of German states – but not with Austria. Initially, Austria saw its own economic interests sufficiently protected through facilitation of trade within its huge empire. Later, it tried to enter the customs union and extend it to its non-German lands, but Prussia foiled these attempts. Customs agreements were one (important) part of Prussian policy, but other areas of cooperation went hand in hand with them. Many of the smaller German states – often hesitantly – adapted their economies to Prussia. Railroad building followed the lines of trade after 1835, and it required substantial negotiation among the German states, too, for example on gauges and schedules. The mind-blowing pace of industrialization in the 1850s and 1860s only increased the demand for such economic and administrative coordination. Prussia, with its heavily industrial West and its separate, more agricultural East, took the lead and dominated this process. In a nutshell, Germany – roughly in the borders of the later Second Empire – was being economically united under Prussian leadership well before 1871. In some regions, particularly the Catholic areas of the South, this process caused considerable discomfort, but it became increasingly obvious for the Prussian government and Prussia's industrial elites that a political unification in the wake of the *Zollverein* made sense in economic and power-political (including military) terms. Meanwhile, Austria jealously and suspiciously watched from the sidelines. Caught in its double role as multinational empire and as German state, Austria hoped to preserve a loosely united confederation in Germany. Such a policy was meant to prevent its rival Prussia from growing too powerful by absorbing much of Germany and to foster ties with German states opposed to Prussian domination. The rulers of these states, keen on protecting their power and privileges, often shared the Austrian desire for weak central control in the German Confederation, but they also had to consider the economic and military power of Prussia. It had become clear already during an international crisis in 1840, when the French government demanded the annexation of all German lands left of the Rhine, that Prussia was much more able and committed to defending the smaller German states than Austria, whose military power was often diverted by its commitments in non-German lands.

The internal and international conflicts came to a head during the 1860s. The momentum came from a Prussia in the throes of internal political crisis. Prussian King Wilhelm I faced massive opposition from a predominantly liberal diet (parliament) over plans for expanding and professionalizing the Prussian army. The liberals opposed some stipulations that would have made the army less of a people's army and more of an instrument under the control of the crown. To get the military budget approved, Wilhelm at the very least needed to make concessions that amounted to sharing more power with parliament. Many liberals in Prussia also desired a more active policy toward German unification, still a central aim of German liberalism. The deadlock with the diet almost triggered the king's resignation. As a last resort, Wilhelm appointed a controversial man as prime minister who promised to overcome the crisis without concessions to the diet. The new Prussian prime minister, Count Otto von Bismarck, was an abrasive and arrogant Junker who had first demanded and then applauded the repression of the Revolutions of 1848 and who hated the Prussian liberals as much as the Austrians. In internal matters, Bismarck ruthlessly encouraged Wilhelm to collect taxes and spend for military enlargement without parliamentary approval, essentially breaking the constitution. In external matters, Bismarck tried to position Prussia as a champion of German unity, not least by embracing the possibility of war. As Bismarck explained to the Prussian diet in one of his early speeches, German unification could not be created by speeches but only by "iron and blood" (which is often misquoted as "blood and iron"). A successful war would be useful in several respects: it might embarrass the liberals who had opposed military spending, and, if it was a war for the cause of German unity, it might separate the moderate liberals from the radical and democratic liberals by attracting the former to the prospect of a unification by war with the help of Prussian arms.

Bismarck was an unlikely promoter of German unification. As a Junker, he belonged to a class that had close ties to the Prussian monarchy and, unlike liberal industrialists, seemed to have little to gain from German unification. Certainly Bismarck was no German nationalist. He believed in a strong Prussian monarchy, but he recognized that a German unification under the auspices of Prussia would strengthen the Prussian crown and state economically, militarily, and politically. He also realized that a unification of Germany under Prussian leadership would contradict above all the interests of Austria and France, and the key problem was to fight these two opponents at different times while keeping out other European powers, particularly Russia. Bismarck also had unconventional ideas about the involvement of the masses in politics, largely inspired by French Emperor Napoleon III who had, like his uncle Napoleon I, established an autocracy that often resorted to popular votes (plebiscites) on a single issue that could be presented to the voters on manipulated and suggestive terms (this system was called Bonapartism). There is no doubt that Bismarck hated democracy, but he believed that charismatic leaders could become popular among the industrial and rural masses; he reckoned that parliaments elected by universal and equal manhood suffrage could be limited in influence and that government propaganda and electoral manipulation would ensure pro-governmental majorities. To Bismarck, universal suffrage offered the advantage of undercutting the power of the liberals, who had a parliamentary majority only by virtue of their wealth (which gave them a vote out of proportion to their actual numbers) and who would almost certainly become a minority in a parliament elected according to universal suffrage. Should universal suffrage produce anti-governmental majorities, however, Bismarck was not afraid of using the basis of conservative power, the army, to dissolve parliament.

Bismarck's skills as a statesman deserve respect even if his ruthless methods and authoritarian goals justify much criticism. In Prussia he was hated by the liberal majority in the diet that he defiantly ignored. Even his position at court was far from secure: some influential advisors of the king were leaning toward compromise with the liberals while others mistrusted Bismarck because of his Bonapartist tendencies. On the German and international stage, Bismarck faced the daunting challenge of winning the confidence of German nationalists and of defeating Austria and France separately – by diplomatic means if possible, by war if necessary – while keeping the other European great powers neutral. This required a remarkable balancing act and a keen sense for good diplomatic opportunities.

The first opportunity arose in 1863, when the Danish king, who had constitutional rights in the mostly German duchies of Schleswig and Holstein, proceeded to make Schleswig an integral part of Denmark by introducing the Danish constitution in Schleswig. Although it was understandable that Denmark, in its own efforts to consolidate its nation state, would want tighter control at least over Schleswig, where a strong Danish minority lived, this move violated an international treaty of 1852. It was an extremely thorny issue for other reasons as well. According to an old treaty the two duchies were considered indivisible. Things were complicated by the fact that Holstein, whose population was entirely German, was part of the German Confederation, whereas Schleswig was not. Some dynastic conflicts also came into play when a German dynasty, which had once renounced its inheritance rights, also claimed rights to the duchies. An earlier attempt by Denmark to better control Schleswig and Holstein had already fanned German nationalist outrage and triggered a war in 1848. Prussia, after having won militarily, had had to concede a diplomatic defeat under international pressure. For all of these reasons, the Danish king's decision to extend the Danish constitution to Schleswig in 1863 triggered a strong reaction in the German lands. The German Confederation called for an all-German war against Denmark. Austria, allied with the German dynasty involved in the dispute, joined in, and Bismarck agreed to have the Prussian army fight side by side with the Austrians in a short, victorious campaign in 1864. This war for a "German" cause boosted Prussia's ambitions to lead Germany, and it went a long way toward mending fences between Bismarck and the largely liberal nationalist movement. The military success, moreover, triggered much enthusiasm among the liberal majority that had blocked the expansion of the Prussian army. Bismarck, by having overridden the majority in the Prussian diet, now seemed vindicated at least in the eyes of the right-wing liberals. As he had anticipated, the successful war drove a wedge into the liberal movement.

As a consequence of the war, Denmark had to bury its rights to the duchies. Both duchies, including Schleswig's regions with a Danish population, were occupied by troops belonging to the German Confederation. After a separate agreement in 1865, Prussia took over the administration of Schleswig and Austria that of Holstein. Prussian-Austrian relations quickly deteriorated, however, and some of this was due to Bismarck. He first frustrated the claims of the pro-Austrian dynasty to the duchies, and then he antagonized the Austrians by infringing on their rights in Holstein. Bismarck recognized that the international situation was becoming favorable for an isolated war between Prussia and Austria. The crucial factor was France. Desiring neither Prussian nor Austrian domination in Germany, France had frequently played out the two powers against each other. As Austria was widely considered the stronger of the two, French support for Prussia seemed more likely than French support for Austria, but it was conceivable that France would help Austria if it were loosing. But in 1866, France was heavily involved in Mexico and unlikely to enter a European war on short notice. Bismarck, moreover, had fostered cordial relations with Napoleon III, partly for pragmatic reasons, and partly because he admired Napoleon's political system. Russia, moreover, was estranged from Austria because Austria had declined to support it against France and Britain during the Crimean War in 1853–6. Russia was also worried about Polish nationalism. The largest part of Poland belonged to Russia, and the Poles had waged several unsuccessful uprisings against Russia in the previous decades. In 1866, another uprising seemed to be brewing. Bismarck, mindful of Prussia's areas with a Polish population, always believed that Prussia and Russia shared a common interest in holding down Polish nationalism, and he made it clear that Prussia would support all Russian actions in that direction. Britain, although the most powerful state, seemed less inclined to intervene in European affairs than in previous decades and did not raise major obstacles for Bismarck. Italy, just united in a war against Austria, was an ally of Prussia because it still coveted the province of Venetia (Venice and its hinterland), which had remained Austrian after French and Italian armies had defeated the Austrians in Lombardy in 1859.

In the spring of 1866 Austria and Prussia were inching ever closer to war. The occupation of Schleswig and Holstein not only exacerbated tensions between the two, it also reopened the larger question of what should happen with the German Confederation, which, after all, had called for the war against Denmark. As the thunderstorm was approaching, Austria and Prussia hastily made one reform proposal for the Confederation after the other, with both powers trying to draft a settlement to their advantage but unacceptable to the other. Prussian policy in this phase was remarkably unsuccessful at wooing the smaller German states. Some of these states, particularly Bavaria and Baden, the predominantly Catholic and more liberal states in the South, felt closer affinities with Austria than with predominantly Lutheran Prussia, but most smaller German states were primarily concerned about their autonomy. They understood that Austria, by virtue of its multi-national empire, had much less interest in a centralized German state than Prussia and was therefore less likely to imperil their autonomy. As a consequence, most German states joined Austria when war broke out between Prussia and Austria in June. This could have been devastating for Prussia, particularly because many states right on the border of Prussia (such as Saxony) and in between the two parts of Prussia (Hannover) sided with Austria. Only a few small north German states joined Prussia. Essentially, Germany experienced a civil war right around the time of the American Civil War! But this civil war was much less acrimonious than the American war largely because Prussia won within a few weeks. The organization and fighting capacity of the Prussian army, modernized by extremely capable generals, foremost Chief of Staff Helmuth von Moltke and War Minister Albrecht von Roon, proved superior to the armies of Austria and the smaller German states. It displayed some very successful ways of using modern technology, particularly the railroads. Already days after the outbreak of war, Prussian troops defeated and occupied some of the smaller states, and in July they won a decisive victory over Austria in Königgrätz (Sadowa) in today's Czech Republic (then Austrian Bohemia). Vienna, the Austrian capital, lay within reach of Prussian troops, but Bismarck, mindful of international complications, asked his king to call them back and to offer a mild settlement to Austria with no territorial gains for Prussia at the expense of Austria. Prussia did go on a wild annexation spree at the expense of other north German territories, however. Hannover, Hessen-Kassel, the city Frankfurt am Main, and Schleswig-Holstein all became part of Prussia, which thereby closed the gap between its two major territories. Saxony escaped Prussian annexation mostly because of French pressure in its favor. The south German states (Baden, Württemberg, Hessen-Darmstadt, and Bavaria) received mild terms. Austria had to cede Venetia to Italy, which had declared war on Austria but lost on the battlefield. Finally, Prussia abolished the German Confederation and began to organize the northern states into a new federation under its own unchecked domination.

The Prussian victory had major repercussions on European politics. First of all, it meant that Austria, for the first time in a thousand years, was excluded from German affairs. Austria thenceforth had to focus on maintaining stability in its extensive non-German holdings. To this end, the Austrian government reorganized the structure of the empire by giving autonomy to its Hungarian half while maintaining the emperor as a common head of state (this settlement, finalized in 1867, was called the *Ausgleich*). The defeat of 1866 did not mean that Austria was excluded for ever from Germany, as some textbooks argue, but it was clear enough that only the collapse of the empire, called Austria-Hungary after the *Ausgleich*, would reopen the question of the place of Austria within Germany, as it promptly did in 1918, when that collapse materialized. Second, the Prussian victory greatly alarmed Napoleon III. It became a crucial objective of French diplomacy in the following years to confine Prussian hegemony to the region of Germany north of the Main River, which goes through Frankfurt and separates the northern two thirds of Germany from the southern third. France, having benefited from German division for centuries, disliked a united Germany under Prussian hegemony. After 1866, France hoped to step into Austria's shoes by becoming the protector of the few remaining independent states in the south of Germany. Third, the south German states faced a changed situation that brought them closer to Prussia, with which they were already linked economically through the *Zollverein*. The support for the Austrian cause in 1866 had been lukewarm in these states. The idea of France, a non-German power, meddling in the affairs of the remaining independent German states stirred up strong German nationalist sentiment there and appeared even less appealing than Prussian domination. Particularly irritating were the repeated claims to German territory by Napoleon III, which reawakened the specter of the French threat of 1840 and made the South Germans wonder whether the wolf was trying to get appointed as the guardian of the sheep. The rulers of the remaining German states therefore saw no alternative to accepting a defensive treaty offered by Bismarck, according to which a declaration of war by a foreign country on one German state would trigger war with all the others. Finally, the victory over Austria gave Prussia the opportunity to establish the blueprint for a united Germany in the regions north of the Main River, which it promptly did by creating the North German Federation in 1867. Its constitution, drafted by Bismarck, prefigured the constitution of the united Germany of 1871. It granted universal suffrage to men above age twenty-five in elections for a parliament (Reichstag) but counterbalanced this democratic element with conservative safeguards. A representation of the member states, the

Bundesrat, consisted of deputies nominated by the state governments, who were of course appointed by the princes. In the Bundesrat, a handful of deputies could veto any legislation coming from the Reichstag; Prussia alone had enough deputies for a veto. Moreover, the constitution of the North German Federation reserved a strong place for the Prussian king as supreme representative of the Confederation and for the Prussian minister president, who became the chancellor of the Confederation in personal union with his Prussian office. Although the Reichstag had the right to vote the budget, the government of the North German Confederation was responsible only to the head of state, the Prussian king. The constituent states with their property-based suffrages, moreover, retained much autonomy, and important areas of state policy did not fall within the reach of the Confederation and its democratically elected parliament.

The victory of 1866 gave Bismarck some breathing space and bolstered his domestic support. The right wing of the liberals formed the National Liberal Party and openly supported him, as did the progressive wing of the conservative party, the Free Conservative Party (the intransigent conservatives still opposed Bismarck, resented his Bonapartist policies, and were unhappy about his establishment of the North German Confederation). With these new parties firmly behind him, Bismarck was finally able to lay to rest the Prussian constitutional dispute over military spending dating from 1862. An indemnity bill passed in 1867 with the votes of the National Liberals and the Free Conservatives declared all of Bismarck's policies legal in retrospect.

Yet German unification remained unaccomplished, and Napoleon III was unlikely to let it happen unopposed. Under increasing domestic pressure, Napoleon III became eager to score a foreign policy success at the expense of Prussia. In 1870 such an opportunity arose when a revolutionary Spanish government invited a cousin of the Prussian king to become king of Spain. This might turn Spain into a Prussian ally through dynastic ties with the Hohenzollern, the Prussian ruling family. Worried about a Prussian hegemony in continental Europe, Napoleon III demanded that the German prince refuse the offer. Clouds of war appeared on the horizon. Bismarck, seeing an opportunity for a successful war against France, encouraged Wilhelm I to support his cousin's candidacy even at the risk of a French declaration of war. Wilhelm I, however, advocated a withdrawal of his cousin's candidacy, and the cousin agreed. This was a major diplomatic victory for France. Napoleon III would have been well advised to leave it at that. However, egged on by a powerful war party at his court, he tried to capitalize on his victory by demanding a guarantee that the Hohenzollern prince would never accede to the Spanish throne. This was an unnecessary and humiliating demand. Bismarck published the diplomatic communication on this matter with a provocative spin – the famous Ems Dispatch; the hawks in the governments of France and Prussia were outraged and demanded war.

What made Bismarck so confident to risk war with the greatest military power of continental Europe from the seventeenth to the early nineteenth century? First, he knew that France was isolated. Napoleon's policies had made most European states nervous, and revelations about French designs on Belgium, played into the hands of the British government by Bismarck, were sure to make Britain unwilling to help France. Italy, which had been France's ally against Austria in 1859, was becoming impatient with the French occupation of Rome, which had kept the Papal State, reduced to a small territory around Rome, outside of Italy (France had occupied Rome in 1848 to protect the Pope against the claims of Italian revolutionaries and nationalists, and Napoleon III had kept the French troops there to placate Catholic opinion in France). Austria had been treated generously by Bismarck in 1866, largely to prevent it from becoming a French ally. Aside from that, the still lingering threat of domestic unrest (particularly in Hungary) as well as the pro-Prussian posture of the Russian government made Austria-Hungary inclined to stay neutral. Russia, where the defeat against France and Britain in the Crimean War was still a bitter memory, was no friend of Napoleon III and remained tied to Prussia through a common interest in Poland. Second, Bismarck was confident that he could provoke a French declaration of war to Prussia, which would activate the defensive treaties he had concluded with the other German states. Napoleon III would not only face Prussia but all the other German states as well. A war against France, harkening back to the memory of the struggle of liberation against Napoleon I, was likely to fan the flames of German nationalism and offer a favorable climate for the unification of the German states. Finally, Bismarck trusted the successful Prussian generals of the earlier wars to mastermind another fast and victorious campaign against a French army that was not prepared for war.

Napoleon III reacted to the Ems Dispatch by declaring war on Prussia on 19 July 1870, expecting a military victory to shore up support for his weakening regime. The French declaration of war immediately activated the German defensive treaties and triggered a massive wave of German national feeling in all German states. When Napoleon received troubling news from the front, he decided to join his main armies. On 1 September, the Prussians defeated a large French army near Sedan, and Napoleon III was taken prisoner. A revolutionary French government continued the struggle but experienced renewed defeats. German troops advanced to Paris and laid siege to the city later in September. Hastily constituted relief armies and irregular combatants (franctireurs) failed to liberate Paris and to hold the German advance elsewhere. In January 1871 Paris capitulated, and a few weeks later the French government signed an armistice. In May, France signed a peace treaty in Frankfurt that gave Alsace and Lorraine to Germany and imposed a large indemnity payment on France.

Just as the fighting around Paris was coming to a close, Bismarck used the nationalist momentum created by the success of the German armies to stage a declaration of the German princes for German unification. In the hall of mirrors in the palace of Versailles, which had been built under Louis XIV in the seventeenth century, the Bavarian king on 18 January 1871 proclaimed Wilhelm I as German emperor, and the rulers of the other German states followed suit. Essentially, the south German states agreed to join the North German Confederation, whose constitution became the constitution of the German Empire with only a few amendments. The Prussian king became German emperor, the Reichstag was enlarged to include deputies from the new territories, and the Bundesrat made room for representatives of the new member states (but not for Alsace-Lorraine, which was administered by the German Empire). In order to overcome the resistance of the kings of Bavaria and Württemberg to German unification, Bismarck had to make some concessions. One of them was the preservation of the state postal services, a delight for stamp collectors now and then but in practice not a very important matter. Bavaria and Württemberg were also allowed to keep their state railroads and some of their diplomatic service. This led to the oddity that in some countries there was a German as well as a Bavarian and Württembergian embassy until 1918. It was only the democratic Weimar Constitution of 1919 that abolished these residues of centuries-long German fragmentation.

In some sense, the unification of Germany on the wings of victory against France was the crowning achievement of Bismarck's career. He had been right in counting on French isolation and the abilities of the Prussian army, he had been successful at harnessing German nationalist feeling, and he had magnified the power of his monarch by making him emperor of Germany. Yet the framework of German unification also shared numerous problematic features, many of which came from Bismarck's staunch conservatism. Bismarck used the groundswell of German nationalist feeling to push the south German monarchs to agree to unification, but he made sure that this unification appeared as a gesture of the princes, not the people (hence the choice of Versailles, the very symbol of royal absolutism). To be sure, the Reichstag suffrage was democratic by the standards of the period (women's suffrage was not yet common anywhere), but Bismarck introduced it not in order to democratically share power but rather in the cynical belief that he could manipulate the working masses in favor of the government and against any remaining opposition from liberals. In any case, the constitution made sure that the Reichstag would only have limited power. The German Empire was still not a centralized state, as crucial powers remained in the purview of the single member states, which all lacked the democratic element of universal suffrage. The armies remained a matter of the states except in wartime, and the budget for the empire covered only a limited range of items and relied mostly on indirect taxes. Finally, the defeat of France left a deep liability for German foreign policy. France could not easily forgive the defeat and the loss of Alsace-Lorraine and was likely to remain an enemy. Bismarck, however, shared less responsibility for this outcome than for the anti-democratic framework of the German constitutional system. He did not push for the annexation of Alsace-Lorraine and even considered opposing it, but he had used up his political capital toward the Prussian generals when he insisted on taking no territories from Austria in 1866. He was unlikely to prevail against the generals a second time, and he expressed some understanding for their arguments that for strategic reasons both Alsace and Lorraine had to be annexed. He did agree that taking German-speaking Alsace and perhaps some German-speaking parts of Lorraine into a united Germany could be justified, but he later considered it a mistake to have taken both provinces to their full extent – including a substantial French-speaking area around Metz. The people of Alsace-Lorraine, despite their predominantly German ethnic background, did not generally welcome their return to the German sphere, to which they had belonged until the seventeenth century. They became one of several national minorities in the new Germany whose deputies in the Reichstag formed their own parliamentary group and fought for their rights (the Poles and the Danes were the other minorities). The integration of these two provinces into Germany never fully succeeded.

In the light of the two world wars, the German campaign against France in 1870 has often been portrayed as the first of three unprovoked German aggressions – as the precedent for 1914 and 1939–40. In the perspective of late nineteenth-century Germans, however, the punctuation of events was different. They tended to perceive the French interest in southern Germany and Napoleon's declaration of war as an extension of a long series of French aggressions against German territories from the conquests of Louis XIV to Napoleon I and in line with the French threat to annex the left bank of the Rhine in 1840. The only truly different feature was that a French invasion this time did not succeed and that France was quickly defeated by German powers without any foreign assistance. It may be a moot point to raise a war guilt question for 1870, but it seems clear that the responsibility was not simply Prussia's. Granted, Bismarck was a promoter of war in the Prussian government, albeit against much resistance from the king and most of his other advisors. But Napoleon III and nationalist circles in France shared much of the responsibility. It was France that pushed too far and declared war, not Prussia. Perhaps the war lasted longer than necessary because the German demands were too harsh for France, but the demand for annexations and reparations was not outrageous at the time; it had been the rule in European warfare. Nobody had ever bothered to ask the inhabitants of conquered provinces to which state they wanted to belong. Although for people in northern France, the three German invasions from 1870 to 1940 formed a continuity of a sometimes harsh conquest and occupation experience, one certainly should not interpret 1870 as a German war of aggression in the style of 1939–40. Nevertheless, the German victory against France and the unification of Germany caused concerns and fears in Europe. Bismarck, although the primary cause of these concerns, became mindful of them and tried his utmost to secure the German position in Europe while reassuring the other powers that he was not interested in further expansion and foreign policy risks.

Was there a credible and desirable alternative to German unification under Prussian hegemony? In view of European integration after 1945, the German Confederation undoubtedly appears as a more attractive model of supranational decision making than it appeared to German nationalist historians of the period before 1945. Maybe it could have been reformed and democratized, emerging into a synthesis of state and international organization such as the European Union since the 1990s, perhaps preserving the richness and diversity of local cultures that had characterized fragmented Germany. Probably such a German Confederation would have appeared less dangerous to the other European powers than the Bismarckian Germany of 1871 – although it can also be asked whether it would have been safe enough from them. But nostalgia for the pre-modern fragmented Germany should not go too far. The rich diversity of states could carry a narrow-minded, provincial flavor. The fragmented Germany also allowed some nasty traditions to persist, such as the crass human rights abuses by princes and social elites that the young dramatist Georg Büchner portrayed so vividly in his pamphlet *Der Hessische Landbote* and his drama *Woyzeck* in the 1830s. The fragmentation of the German-speaking lands could be attractive to intellectuals persecuted in one state and able to go somewhere else, but this would not have been an easy option for the majority of people who still had ties to the land. If in cultural terms German unification may have been a loss, there is no doubt that it made perfect sense in economic terms. In a rapidly industrializing economy the elimination of tariffs was a small achievement if not followed up by co-operation in other spheres. Unlike in the European Union of today, the people in the German Confederation (with the exception of some pockets of non-Germans) spoke a common language, albeit in different dialects, and generally felt that they belonged to a common cultural sphere. Forming one state out of the many made sense to them. A reformed, democratized German Confederation of independent states on the lines of later European integration would have seemed an oddity to most observers in the nineteenth century. The Confederation appeared to be too much of a princely construction – something Bismarck tried to replicate in the pathetic proclamation of Wilhelm as German emperor in Versailles – to make sense as a people's state. Any democratization of the German Confederation would have been fiercely resisted by the princes and, not least, by Austria. In the heady days before the outbreak of the war of 1866, for example, Bismarck proposed a Confederation parliament elected according to universal male suffrage. Even though this suggestion included all the typical Bismarckian safeguards against democracy, it drew massive opposition from Austria. Although the German Constitution of 1871 had severe deficits, it did include some important democratic innovations, particularly universal male suffrage, and it protected basic human rights better than they had been protected in some member states of the German Confederation before 1866.

Map 1 Germany in 1871.

–3–

Germany under Bismarck

For better or worse, Bismarck dominated political life in Germany until his resignation in 1890. Bismarck's initiatives, although not always successful, set the direction of politics. This was due largely to the enormous prestige that he had built up during national unification, but it was not a given in the light of the constitution and the dynamics of political life. Essentially, the supreme power according to the constitution was the emperor. He had the right to dismiss the chancellor and the ministers, and he had the supreme command over the army. As Prussian king, the emperor also was the highest authority in by far the most powerful single state. Emperor Wilhelm I, however, had little interest in the exercise of his power. Before 1871, he had repeatedly disagreed with Bismarck and expressed concern about the risk associated with his plans, as during the Spanish succession crisis, but after 1871 he gave Bismarck much latitude. Some historians ascribe this fact to a certain tiredness associated with Wilhelm's age (he was born in 1797 and ruled until 1888); others see it as a sign of admirable restraint. The big worry for Bismarck, and the big hope for many of his opponents, however, was what would happen after the death of Wilhelm I. The political ideas of the heir to the throne, Prince Friedrich Wilhelm, were perhaps obscured by his dreamy romanticism, but there was no doubt that he shared some liberal views. Friedrich Wilhelm had been a vocal critic of Bismarck during the wars of unification. He was worried about the brutal and highhanded way in which unification was achieved, and he suffered from the resulting negative image of Germany in France and elsewhere. Friedrich Wilhelm was married to Princess Victoria, daughter of English Queen Victoria. This dynastic marriage alliance had been shaped in the late 1850s as a step toward a rapprochement of Prussia and Britain and perhaps as a sign of reconciliation of the Prussian monarchy with the liberals, who looked to Britain as a political role model. To Bismarck, the prospect of serving under a liberal emperor with an assertive and politically interested wife (who kept an intense correspondence with her mother) was a nightmare. He did not get along with Friedrich Wilhelm and Victoria and feared that Friedrich Wilhelm, if not dismissing him outright, would certainly not allow him the free rein he had under Wilhelm I. In the 1880s, as news spread that the crown prince's health was in danger, Bismarck cultivated close relations with the oldest son of Friedrich Wilhelm and Victoria, Wilhelm, blatantly encouraging the young man's rebelliousness against his parents.

Figure 3.1 The proclamation of Wilhelm I as German Emperor in the Hall of Mirrors of the French royal castle in Versailles (drawing by Anton von Werner, 1871). (Kaiserproklamation, Inv.-Nr.: 1988/532, Anton von Werner © DHM, Berlin).

This scene represents Bismarck's idea of the German Empire as a union of princes. Bismarck, the main engineer of unification, is in the center of the picture but leaves the elevated main stage to the princes. The people in the drawing probably heard the thunder of cannons from nearby Paris, which was still besieged. Although German unification was the result of three wars, Bismarck envisioned the new empire as a force for stability and peace. However, the defeat of France proved to be a major liability for his foreign policy.

That Bismarck dominated politics in the first two decades of united Germany is not to say that he established a dictatorship, as some historians argue. The period 1871–90 also saw the maturation of a modern German party system, and the balance between Reichstag, Bundesrat, and Bismarck as chancellor remained volatile. Historians have often criticized the German parties for not having done enough to establish a more democratic parliamentary system and constitutional order. This reproach targets particularly the liberal parties, given that the conservatives were not at all interested in furthering a parliamentary system. However, Bismarck's relationship with the leading parties in the Reichstag was one of give and take, and the parties were far from just taking his orders. Bismarck, having no firm party base himself, worked with different party alignments over the years. He did influence elections by dissolving the Reichstag and calling new elections on his own terms, and he toyed with the idea of a coup d'état whenever the Reichstag failed to support his policies. In sharp contrast to the American and French political cultures, in which constitutions were directed "by the will of the people," Bismarck saw the German constitution and the Reichstag as granted by the German princes, a "gift" to the people that the princes could always take back and revise if the people proved not to be appreciative enough. However, Bismarck's control was not complete, and he never attempted a coup d'état even though the alignments of parties supportive of his policies suffered severe defeats, notably in 1881 and 1890. Much of his intense frustration resulted precisely from his experience that he could do little without support of the Reichstag. Given Bismarck's strategically timed dissolutions of the Reichstag and the populist aspects of his politics, historian Hans-Ulrich Wehler has called Bismarck the first charismatic leader in German history.[1] A charismatic leader tends to have an insecure institutionalized power base but draws strength from continuous appeal to the people through successful populist initiatives. Much of this definitely applies to Bismarck, although it would be too simple to see all of his policies as primarily motivated by manipulation of public opinion.

Which were the leading parties under Bismarck? For much of Bismarck's career, the liberal parties were the strongest force in parliament, even after universal suffrage undermined their position. But the liberal spectrum was highly volatile. Parties split and united in different configurations. Left-wing liberals embraced democratic policies whereas right-wing liberals drew closer to the conservatives. The principal support for the liberals came from the upper middle classes including industrialists and businessmen as well as from the educated groups in the cities. The Progressive Party, founded in Prussia in 1861, was the main liberal force and dominated the Prussian diet at the time of Bismarck's appointment as prime minister. In reaction to the Prussian victory against Austria, however, the right wing of the party broke off and constituted itself as the National Liberal Party, which supported Bismarck and helped to legalize in retrospect his defiant actions regarding the Army Bill. The National Liberal Party, loosely organized and dominated by industry and business, initially was the strongest party in united Germany. From 1871 to 1877, it won roughly one-third of the seats in the Reichstag, but it suffered severe defeats in 1878 and 1881, when Bismarck sought help from other quarters and when the party was widely seen to have compromised its liberal credentials. This feeling led to the secession of the party's left wing, which later merged with the Progressive Party. Only slowly did the National Liberal Party recover during the 1880s. The Progressive Party did well in the elections of 1871 and particularly in 1881, when it won approximately one-quarter of the Reichstag seats. It drew closer to Bismarck in the 1870s but usually found itself on a course of confrontation with him after 1878. Other parties also left a mark in the liberal spectrum, for example the German People's Party, a democratic party based in Württemberg.

The Center Party was the second strongest force in the Reichstag after the National Liberals in the 1870s and even rose to first place during the 1880s. It was the party of political Catholicism, which had its roots in the romantic movement early in the nineteenth century. The Center Party aimed to defend the Catholic Church and Catholic institutions. After the defeat of Austria in 1866, the Catholic Church in the German lands felt threatened by the Protestant Prussian monarchy and the predominantly Protestant liberal movement, which wanted to secularize education and marriage, restrain the Jesuit order, and abolish the traditional privileges of the Church. During the 1870s, Bismarck's anti-Catholic policies boosted the Center Party vote and, ironically, helped the party to consolidate itself. But the Center Party housed different, even contradictory, tendencies under its wings. It was a federalist party, supporting the rights of the predominantly Catholic states and regions, which had lost Austria as their traditional patron within Germany in 1866. The Center Party was also anti-liberal and interested in social reform. Aside from being almost completely Catholic, it attracted a fairly representative spectrum of German society – from aristocrats to industrial workers (there was a Catholic worker's movement organized in connection with the Center Party). Some groups in the Center Party were democratic, others authoritarian. Considering these differences, it is remarkable that the party's share of the vote remained comparatively stable until the First World War and even beyond – around 20 percent (Germany's Catholic population made up approximately one-third). Even after 1880, as Bismarck's anti-Catholic policies wound down, the Center Party drew much strength and cohesion from the memory of the repression in the 1870s. It was better organized than the liberal and conservative parties and always benefited from the mobilizing power of the Catholic Church and its vast network of allied organizations. In the Catholic states, particularly Baden and Bavaria, the Center was the predominant party, and it also held a strong position in Prussia's Catholic provinces (for example the Rhineland and Silesia).

The conservative spectrum in German politics was shaped mostly by the aristocracy, although the conservative parties attracted a broader group of voters than just the aristocrats. The conservative parties were slow to build up a grass-roots organization but derived much power from their connections to the various German royal courts and their leaders' aristocratic privileges, for example membership in the hereditary upper chambers of the German states and access to the highest careers in the state and the military. First conservative party groupings date back to 1848. During the 1850s, the conservatives were a strong force in the Prussian diet, and Bismarck was one of them. Like the liberals, however, the conservatives split over Bismarck's policies in the 1860s. One group, initially called the Old Conservative Party, opposed German unification as masterminded by Bismarck and found the Bismarckian constitution much too democratic. Only in 1876 did these conservatives reconcile with Bismarck, changing their name to German Conservative Party. The other group, the Free Conservative Party, approved Bismarck's course toward German unification and became a generally reliable supporter of his policies in the Reichstag for most of his career. Despite their narrow social base, the electoral strength of the two conservative parties was impressive. In the 1870s, both parties won approximately 10 percent of the Reichstag seats each, and in the 1880s they at times managed to hold almost a third of the seats (with the German Conservative Party becoming about twice as strong as the Free Conservative Party). Two factors explain the strong Reichstag representation of the conservative parties: first, the conservative landowners in the eastern regions of Prussia were able to manipulate the popular vote in their districts. Before 1903, secret ballot boxes were not standard, and aristocratic landlords often stood by and watched the choices of "their" rural laborers. Even after 1903, a landlord, seeing on the official lists that there were some left-wing votes in his district, could seek ways to punish the suspected "perpetrators." Second, conservative resistance in the bureaucracy and the government effectively blocked the redrawing of the voting districts until the revolution of 1918–19. Already by the 1880s, massive migration from rural areas to the industrial cities had created a significant imbalance, and by the 1890s some urban districts had several times the number of voters than some rural districts. Since each district still elected only one representative, the existing system strongly benefited the more rural-based parties, above all the conservatives and the Center Party. The conservative parties therefore won more votes than they would have received in truly secret elections (until 1903), and their rural base gave them a disproportionately large number of Reichstag seats.

Several smaller parties existed outside the liberal, conservative, and Catholic spectrum. The national minorities in Prussian Poland, Alsace-Lorraine, and northern Schleswig all sent deputies to the Reichstag, where they often aligned loosely with the Center Party – attracted by its federalist stance and, in the case of Alsace-Lorraine and Prussian Poland, its Catholicism. A small but long-lived party represented the Welfs, a German minority unhappy about the absorption of Hannover into Prussia in 1866. In the later 1870s, some parties constituted themselves on the basis of anti-Semitism. The most notable of them was led by Adolf Stoecker, the official chaplain at the Prussian court, who aimed to combine anti-Jewish resentment with social reform. But none of the anti-Semitic parties had much success at the polls. In the 1890s, their modest share of Reichstag seats melted away.

In the long run, the most important smaller party under Bismarck was the Socialist Workers' Party (SAP), which renamed itself Social Democratic Party of Germany (SPD) in 1890. The SAP, founded through a merger of small working-class parties in 1875, forged a compromise of Marxist-revolutionary and reformist or trade-unionist elements. It was committed to democracy, universal, equal, and secret suffrage in all elections, a range of social reforms, freedom of speech and publication, and a people's militia – a demand inspired by the defeat of revolutionaries by reactionary professional armies in 1848–49. In some respects, the SAP echoed liberal concerns, as in its demands for a fully secular, state-supported education, but its claims for protective legislation for workers and its revolutionary rhetoric alienated the liberals. The SAP did not receive a strong representation in the Reichstag until 1890, but its vote grew rapidly and was always much stronger than its share of

Reichstag seats. In 1890, for example, the SAP received almost 20 percent of the popular vote – more than any other party – but less than 10 percent of the Reichstag seats. This discrepancy came from the fact that the industrial workers, the main support of this party, were concentrated in a few densely populated urban voting districts. Another factor was the SAP's radicalism, which at this time precluded it from forming alliances with other parties. This was important because the constitution stipulated that districts without an absolute majority for one candidate had to hold a run-off election during which the candidate who received a plurality of votes would win. For these run-off elections parties negotiated agreements to put a combined vote behind one party's candidate in exchange for a combined vote for the other party's candidate in another district. Before the 1890s, the SAP rarely benefited from these alliances because other parties tended to treat it as a pariah and often pooled their votes to prevent an SAP candidate from winning a contested seat. Despite the weakness of the SAP's representation in the Reichstag, Bismarck watched the rise of this party with growing concern. Since the 1860s, he had hoped to neutralize the rising socialist movement through the promise of social reform, but the open democratic demands of the SAP alarmed him. Already in 1878 he won a Reichstag majority in favor of outlawing most of the SAP's activities. The party's candidates were allowed, however, to participate in elections and serve in the Reichstag even as their newspapers and election posters were illegal.

The regional division of the German Empire overlapped with its division according to party lines. There is no doubt that Prussia dominated united Germany. Prussia, boosted by its annexations of 1866, had nearly two-thirds of Germany's population and territory and by far the most powerful army and economy. Prussian and German politics were closely interwoven. At the top was the personal union of Prussian king and German emperor. The Prussian minister president and the German chancellor were also one and the same person – although this was not demanded by the constitution (Bismarck for a while gave up the office of Prussian minister president but reversed his decision when he realized how much power the Prussian minister president, who was also president of the Bundesrat, possessed; in 1917–18, the offices were separated again under very different conditions). A symbiosis of Prussian and German politics also existed at the middle and lower levels of the political structure. Most national business was initially conducted by Prussian ministries, and when Bismarck began building up a German national administration, he drafted most personnel from the Prussian administration. The preponderance of Prussia in the national administration did not weigh too heavily, however, because the separate states retained much autonomy and because the national administration was not yet very powerful. Tax authority, for example, still rested predominantly with the single states. Although a national German law code was developed, the courts, the police, the universities, and in some way the armies (at least in peacetime) remained within the purview of the states. Historians have also pointed out that the identity of most Germans remained focused on the region (even below the level of the states). This was particularly relevant in Prussia, which contained a conglomerate of territories acquired fairly recently (in 1815 and 1866).[2] As a consequence, a sense of "Prussian" identity, as far as it existed, was confined largely to the old territories of Prussia around Berlin and in East Prussia. The largest and most powerful German state thus also harbored some of its own particularist movements, such as the above-mentioned Welfs in Hannover.

In this context, it has to be considered that the German Empire of 1871 was not at all congruent with the area of ethnic German settlement in Europe. It included national minorities and excluded millions of Germans. Inside the empire, the Poles were by far the largest national minority (approximately three million in a population of fifty million in 1890). In eastern Germany, some areas were inhabited predominantly by Poles, and large areas had mixed Polish and German settlement. Germans tended to predominate in the cities; Poles in the countryside. There was much Polish migration into Germany, as thousands of migrant workers crossed the border to provide cheap labor to Prussian landlords in the east; many of these migrant workers sooner or later decided to remain in Germany, often leaving the backward East to work for German industry in the West, particularly in the Ruhr Basin. Whereas many Poles were receptive to Polish nationalism, some Polish groups such as the Protestant Masurians in East Prussia embraced Germanization. The nationalist Poles tried to protect their language and cultural institutions against the repressive policies launched by Bismarck, which targeted the Poles both as a national minority and as Catholics. Under Bismarck, who felt contempt for Polish culture, the use of the Polish language in the schools, the courtrooms, and in all official business was restricted and ultimately banned. In 1885, 48,000 Poles who had no German citizenship papers were expelled across the border into the Russian Empire. The situation of the Poles was particularly frustrating considering that they had no state of their own that they could have joined. The majority of ethnic Poles lived under Russian rule, which was considered even worse than Prussian-German rule.

The small Danish minority in northern Schleswig had a state outside Germany and faced less oppressive measures than the Poles, but it also had to organize itself for the protection of its language and institutions. Although there was a belt of mixed settlement, the bulk of Germany's Danes lived in an area right on the border to Denmark. If given the choice, they would probably have opted to secede from Germany and joined Denmark (as they did during the plebiscites following the First World War). A slightly different situation existed in Alsace-Lorraine. Aside from a strong minority of French-speakers particularly in Lorraine, most people in Alsace-Lorraine spoke (and still speak) a southwest German dialect and were therefore considered ethnic Germans. Alsace-Lorraine was governed as a conquered territory by the German Empire after 1871. Until 1911, it had no representation in the Bundesrat. The people of Alsace-Lorraine therefore often felt that they were considered second-class German citizens. There are signs indicating that loyalty to

Germany increased over time. Initially, the province elected only separatist deputies to the Reichstag, but after 1890 some German parties made significant inroads into the electorate of Alsace-Lorraine. Still, it is probably fair to say that a majority in this province continued to favor France over Germany. When Alsace-Lorraine changed hands again in 1918, a few people emigrated to Germany, but the vast majority made possible a smooth reintegration into France.

Millions of ethnic Germans lived outside the new Germany, mostly in Austria-Hungary. There was a continuous area of ethnic German settlement from parts of South Tyrol (now in Italy) through today's Austria into the entire periphery of Bohemia (today's Czech Republic). There were also large groups of Germans in Prague and other cities surrounded by non-Germans, and pockets of German settlement existed all the way along the empire's long frontier zone across the Balkans, from Slovenia to Transylvania. Only few of the Germans in Austria-Hungary considered unification with the German Empire a priority, but this could easily change if the empire collapsed. Although historian Joachim Remak has argued that Austria-Hungary was by no means a doomed empire, there is no doubt that it was becoming increasingly hard to govern as separate nationalisms began to tear it apart.[3] The striving for Czech autonomy, in particular, triggered a militant response among many ethnic Germans in the empire. Bismarck and all of his successors considered the existence of Austria-Hungary essential for German security, so much so that the German government risked the outbreak of a general war in 1914 to maintain its stability. The more radical German nationalists believed that the ethnic German lands adjacent to Germany should be joined with Germany, but this was never one of Bismarck's goals. It would have disturbed the precarious constitutional balance in the German Empire and brought a large number of Catholics into Germany – certainly no desirable outcome in Bismarck's eyes. Other significant pockets of German settlement existed in many regions of Eastern Europe, even deeply inside Russia, but these areas were too dispersed to offer themselves as targets of any but the most fanciful annexation plans.

Another important fault line in Germany was religion. This aspect was connected with the long fragmentation of Germany. France, which had been divided on religious grounds in the sixteenth century, was made into an overwhelmingly Catholic country by the centralizing royal administration under Louis XIV – at the price of bloody persecution of other religious groups (particularly the Protestant Huguenots). In Germany, the religious peace of Augsburg (1555) had recognized the right of the territorial lords to determine the religion of their states. Given its territorial fragmentation, the Holy Roman Empire became a complex puzzle of different religious areas. Tolerance for religious minorities became more common in the eighteenth century, so that some religiously mixed areas developed. Generally, the South and West of Germany remained predominantly Catholic (with some strong Protestant pockets particularly in Württemberg and with much mixing in the cities), whereas the East and North remained largely Protestant (with the exception of Silesia, which Prussia took from Austria in 1740, and also with much mixing in urban areas). Although organized religion lost importance for many Europeans in the second half of the nineteenth century, the religious divide in Germany was a liability for a unified state because it also meant different cultures, mindsets, and value systems. The growth and persistence of the Center Party shows how strongly the religious dividing line between Protestants and Catholics influenced the political landscape of the German Empire.

One specific religious minority deserves separate mention: the Jews. In 1867, the constitution of the North German Confederation granted Jews equal civil rights (which had happened earlier in some of the southern states). Most of Germany's Jews were already on the way to assimilation by that time. Conversions to Christianity and mixed Christian-Jewish marriages were common, and many Jews, like urban German non-Jews, gave less importance to their religious affiliation than previous generations had done. There was some immigration of poor, Orthodox Jews from Russian Poland, but these newcomers were generally seen as foreigners by the German Jews, too. Many German Jews belonged to the middle classes and were strongly represented among the economic and cultural elites despite discrimination in some careers (judges, officers, higher administrators). Anti-Semitism was widespread, though not more so than in most other European countries. It intensified in the wake of the economic crisis beginning in 1873, when Jewish bankers and businessmen received much of the blame for unemployment and the failure of small businesses. Several theorists, such as Paul de Lagarde and Wilhelm Marr, who coined the word anti-Semitism, justified resentment of Jews on the basis of alleged racial instead of religious characteristics. But parties that made anti-Semitism their central cause quickly failed after modest electoral gains in the 1880s. The German state did not condone anti-Semitic violence. During an anti-Semitic riot, the army protected Jews without question.

The political, ethnic, and religious divisions in the new Germany all helped to shape the dynamics of German politics until 1918 and partly beyond, but they were hardly fatal and hardly more divisive than political fault lines in other countries. One social division, however, was more difficult to tackle. In social terms, Germany is considered to have been divided roughly along the Elbe River – a line from Dresden to Hamburg. East of this line, middle to large landholdings under powerful landlords were common. These mostly aristocratic lords had until not too long ago benefited from serfdom and later from feudal services of "their" peasants. Although the peasants had been liberated in 1848, many lords still cultivated an air of superiority and control over the largely poor peasants. The lords also benefited from the deal that the Prussian king had given them in the Prussian Constitution of 1850: they controlled a disproportionate share of the Prussian diet right up to 1918. Although these lords modernized their holdings and increased output and efficiency, they increasingly felt the pinch of international agricultural competition. With their entrenched political power and close connections to the crown, the landlords stubbornly defended their privileges and opposed modernization and democratization. In the west of Germany, most peasants had been freer and owned small to mid-size landholdings. Urbanization was higher in Germany west of the Elbe, and this half of Germany also contained the largest industrial area, the Ruhr Basin. Mentalities and culture to some extent also differed. East Elbian Germany was a more thoroughly Protestant region that had never been romanized. Germany west of the Elbe had largely been conquered by the Romans, was more Catholic, and had seen much stronger French and Western influence. This line can perhaps be compared to the fault line dividing the northwest of Yugoslavia from the rest of the country and perhaps also to the line dividing northern Italy from the South. Referring to the case of Yugoslavia, historian Gale Stokes argues that state building across this line has always been a difficult undertaking; the cases of Italy and Germany tend to underscore his point.[4] Of course, dividing Europe into a more urbanized, more commercial, and more enlightened west and a backward east would overlook many shadings of development in different parts of the continent. But it is hard to refute the point that the east Elbian region of Germany was based on a different social structure from the region west of the Elbe and that this had important political repercussions, just as the north-south divide has left a complicated legacy in Italy. In East Elbia, traditional privileges and mentalities persisted much longer, and this provided an important impediment to all efforts for the democratization of the German Empire.

The consolidation of Germany's political system took place amid a not-too-favorable economic framework. After a boom period fed largely by the French payments in 1871–3, Germany began to feel the effects of a Europe-wide economic crisis that lasted until the mid-1890s. Financially unsound schemes for railroads played a role in triggering the crisis, as did over-production in industry and agriculture. German industrial products, though generally still successful, faced much international competition, while cheap food imports from the United States and Russia put pressure on German agriculture. This economic crisis should not be imagined as a dramatic downturn such as the Great Depression in 1929 and the 1930s. Industrialization continued in Germany as elsewhere in Europe, albeit with a slower rate of growth. But contemporaries experienced the beginning of the crisis, which brought unemployment and initially many business failures, as a dramatic event, and fears of recession and insurmountable trade barriers lingered on into the 1880s.

The big parameters of Bismarck's domestic politics were repressive policies against Catholics, Social Democrats, and Poles as well as a gradual alienation from the National Liberals and rapprochement with the conservatives. Until 1878, Bismarck relied largely on National Liberal support in the Reichstag, and even the left liberal parties mounted little opposition to him at this time. Through national unification, Bismarck had fulfilled a long-standing dream of German liberals. Moreover, Bismarck's initial commitment to free trade pleased them, as did his support for a uniform German law code, which was being drafted during his tenure in office although it was not passed by the Reichstag until 1896. Another policy also won liberal support although it threatened to compromise liberal principles: the struggle against the influence of the Catholic Church, *Kulturkampf* in German, which means "struggle about culture" or "struggle of cultures." The *Kulturkampf* was part of a wider European phenomenon. In several countries, governments influenced or dominated by liberalism challenged the traditional role of the Catholic Church in society. Battlefields were, among others, the role of the Church in education and marriage, the appointment of bishops, as well as the status of the Jesuit order, which was considered to be the most reactionary force of the Church. In Switzerland, this issue had led to a civil war of Catholic against Protestant cantons in 1847, which was won by the Protestants. In France, the struggle had begun after the revolutionary government took control of the Catholic Church in 1791, which triggered a conflict with the Papacy and split the French clergy and parishioners into a group loyal to the state constitution and a refractory group loyal to Rome. Although Napoleon I calmed the troubled waters through a concordat (Church-state agreement) with the pope, the conflict dragged on until the early twentieth century, when it resulted in a liberal victory – the complete separation of state and church in 1905. In Italy, the issue was complicated by the fact that Italian unification had gradually robbed the pope of his own state, which until 1860 had included large territories in central Italy. Until 1870, the pope held on to a territory around Rome, which was guarded by a French protection force. In 1870, however, the French withdrew their troops because of the Franco-German War, and Italy annexed Rome and its surroundings. The Vatican did not forgive this, and the liberal Italian republic and the Church never really made peace; it fell to the fascist regime of Benito Mussolini to accomplish that feat through a concordat in 1929.

Following the unification of Italy as a liberal state, the Vatican became more aggressive in taking on the liberal challenge across Europe. In 1864, Pope Pius IX issued the *syllabus errorum*, a document sharply condemning liberalism, and in 1870, the First Vatican Council adopted the doctrine of papal infallibility. This radicalization of papal policy created unrest in the Church and provoked mistrust in liberal circles. Catholic bishops and priests were now often called "ultramontane" in Germany, implying that their primary loyalty was "across the mountain" (meaning the Alps) to Rome and not to the new German state. This was not entirely fair given that the German bishops had opposed the doctrine of papal infallibility and fought for a more moderate line. The foundation of the Center Party and the fact that it collaborated with the national minorities in the Reichstag convinced Bismarck that Catholics represented a hostile element in his new state and that only an attack on their organizations would create the preconditions for integrating them. This attack drew much liberal support because it led to a greater secularization of the school system, mandatory civil marriage, the repression of the Jesuit Order, and a greater role of the state in the appointment of bishops. Some of this legislation, however, compromised the liberal commitment to freedom of expression. A law of 1871, for example, forbade criticism of the state in a sermon, and several other laws against priests violated civil liberties and led to the expatriation of priests on questionable legal grounds.

It is doubtful that Bismarck could have avoided the struggle with the Catholic Church altogether. There was too much flammable material. How, for example, should the German states react if, as happened repeatedly, the Vatican threatened theology professors at the state universities with prohibition from teaching or, worse, excommunication because they refused to accept the dogma of papal infallibility? A modern nation state, moreover, could hardly tolerate teachings in elementary schools and at theological faculties of its universities that were hostile to the state and its values. Nor could the domain of marriage be left within the purview of the Church at a time when liberal law codes increasingly digressed from traditional Church morality. The collision was bound to happen, and Pope Pius IX's intransigent policies only helped to accelerate it. Yet Bismarck could have exploited the divisions within the Church. It was obvious that many, perhaps most, German bishops and priests did not condone Pius' radicalism. A less aggressive course against the Church could have drawn more support from German Catholics and perhaps led to a more moderate secularization acceptable to both sides (even if opposed by the Pope). Instead, Bismarck was deliberately confrontational and gave free rein to radical anti-clerical liberals in the Prussian state administration. The result was an impressive strengthening of political Catholicism. The vote of the Center Party increased, and state repression created many popular heroes among the Catholic clergy. Although the Catholic Church initially seemed to split as it had under the pressure of the secularizing French state in 1791, the antagonistic state policies in the long run increased Catholic solidarity and created an increasingly stable bulwark among German Catholics. If the goal of the *Kulturkampf* had been to integrate German Catholics into the new state, it failed. Catholics, in a defiant siege mentality, were integrated into the Center Party and other Catholic organizations but not (yet) into the German state. Bismarck acknowledged this outcome when he toned down the *Kulturkampf* in 1878. He was helped by a new pope, Leo XIII, who was willing to mend fences and seek out a compromise. In the following nine years, the most objectionable *Kulturkampf* laws were repealed or mitigated; only the anti-Jesuit law remained valid until 1917. Historian Hans-Ulrich Wehler appreciates the modernizing achievements of the *Kulturkampf* while deploring its anti-liberal excesses and the painful legacy they left for German Catholics as well as for Germany's political culture until 1945. He detects a pervasive siege mentality in German Catholicism that strengthened pockets of anti-modern cultural resentment and made many leading Catholics obsessed with supporting almost every government in order to prevent a repeat of state-sponsored persecution (most fatally so in 1933 after the appointment of Hitler). He further argues that many Catholics felt compelled henceforth to prove their loyalty to Germany through excessive and blind nationalism.[5] To be sure, the *Kulturkampf* should not be imagined as a bloody repression with the help of a sinister and mean police force. It generally progressed in legal channels and at worst brought prison terms or expatriation to recalcitrant priests. The Center Party was able to organize itself and participate in elections – quite successfully. Still, the *Kulturkampf* for generations made Catholics feel that they were second-class citizens who had to prove their loyalty to Germany, and it compromised many German liberals, whose anti-clerical zeal overrode their commitment to the state of law and to civil liberties.

The year 1878 not only marked a break in Bismarck's handling of the *Kulturkampf* – it also indicated a more profound change in his policy. After long hesitation, Bismarck finally committed himself to protective tariffs for German industry and agriculture. The onset of the economic crisis in 1873 had nurtured doubts in the advantages of free trade, and liberals of all shadings encountered increasing popular resentment against their support for free trade. Bismarck began supporting tariffs for a variety of reasons. He probably believed they had economic benefits, but they suited him for other reasons as well. One reason had to do with the financial basis of the German Empire. Since direct taxation was a matter of the single states, the empire was largely dependent on some indirect taxes and on voluntary contributions from the single states. Tariffs would increase imperial revenue and make the imperial government less dependent on the states. Tariffs also would ease a rapprochement between Bismarck and those Prussian conservatives who still opposed him. Most conservatives desired tariffs on agricultural imports in order to protect their own economic position; given that Prussia had a property-based suffrage, an economic decline of the big landlords also meant that they would weaken politically. Tariffs were popular in the later 1870s, and they were not anathema to the Center Party with its strong rural base. Bismarck therefore saw the introduction of tariffs as a way of forging a new support base around both conservative parties and with tacit support from the Center Party, which had, of course, an interest in mellowing out the *Kulturkampf*. This power base would be independent of the liberals whose popularity was waning in any case. After the liberals lost many seats during the elections of 1878, Bismarck managed to pass the tariffs through the Reichstag, even drawing some support from National Liberal deputies worried about foreign competition for German industry.

Bismarck also needed a new power base for a crucial policy of his later years: the repression of socialism. He was not opposed at all to the idea of social reform. In the 1860s, he had fostered contacts with moderate socialist leader Ferdinand Lassalle, who advocated relief through social legislation by the state. Lassalle, however, was killed during a duel, and the socialist movement in Germany had become influenced by more radical socialists. When the workers of Paris rose up in 1871, forming a socialist "Paris Commune" in the wake of the French defeat, they sent a shockwave through much of Europe. Although the Paris Commune was much less radical than its brutal oppressors made the world believe, the specter of revolution and anarchy that seemed to have been banned in 1849 was rising again. When German socialist leader August Bebel condemned the annexation of Alsace-Lorraine and praised the Paris Commune, he was sent to prison. Bismarck was greatly alarmed to see men like Bebel at the head of the rapidly increasing German socialist movement. Continuing industrialization and the growing disenchantment with free trade boosted the socialists, who founded their united party, the SAP, in 1875. Like Catholicism with its ties to the national minorities and to a power center outside of his control, the socialists now appeared to Bismarck as a monster with many vile heads. He feared their commitment to democracy, their potential for revolutionary action (although with little reason), and their excellent prospects for increased electoral strength offered by continued industrialization and the growth of the industrial working class. Bismarck repeatedly tried to initiate legislation restraining socialist propaganda, but the liberals blocked almost all of his initiatives out of concern for civil liberties – at the same time as they compromised their stance on civil liberties in the *Kulturkampf* legislation. Yet even the liberals became worried when in the elections of 1877 the SAP received 9 percent of the national vote and increased its Reichstag group from 9 to 12 seats. Finally, in May 1878, Bismarck believed he had found the decisive excuse for pushing through a restrictive anti-socialist law: Max Hödel, an artisan who had once been an SAP member, opened fire on Kaiser Wilhelm I. The Kaiser, who was riding through the center of Berlin in an open coach, was not hit. Bismarck immediately claimed that the socialists had inspired the would-be assassin. The truth was that no connection existed between the SAP and Hödel's assassination attempt. Hödel had been expelled from the SAP because he had embezzled party funds, and he had subsequently joined the Christian Social Party led by Adolf Stoecker, the court chaplain! Moreover, the socialists, unlike the anarchists, did not condone political assassinations. But Bismarck, who had a tendency to lump all revolutionary movements together, tried to capitalize on public outrage at the assassination attempt on the popular Kaiser by presenting the Reichstag with a sharp anti-socialist bill. However, the bill violated so many fundamental laws that a vast majority in the Reichstag, including the liberal parties, defeated it. Bismarck had barely digested this parliamentary defeat when another assassination attempt on the Kaiser triggered even more outrage and provided him with a welcome excuse for dissolving the recalcitrant Reichstag. This time, the Kaiser was seriously wounded and had to hand over power to Crown Prince Friedrich Wilhelm for a couple of weeks while he was recovering. Bismarck spread rumors that the perpetrator of the second assassination attempt, Dr. Karl Nobiling, was a socialist. The truth was, and Bismarck knew it well, that Nobiling was a mentally deranged farmer with no connection to any socialist party. With speeches and newspaper articles filled with fiery rhetoric against the socialists, Bismarck put pressure on the liberals, who were already on the defensive because of the economic downturn. He depicted the socialists as a band of murderers and robbers and argued that all means were justified to annihilate these "rats" that had declared war on the state.[6] The result was an electoral victory of the conservative parties and a crushing defeat for the

National Liberals and the left liberals. The humbled National Liberals now proved willing to override their liberal principles and to vote for the proposed anti-socialist legislation, which passed with their votes and the support of the conservative parties. The left liberals and the SAP voted against, as did, Bismarck's conciliatory moves on the *Kulturkampf* front notwithstanding, the Center Party, the most recent victim of discriminatory legislation.

The anti-socialist laws outlawed a broad range of socialist organizations including the SAP. They forbade socialist assemblies, newspapers, and speeches. Violators received prison sentences and could be expelled from the country, as had happened to refractory priests only a few years earlier. The laws did not bar socialists from participating in elections and from sitting in the Reichstag. The SAP actually built up a clandestine support network and smuggled its pamphlets and newspapers to Germany from print shops established in liberal Switzerland. Except for a setback in 1881, its Reichstag group kept growing at an impressive pace. The time of the anti-socialist laws, which were renewed several times until 1890, was to the socialist movement what the time of the *Kulturkampf* was to many activist Catholics. The repression was generally not traumatic; it bolstered group solidarity and inspired many personal stories of heroic escape and defiance. It also reinforced a profound distrust of the state authorities and the sense that socialists were second- or even third-class citizens in Germany. In some ways, the socialists learned during the period of repression that they had to rely on themselves, and this helped promote the buildup of a powerful socialist network after 1890, which became something of a state within the state. Some historians also argue that the repression made the socialists so reluctant to envision participation in state governments that they were poorly prepared when power fell into their laps in 1918. In terms of Bismarck's goals, the anti-socialist policy was a failure that produced, like the *Kulturkampf*, the opposite of what it was meant to achieve. The repression by the state was harsh enough to enhance group solidarity and give credibility to the socialists' revolutionary rhetoric about a repressive state in the service of the upper classes. But it was not harsh enough to destroy the SAP network. The SAP, like the Center Party, became stronger, not weaker.

After having driven the SAP into illegality, Bismarck made one of his unorthodox moves, in line with the introduction of universal suffrage in the North German Confederation: he began pushing for social reform. Bismarck's Christian faith may have made him receptive to calls for an improvement of the situation of the working class, but he also believed that social reform could woo the workers away from the socialism sponsored by a now repressed party hovering in the underground. Throughout the 1880s, Bismarck introduced various social security bills in the Reichstag, which usually passed after heavy debates and in the face of much opposition from the liberals. Bismarck's social legislation is considered so path-breaking that the United States Social Security administration features a picture of Bismarck on its website.[7] The landmark legislation was a health insurance bill

(1883), an accident insurance bill (1884), and an old-age and disability bill (1889). Historians argue over the merits of this legislation. The benefits were small, and not all workers qualified for them. The old age bill, for example, applied only to male workers who were at least seventy years old, but in the 1880s barely a quarter of all men reached that age! Still, these laws were an important start. Legislation implemented after Bismarck's tenure in office created a more comprehensive social security network on the basis of what he had done. As a political strategy, however, the social security laws failed. Most workers resented the paternalist approach by the same state that was repressing their organizations. They generally did not want handouts from the state; they wanted to fight for what they considered their rights. The social security laws were as ineffective as the anti-socialist laws in stemming the tide of socialism in Germany.

On balance, Bismarck left a mixed record in domestic policy. One thing he did well was to manipulate and preserve his own power, but this was also a problem. His special legislation against Catholics, socialists, and Poles compromised or at least tarnished the law even while binding different party coalitions to him. Against his perceived and real opponents, he often was petty and jealous, thinking in categories of black and white and thus failing to recognize and exploit their internal differences. But he was also able to tone down his hateful rhetoric and woo his opponents; he did so with the Center Party, and there are signs that he might also have considered some arrangement with the socialists had he stayed in office longer. He tried everything he could to restrict the power of the Reichstag and sometimes entertained the idea of an authoritarian government with the help of corporations, institutions representing the groups involved in the national economy – essentially an idea foreshadowing fascism. Many historians believe that he delayed the democratization of Germany and prevented a more liberal state order. But is this a justified reproach? Bismarck was a man of the nineteenth century, a conservative, and somebody whose political outlook had been shaped during the age of reaction before 1848. How much latitude would have been available to him had he really wanted to create a more liberal and democratic Germany? After all, he was the prime minister of a king who could always dismiss him. He could perhaps have avoided duplicating that arrangement in the constitution for the German Empire, but would he have received the support of the king? Bismarck had too much trouble pushing his policies through against the opposition from his own political quarters, the conservatives, to be more of an innovator than he already was. His two most unorthodox measures – unorthodox for a conservative – were perhaps his most successful in the long run: the introduction of universal suffrage and the social security legislation. Both measures were motivated by dubious power schemes, the former against the liberals and the latter against the socialists, but they did create the foundations for a democratic and social state, even if that was squarely against Bismarck's intentions and even if it took much more work to raise a building on Bismarck's foundations. Universal suffrage was difficult to take away. More and more Germans demanded that it be applied to all state and local elections as well, and some Germans demanded that it be granted to women. A Reichstag majority legitimized by universal suffrage was difficult to ignore even if Bismarck's constitution did not allow the Reichstag to overthrow the chancellor and his government. The social security system provided the basis for a German social welfare state. This is an important issue. No government after Bismarck really tried to reverse this achievement. Instead, the social security network became tighter and better over the decades. One of the crucial elements of Hitler's initial success came from his efforts to build on the foundation that Bismarck had laid. After 1945, there was no going back either. Both German states founded in 1949 made social welfare their central concern.

How did Bismarck fare as a foreign policy maker? He was, in personal union, German chancellor and foreign minister for most of his period in office. Many political scientists and historians see his foreign policy as a success story. The term *Realpolitik*, meaning an unemotional foreign policy strictly focused on reality and national interest rather than on ideology and morality, is connected with Bismarck's name. Yet it has to be noted that Bismarck did not consider foreign and domestic policy as separate. He often tried to use a foreign policy success to his advantage in domestic policy, which was a modern feature at a time when a nationalist mass public was just beginning to form, and it was again an approach he had seen practiced by Napoleon III. Using success in foreign policy for domestic advantage had been on Bismarck's mind already during the wars of unification: the expectation that successful wars would overcome the constitutional conflict with the liberal majority in the Prussian diet and split the liberal movement was part of his overall plan. The foreign policy after 1871 often had a domestic aspect, too. The only difference was that Bismarck no longer resorted to war after 1871. Why not?

Bismarck held that Germany was a satiated state and, unlike Hitler in the late 1930s, he meant it. He had absolutely no interest in bringing "home" the millions of Germans living outside his empire by conquest and annexation or by any other means. This does not mean that Bismarck suddenly turned into a pacifist; no, he was still willing to go to war and on some occasions used the threat of war for diplomatic ends, but he made it very clear that he would not wage a war of conquest. Maybe it was his greatest achievement that he did not push for further expansion after 1871, except for the acquisition of colonies, in which he did not fully believe. Bismarck always displayed a keen sense for the vulnerability of Germany in the center of Europe, surrounded by the other great powers and with borders that were difficult to defend. His foreign policy was as manipulative as his domestic policy, but it served a purpose that received increasing recognition in foreign capitals: the preservation of stability and security around Germany. Bismarck was bothered by the fact that one of the great powers, France, was for the near future implacably hostile to Germany. His priority therefore was to prevent France from winning allies that could pressure Germany and perhaps help France in a war to avenge its defeat and loss of Alsace-Lorraine. To this purpose, he constructed a delicate system of alliances and encouraged French colonial expansion so as to divert French resentment away from Alsace-Lorraine and to keep France on a conflict course with other colonial powers.

The cornerstone of Bismarck's security system was an alliance with both Austria-Hungary and Russia. This triangular alliance had famous precedents, such as the agreements resulting in the partition of Poland in 1772 to 1795 and the Holy Alliance concluded at the Congress of Vienna, and it rested on some community of interest. All three empires were conservative and anti-democratic, and they all held a share of Poland and therefore had no interest in reviving Poland as a nation. Germany and Russia had no border disputes and no conflicting interests in overseas regions. Austria-Hungary still resented the defeat of 1866 but was too afraid of Russia to take a clear anti-German stand in 1870. That Austria-Hungary had been treated generously by Prussia after the war of 1866 helped pave the way for a mutual understanding. Bismarck, who had often expressed contempt and hatred for Austria before 1866 now considered friendship with Austria-Hungary essential for German security – as long as that friendship did not come at the expense of German-Russian relations. He consequently took a strong interest in the stability of Austria-Hungary. A disintegrating Austria-Hungary would conjure up instability and the danger of Russian expansion. Remaining on good terms with Austria-Hungary and Russia at the same time was no simple feat, however. The two empires were fierce rivals in the Balkans, where the declining Ottoman Empire was leaving a power vacuum. Russia was interested in expanding toward Constantinople (today's Istanbul) and the Dardanelles, the connection between the Mediterranean Sea and the Black Sea. Russia had few ports that were free of ice all year long, and most of them were in the Black Sea. However, Russian sea traffic had to pass the Dardanelles if it did not want to be confined to the Black Sea, and Russian warships were not allowed through this sensitive passage, which went right through Constantinople, the Ottoman capital. Austria-Hungary's interests in the Balkans were more defensive than Russia's. Conquering more territories with a predominantly Slavic population did not seem desirable because it might increase instability within the empire. On the other hand, Austria-Hungary had an interest in preventing a hostile and strong Slavic power, especially Serbia, from emerging because it could become a rallying point for the many South Slavs (Yugoslavs) in the Austro-Hungarian Empire. For the time being, Austria-Hungary managed to foster good relations with a weak Serbia, which was dependent on the Austrian market for its principal exports, pork and fruit. Russia, however, was stoking the fires of Southern Slavic nationalisms, making use of the linguistic, cultural, and religious (Christian Orthodox) affinities between Serbia, Bulgaria, and Russia. The Balkans was not the only avenue of Russian expansionism in the late nineteenth and early twentieth century, but Russia's interests in Persia and northeastern China did not threaten Austria-Hungary and had the benefit of keeping Britain worried about Russia. Britain also opposed Russian expansion on the Balkans because it did not want a Russian naval presence in the eastern Mediterranean, which would materialize if Russia gained control of Constantinople.

Bismarck sounded out the prospects for an alliance with Austria-Hungary and Russia soon after the foundation of the German Empire. His efforts led to an agreement in 1873, when the three monarchs concluded the League of Three Emperors in Vienna. This treaty was a commitment to consult with each other and to work toward the prevention of war in Europe. It was important for Bismarck because it helped mitigate tensions between Austria and Russia, but it was not a close-knit alliance. Its limitations became clear during an international crisis in April and May 1875, when the German General Staff, worried about the speed of the French economic and military recovery, began talking about the threat of a French attack and the possibility of a preventive war against France. Bismarck probably did not want a preventive war, but he decided to test the waters by inspiring two newspaper articles that openly hinted at that possibility. The outcome of this "war in sight" crisis was sobering for Bismarck. That the press reaction in France was hostile could have been predicted, but the British press also acted in an outraged and alarmed manner. Worse, the Russian and British governments both made it clear to Bismarck that they would not tolerate a further weakening of France (although it is by no means sure that this would have been the outcome of a Franco-German war in 1875; France was militarily better prepared than Germany at this time). It was painfully obvious that the European powers, perhaps with the exception of Austria-Hungary, were seeing the new Germany, and no longer France, as the primary potential threat to the balance of power in Europe. Even Russia, the Three Emperors' League notwithstanding, would likely have declared war on Germany had it attacked France. Bismarck, who claimed to have sleepless nights and nightmares about hostile coalitions, saw his worst fears confirmed. Any threat by Germany would probably foster an alliance of France, Russia, and Britain.[8] It speaks for Bismarck, however, that he learned his lesson and quickly poured oil over the troubled waters.

The "war in sight crisis" had barely passed when a new conflict in the Balkans provoked tensions between Austria-Hungary and Russia. It began with an uprising of Serb-Orthodox and Muslim peasants against Muslim landlords in Bosnia-Herzegovina, which belonged to the Ottoman Empire. The uprising soon took on a religious character and led to mass killings of Muslim peasants by Orthodox Serbs in eastern Bosnia. At the same time, a popular uprising in Bulgaria, also within the Ottoman Empire, was brutally repressed by the Ottomans. Austria-Hungary and Russia watched each other with suspicion as the crisis dragged on and as the Ottomans began crushing Bulgarian and Serbian resistance. At the behest of Bismarck, however, Austria-Hungary and Russia negotiated an agreement in 1877 that sanctioned a Russian military intervention against the Ottoman Empire while giving Austria-Hungary the right to occupy Bosnia-Herzegovina, which geographically was like a wedge reaching into Austro-Hungarian Croatia. Russian armies attacked and quickly defeated the Ottomans, pushing on toward Constantinople in the winter of 1877–8. After this victory, Russia forced the Ottoman Empire to sign the Treaty of San Stefano, which recognized the independence of Russia's allies Serbia (which had enjoyed de facto independence since 1815) and Bulgaria while giving them generous territorial enlargements. This treaty, however, was not preceded by consultation with any other power, and it went beyond the Russian agreement with Austria-Hungary from 1877. Austria-Hungary was outraged, as was Britain. International pressure compelled Russia to agree to a conference that would revise the Treaty of San Stefano. It speaks for Bismarck's international prestige at this time that the European powers agreed to call him as a mediator and to convene a congress in Berlin.

During this conference, Bismarck tried hard to act as an "honest broker," aware that Germany had no direct interests in the Balkans and that its security was best served by preserving peace between its allies Austria-Hungary and Russia. Russia succeeded in getting international recognition for Serbia's independence (as well as for the independence of Montenegro, which had, like Serbia, enjoyed de facto independence for many decades). But Russia had to concede the division of Bulgaria, whose northern half became independent while its southern half remained under Ottoman rule. Austria-Hungary was allowed to occupy but not to annex Bosnia-Herzegovina, which was henceforth administered jointly by Austrian and Hungarian officials. Although the agreement preserved peace between Austria-Hungary and Russia, Bismarck's primary concern, it did lead to a cooling in German-Russian relations. Russia was thoroughly frustrated because it had to renegotiate a peace agreement after a military victory and make significant concessions. British diplomats, who were deeply suspicious of Russian intentions in the eastern Mediterranean (Britain took Cyprus in order to bolster its strategic position in this region), were probably more responsible for the outcome than Bismarck, but Russian diplomats were disappointed that Bismarck did not support their claims more warmly and gave him much of the blame for the unsatisfactory result. Russia therefore refused to renew the Three Emperors' League, which ran out in the same year. In domestic politics, however, the Congress of Berlin was a great success for Bismarck. He gained respect for his role as leading European statesman, and his obvious international prestige reaffirmed during the congress is widely believed to have improved the electoral showing of his allies, the conservative parties, in the Reichstag elections of 1878.

In international politics, Bismarck next secured a closer alliance with Austria-Hungary. In October 1879, Germany and Austria-Hungary signed the Dual Alliance, which committed both states to helping each other in case of a Russian attack and to observing benevolent neutrality in case of an attack by another power. The terms of the alliance were secret, but it was agreed that they would be made public if Russia threatened either power with war. Wilhelm I, in one of his last disagreements with Bismarck, opposed the Dual Alliance because of its anti-Russian orientation. He gave in only after Bismarck threatened to resign. Bismarck's motives and the wisdom of this treaty for Germany have provoked much debate. To be sure, Germany and Austria-Hungary had had good relations in the preceding years. That Austria-Hungary, given its Balkans rivalry with Russia, had much to gain from a defensive alliance with Germany was clear. But what did Germany have to gain from an alliance with Austria-Hungary, considering that Russian interests, as shown above, did not conflict with German interests? Granted, the Dual Alliance committed Austria-Hungary to neutrality in case of a French attack on Germany, but did Germany have to pay a price for this? During the "war in sight crisis," Austrian policy had been very restrained. The threat from Russia seemed to be sufficient to make Vienna inclined toward neutrality in case of a new Franco-German war. Historians have argued that Bismarck wanted the Dual Alliance as a tool to influence and restrain Austrian policy toward Russia or that he believed that Germany would sooner or later dominate and control a disintegrating Austro-Hungarian empire. The first thesis makes more sense than the second because Bismarck repeatedly stressed the value of a stable Austria-Hungary as an ally of Germany. But the second thesis may also have been in the back of his mind as an alternative plan in case Austro-Hungarian stability could not be maintained. What is most important, however, is that Bismarck did not consider the door to an agreement with Russia closed. For the time being, Russia was frustrated by the Congress of Berlin and by the introduction of protective tariffs in Germany, which hurt its agricultural exports. But Russia, which remained an imperial rival of Britain and could not yet envision an alliance with republican France, soon concluded that an agreement with Germany and Austria-Hungary might serve its interests better than confrontation with the Dual Alliance, particularly in the light of a possible Austro-British alliance. Bismarck therefore succeeded in brokering a new Three Emperors' League in 1881, renewable every three years. This agreement committed the contracting powers to neutrality in case of war between one of them and a fourth power and stipulated that the signatory powers would consult with each other on all territorial changes affecting the Ottoman Empire. Russia agreed that Austria-Hungary would be allowed in the future to annex Bosnia-Herzegovina, and Austria-Hungary agreed to support the reunification of Bulgaria. The neutrality clause was important for Germany because it kept Russia out of a Franco-German war and did not commit Germany to Russia in case of a war between Britain and Russia. Some German foreign officials worried that the terms of the Dual Alliance and the Three Emperors' League might be contradictory. Indeed, during the negotiations for the new Three Emperors' League, Bismarck had consciously deceived the Russians about the German obligation to defend Austria-Hungary against an attack by Russia according to the Dual Alliance. Bismarck was aware of the tensions between both treaties, the first of which was an alliance against the third power involved in the second treaty, but he continued to believe that a close connection between Berlin and Vienna was the best way of keeping Russia attached to both.

Meanwhile, the French declaration of a protectorate over Ottoman Tunisia in 1881 provided Bismarck with an opportunity to broaden the Dual Alliance. Italy had its own designs on the Ottoman territories in north Africa, including Libya and Tunisia. The French protectorate frustrated Italy's colonial ambitions and made it inclined to conclude an anti-French alliance with Germany and Austria-Hungary. The Dual Alliance was therefore complemented by a Triple Alliance in 1882, which promised Italy support in case it was attacked by France and committed Italy to assist Germany and Austria-Hungary in case they were attacked by two other powers, presumably Russia and France. These scenarios were perhaps not very likely in 1882, but the crucial motive for Bismarck was to secure Austria-Hungary against the Italian claims to territories with Italian minorities in South Tyrol, Istria, and along the east coast of the Adriatic Sea (in today's Slovenia and Croatia). He was worried that Italy might attack Austria-Hungary in case of an Austro-Russian war. The French consolidation of a colonial empire in northern Africa kept angering Italy for the next twenty years, but the Triple Alliance did little to assuage Italian desires for Austro-Hungarian territories. It was probably good to have Italy allied with its former enemy Austria-Hungary rather than having to worry about Italy joining France or Russia, but the Triple Alliance was worth very little. In 1902, Italy signed a secret agreement with France, winning French support for the Italian claims to Libya in exchange for Italian recognition of the earlier French acquisitions in northern Africa, and in 1914 the Triple Alliance did not matter at all even though it was still valid. In April 1915, Italy joined the war on the side of France, Russia, and Britain in order finally to satisfy its claims to Austrian territory.

In 1884, Bismarck agreed to establish German colonies in Africa and in the Southern Pacific. This was a surprising move, given that he had previously expressed doubt about the value of colonies. He argued that they would bring little economic benefit and embroil Germany in conflicts with other powers. Since 1881, however, Britain and France had become more assertive in claiming new territories in Africa and Asia. The French protectorate over Tunisia was a reaction to greater British engagement in Egypt, which frustrated France's plans for a great north African empire. In 1884, Britain had concluded a treaty with Portugal regarding rights in the Congo Basin, a land desired by various European powers because of its rich rubber and mineral resources. Colonial expansion became a more popular claim in Germany as well. In this situation, Bismarck called another conference to Berlin. At this second Congress of Berlin, Africa and parts of Asia were divided into zones of influence for the European powers. Although some territories remained disputed, this conference was a milestone in the cynical and arbitrary division of lands by the European powers, who had at this time an enormous advantage in weaponry over the peoples of Africa and most of Asia. The second Congress of Berlin, unlike its predecessor, brought Germany large gains. Within a few days, a German colonial empire emerged that was several times larger than Germany itself – although only with a third of its population. In Africa, Germany acquired Togo, Cameroon, Southwest Africa (today's Namibia), and East Africa (today's Tanzania with Burundi and Rwanda). In the Pacific, Germany received the northeastern part of New Guinea as well as several island groups. With some small exceptions (the Chinese territory of Kiao-Chow was leased by Germany in 1897 and Cameroon was enlarged in 1911 at the expense of neighboring French territories), Bismarck therefore established the German colonial empire. What motivated him?

Historians have not reached a consensus, but it is safe to say that a combination of foreign and domestic factors weighed on Bismarck's mind. He definitely tried to capitalize on French anger at the British involvement in Egypt and consistently encouraged French colonial claims. He may have wanted to show to France that an alliance or at least a rapprochement with Germany would result in colonial benefits, which was no small prize at a time of increasing popular pressure for colonies. As a side benefit, a France heavily engaged in imperialist pursuits might become less concerned about Alsace-Lorraine and seek glory elsewhere. Other historians believe that Bismarck's colonial engagement was primarily meant to increase tensions between Germany and Britain, the pre-eminent colonial power, in order to tie Friedrich Wilhelm's hands toward Britain should he succeed Wilhelm I soon. But this interpretation does not square well with Bismarck's occasional comments that he would be happy to trade in the new German colonies for advantages in Europe, indicating that he did not want a deeper alienation of Britain. Still, domestic motives did influence Bismarck. He must have realized that the colonial hype had reached Germany. German traders had been engaged in most of the territories Germany was awarded at the Congress of Berlin, and these traders demanded state protection against the native population and against the claims of competitors from other European countries. These claims had elicited some supportive public response in Germany. Given that 1884 was an election year, Bismarck expected a fallout from a successful colonial settlement to benefit the parties supportive of his policies and to give the left-leaning Reichstag of 1881 a correction to the right. Some historians also see Bismarck's colonial policy as a plot to unite the German people and thereby to undercut demands for domestic reform, but this appears a bit far-fetched. In 1884, the socialists and the left liberals opposed colonial acquisitions, and it would take a long time to reconcile some of them to colonies. The second Congress of Berlin helped in particular the Free Conservative Party, which always stood behind Bismarck, to win Reichstag seats at the elections of 1884.

Trouble in the Balkans, however, put renewed pressure on Bismarck's foreign policy. A war between Bulgaria and Austrian-backed Serbia in 1885 ended in a defeat of Serbia. Austria-Hungary, as Serbia's ally, was determined not to let Bulgaria, which was under the influence of Russia, exploit this victory, and Austria-Hungary and Russia were inching closer to war. Britain, too, was growing alarmed again about an expansion of Russian influence on the Balkans and hoped for Bismarck to remedy the situation. Bismarck, mindful of how the Congress of Berlin of 1878 had affected German-Russian relations, tried to keep his head above the troubled waters, warning Vienna that Germany would not let itself be embroiled in a war with Russia. Bismarck was particularly worried at this time because a populist French politician with far-reaching political and military ambitions, General Georges Boulanger, had just become French defense minister and was building up much popular momentum for a dictatorship and potentially a war against Germany. Boulanger blundered away his strong position and had to go into exile the following year, but the ease with which he rose, and the popular response elicited by his revanchist rhetoric, made Bismarck more skeptical about the possibility of a Franco-German rapprochement and motivated him to redouble his efforts to prevent an understanding between Russia and France. In the short run, Bismarck succeeded in deflecting tensions by mediating an agreement between Austria-Hungary and Russia to again divide the Balkans into spheres of interest. He also inspired a defensive agreement between Italy and Spain that was meant to isolate France, whose ambitions for a north African empire caused concern in both states. The Three Emperors' League was dead, however. Tsar Alexander III was even insecure whether he wanted any understanding with Germany. A strong Pan-Slavic group at the Russian court believed in an inevitable, racially motivated struggle between Slavic and Germanic peoples and therefore rejected any understanding with Germany or Austria-Hungary. For the time being, however, the Pan-Slavic pressure was kept in check and Bismarck negotiated a bilateral Reinsurance Treaty with Russia in 1887. This treaty, valid for three years, committed both countries to neutrality in a war with a third power unless Russia attacked Austria-Hungary or Germany attacked France. Germany recognized Russian influence in Bulgaria and promised Russia to consider the passage of a navy hostile to Russia through the Dardanelles as a hostile act against itself. Historical opinion on the wisdom on this treaty is sharply divided. Its secret clauses represent to some historians an irresponsible contradiction to the Dual Alliance with Austria-Hungary of 1879, whereas other historians, without always denying that there were contradictions, consider it a crowning achievement of a delicate foreign policy meant to preserve peace.[9] The problem was, however, that the treaty failed to bring stability to the Balkans and to Russian-Austrian relations. To discourage Russia from rearming for a war with Austria in the following years, Bismarck decided to prevent Russian borrowing from German banks, thereby making Russia financially more dependent on France and, in the long run, more inclined to accept the alignment with France Bismarck wanted to prevent. Still, authoritarian Russia was not yet willing to ally itself with republican, democratic France, its antipode in domestic politics, and the tsar offered to renew the Reinsurance Treaty indefinitely when it ran out in 1890. But negotiations were thwarted by Bismarck's resignation in March 1890.

In retrospect, Bismarck's resignation appears to be a fatal and decisive date in German history. Many books carry titles or subtitles such as *Germany After Bismarck*, and the opinion is widespread that Germany went astray once the wily old statesman left the stage. The famous caricature "Dropping the Pilot" of the British satirical magazine *Punch* expressed this feeling already at the time: a wise statesman and experienced pilot leaves the ship, watched by an arrogant young emperor Wilhelm II. Without doubt, there is some truth in this picture. Bismarck's complex diplomatic web tore apart with his fall, and Germany without him at the helm over the years became more threatening and less calculable to other powers, encouraging a web of hostile agreements and alliances. The leadership qualities of Wilhelm II, who aspired to take the governmental authority that Bismarck had monopolized for so long under Wilhelm I, were miserable, and no statesman appointed by Wilhelm II ever garnered (and deserved) the respect Bismarck had acquired on the international stage after 1871. Bismarck's successors led Germany into growing isolation, which ultimately provoked the mixture of aggression and anxiety that helped to trigger World War I. The image of 1890 as a fatal watershed, however, rests too much on a foreign policy view and considers Bismarck too much in the light of the weakness of Wilhelm II and his successors. Moreover, some trends in the diplomatic situation arose from factors outside the control of Bismarck's successors and would have been difficult to avoid even for Bismarck had he stayed on any longer. Finally, Bismarck's resignation is often misrepresented as a *dismissal* of a well-meaning statesman by an arrogant, blasé, and inexperienced emperor. The truth is that Wilhelm II simply accepted Bismarck's resignation instead of giving in to his wishes and imploring him to stay, as his grandfather would have done. Moreover, good intentions, arrogance, and lust for power were divided more equally than the common picture suggests.

The root of the conflict leading to Bismarck's resignation lay in the power of the monarch granted by the Bismarckian constitution. In essence, the monarch, as German emperor and Prussian king, was the supreme authority with the power to control all top-level appointments and to decide about war and peace. Wilhelm I had not claimed the full range of the power at his disposal, trusting Bismarck instead and letting him direct foreign and domestic policy without much interference. Bismarck always feared that he might not be able to count on such a pliant monarch after the death of Wilhelm I, and we have seen how some of his policies aimed at limiting the political options of the liberal crown prince and making himself indispensable. When Bismarck became aware of the fragile health of the crown prince he also made a seemingly successful effort to win over young Prince Wilhelm, the oldest son of the crown prince. When Wilhelm I died in March 1888, Friedrich Wilhelm assumed power as Emperor Friedrich III, but he was already terminally ill and died just three months later. Power fell into the lap of Prince Wilhelm, now Kaiser Wilhelm II, at age 29. Wilhelm II admired Bismarck but was also keen on filling out the big power range that Bismarck's constitution gave to the monarch. A conflict with the chancellor was inevitable as soon as opinions began to differ, and this did not take very long given that Wilhelm II initially wanted to be well liked by all Germans and therefore felt uncomfortable with some of Bismarck's less popular policies. To some extent, Bismarck's resignation was simply an outcome of a power struggle at the top. Wilhelm II insisted on his right to consult with his ministers even without Bismarck's presence. Bismarck, seeing this step as a provocation and attack on his prerogatives, submitted his resignation.

There were deeper and more substantial issues at stake, however. The most important one was that Bismarck intended to renew the anti-socialist laws in the face of strong opposition from the Reichstag. Bismarck felt so strongly about this that he even hinted at a coup d'état should the Reichstag reject a renewal. Given his desire for broad popularity, Wilhelm II did not support this aim. He had backed proposals for labor reform that increased entrepreneurs' responsibility for worker safety and were avidly fought by Bismarck. At the time of the decisive confrontation, Bismarck's position was damaged by a Reichstag election on 20 February 1890 that strengthened the Social Democrats, the Center Party, and the liberals while weakening all the parties behind Bismarck himself. An attempt by Bismarck to enlist support from the Center Party in exchange for the revocation of some *Kulturkampf* measures provoked an angry showdown with the Kaiser, who resented not having been consulted and whose advisors were not ready to make immediate concessions. Bismarck, seeing his parliamentary position impaired and realizing the emperor's constitutional strength, submitted his resignation. Foreign policy differences also played a role, although less so than widely assumed. Bismarck wanted to negotiate a renewal of the Reinsurance Treaty with Russia, whereas Wilhelm II and influential members of the Foreign Office preferred a rapprochement with Britain instead of an alliance with Russia. But foreign policy issues did not influence Bismarck's fall. The decisive issues were the controversy about the anti-socialist laws and the struggle over Wilhelm's prerogative to interview his ministers himself and without the presence of the chancellor.

Although Bismarck's fall in retrospect appears as a fateful break in German foreign policy, it can also be seen as the fall of a stubborn, power-hungry man whose manipulative acumen had run dry. With all of his connections to the press and the parties, with all of his power over the civil service, and with his cynical talent for power mongering, Bismarck simply could not go on controlling the affairs of state at all levels. New trends, particularly the rise of an organized labor movement, had made his constitutional framework ever harder to control, as he understood even before his conflict with Wilhelm II came to the fore. As a consequence, Bismarck talked about a coup d'état with increasing frequency toward the end of his tenure in public office. The German princes, he suggested, should simply convene and revoke the constitution they had so generously granted the German people in 1871. A new constitution on more authoritarian terms should then be forced on the people, if necessary with the help of the army. Nothing came of these plans, not least because of Wilhelm II's opposition, but they indicate how disillusioned and frustrated Bismarck had become with his own creation. Only five years after his resignation, Bismarck had become a highly popular critic of the German government and an object of nostalgia, but in 1890 not many Germans seem to have been upset by his fall. He had held political life in an iron grip, and there was widespread relief in many parties after his departure. A large shadow seemed to have been lifted. The young Kaiser seemed well intended and better attuned to the changing times, and new political opportunities appeared to open up. Although there is no question that Germany's diplomatic situation deteriorated after 1890, it is by no means certain that Bismarck could have prevented this. The road to the First

World War was long, and there was no inevitability about it, at least not in 1890. Clearly, Bismarck was stubborn and had become obsolete by 1890, and thére were many good reasons for letting him go. It was above all the failures of his successors that helped feed a Bismarck nostalgia and an increasingly powerful Bismarck cult.

−4−

Wilhelmine Germany

The basic problems of Bismarck's Germany did not go away when Bismarck left the stage. In foreign policy, it had proven a nearly Herculean task for many years to keep Austria-Hungary and Russia on peaceful terms and to secure the friendship of both. Bismarck's alliance framework, as we shall see, fell apart very quickly and left Germany in a less secure, increasingly isolated position, which German diplomats later on worsened through their attempts to split the hostile alignments. The country still experienced high, even growing, tensions between a modernizing, very dynamic industry and an ailing, though also modernizing agriculture, between a democratically oriented population sector and conservative elites clinging to their privileges, and between avant-garde and traditionalist cultures. A contradiction seemed to haunt Wilhelmine Germany. It was the place where the car was invented and the first electric trains were built. It was the place where Albert Einstein developed his relativity theory, painters made decisive steps toward abstract painting, and workers built up the largest socialist party and trade union network of the world. Yet, the same country had a political system in its constituent states that preserved semi-absolutist features and secured the old prerogatives of a landholding aristocracy. These conservative forces had a fearsome power base in the army, the strongest in the world, which was under the supreme command of the Kaiser and led by a still largely aristocratic and staunchly conservative officer corps bent on excluding democrats, socialists, and Jews from its ranks. Germany's emperor in many ways represented the contradictions of his country; whereas he was deeply committed to modern technology and interested in the mass media, he still believed in the divine justification of his rule and cultivated a quasi-Byzantine court ritual.

Some historians therefore see Wilhelmine Germany as fundamentally flawed and tend to interpret its history a succession of awkward coping attempts that ultimately resulted in a drastic step: the flight forward into a world war that was meant to stabilize an outdated social and political arrangement but instead destroyed the Wilhelmine state and much, much more. Other historians point out that many contradictions of Wilhelmine Germany were typical for rapidly industrializing countries and tend to interpret the outbreak of war in 1914 in a more international frame of reference. On closer inspection, the dichotomy between modernity and traditionalism tends to blur. On many fronts, for example in supporting fleet building and hyper-nationalist imperialism, conservative and modern mindsets often found themselves on the same

Der Kaiser mit seinen 6 Söhnen.

Figure 4.1 The Kaiser and his six sons in front of the Imperial Castle in Berlin, 1913. (Kaiser Wilhelm mit seinen Söhnen, Inv.-Nr.: F 66/3245 © DHM, Berlin).

The Kaiser symbolized the contradictions and tensions in Germany during his reign. On the one side, he still believed in the divine justification of his rule and drove the traditional court ceremonial to absurd extremes. On the other side, he was fascinated with modern technology and founded a society for the promotion of modern science. Albert Einstein played an important role in it, as did many other Nobel Price winners.

side. The modern industrial and administrative bourgeoisie in the towns, it has been claimed, desired to imitate aristocratic life forms, while aristocrats sought to imitate bourgeois and urban life forms. Whereas the dichotomy between the modern and the traditional is therefore often less sharp than expected, we find a very diverse field of opinion in Wilhelmine Germany, from pacifists, nudists, feminists, and vegetarian life reformers all the way to died-in-the-wool traditionalists who upheld the right of the monarch to absolute rule and extolled the power of the Church to direct all matters of life. Such diversity of opinion, of course, can be considered a hallmark of a modern society.

There is no doubt that we are dealing with a highly dynamic economy and culture. When the worldwide economic slowdown was over, roughly by 1896, Germany began rivaling, and in some aspects overtaking, Britain in the traditional sectors of heavy industry, coal and steel. It also ventured into new fields and became a leader in the chemical industry (particularly artificial fertilizers, dyes, and pharmaceuticals) and in electric motors and appliances. Its scientists won the lion's share of Nobel Prizes. Its artists, writers, and composers ventured into new forms of expression that fundamentally questioned or broke up old paradigms. The fast pace of developments in the economy and culture naturally caught many people off guard and produced a nostalgia for a preindustrial romanticized past, obvious for example in the plush, dark interior decoration of bourgeois homes during the Wilhelmine period. Not only in Germany, the achievements of modern technology and the industrial revolution triggered both fascination and anxiety and threw open haunting questions on the meaning of life.

Let us look at the political developments first. Although Wilhelm II's intentions may have been good at the beginning and although he had shown political acumen in ousting Bismarck, his deeply contradictory and troubled personality was his worst enemy. Wilhelm II's psychology has been studied extensively, and we know much about his disturbed feelings about his value, not least because of his stunted left arm, the effect of a difficult birth. He was intelligent, sometimes brilliant, and he could be very charming. But he also had a rash and rude streak, was unable to focus on anything for a longer period and could be cruel, arrogant, and undiplomatic. Despite his intelligence, he never grew beyond the emotional maturity of an average thirteen-year old. Under different circumstances, he would have been an embarrassment for the monarchy without deeper consequences, but the problem was that he had the supreme authority of the strongest military state in Europe – an authority he was determined to use to the fullest extent possible. Wilhelm quickly found out, however, that his power in reality was more constrained than he expected (not least because of his own weaknesses), and he became enveloped in a flattering circle of advisors who often used their influence on him in their favor. In the end, Wilhelm II succeeded only in destroying the governmental coherence that Bismarck had built up in some ways against the spirit of the constitution, but he was unable to fill the resulting power vacuum at the top and to set clear and viable priorities. German policy therefore came to be perceived as the maneuvering of a powerful but rudderless ship, as Chancellor Bernhard von Bülow, a late critic and perpetrator in one, admitted in retrospect. The awkward attempts by Wilhelm II and his courtiers to establish a "personal rule" of the monarch clashed with a changing political landscape that probably made it harder to govern by 1914 than it had been in 1890.

The predominant feature in political developments between 1890 and 1914 was the rise of the SPD. Freed from the constraints of the anti-socialist laws, which had failed to prevent its growth in any case, it became a true mass party with a nationwide party bureaucracy, a disciplined membership paying its dues, and an extensive network of support and leisure organizations. The growth of the SPD was impressive and seemingly unstoppable. The SPD fared very well already in 1890, attracting 19.8 percent of the national vote, twice its share from the 1884 and 1887 elections. By 1912, it received 34.8 percent of the votes after an almost uninterrupted growth, and it became by far the strongest party in the Reichstag, albeit still massively underrepresented in terms of seats due to the unchanged electoral districts. The SPD scored best in the big industrial sectors in the Ruhr valley, Saxony, and around Berlin, and it was also very strong in large cities. The growth of the SPD was no doubt fuelled by the increased pace of industrialization and the growth of the industrial working class. But recent research by Jonathan Sperber also points out that its appeal was far broader; it seems that the SPD developed into a mass party for democracy, social justice, anti-clericalism, and women's rights, and these causes drew support also from left-wing circles of the bourgeoisie.[1] Parallel to the SPD, the so-called free trade unions, usually allied with the SPD, also grew by leaps and bounds, becoming the largest mass organizations in Wilhelmine Germany with 2.5 million members by 1914 – twice the number of SPD members.

The SPD was a distinctive party. Ironically, it seemed almost like a mirror image of the Prussian state: bureaucratically organized, disciplined, hierarchic (though more democratic), with a venerated leader at the top. August Bebel, the party chief, was often called the "workers' kaiser." Whereas most bourgeois parties were rather informal associations with few permanent members and a minimal bureaucracy, the SPD became a home to its members and, together with the free trade unions, formed a state within the state. The SPD and the trade unions built up an extensive bureaucracy and created an alternative cultural and social network. Working men and women joined socialist clubs, sports teams, men's and women's choirs, and poetry groups; socialist associations and institutions existed for almost everything, from party or union-sponsored child care centers to funeral homes; SPD voters read the party newspaper and many of the theoretical works by their leaders printed by socialist publishing houses; whenever they felt that the state-supported social security system proved insufficient they could join the union's health and accident insurance or draw from the union's poverty funds. This alternative structure was made possible because members of the SPD and the free trade unions were willing to sacrifice time and money for the sake of the whole organization. It reflected the exclusion of the socialists from the regular channels of political power in the Bismarckian and Wilhelmine period. The bourgeois parties formed alliances against the SPD, the conservatives mobilized the countryside against them, and the Catholic Center Party attacked them as a godless party. Wilhelm II and his government chastised them for allegedly denying and betraying their fatherland, and careers in the bureaucracy and army were almost impossible for socialists. Even when the SPD became stronger in the Reichstag and local parliaments, there was no question of letting it participate in government.

Discrimination was widespread, but one must also admit that the SPD's own revolutionary rhetoric and internationalist posture were often irresponsible and needlessly antagonizing toward the bourgeois parties and state authorities. The party program (1891) had two parts: a declaration of principle and a practical plan. These parts, written by different party leaders, contradicted each other, at least in political practice. The first was Marxist. It aimed at the socialization of the means of production and a classless society. The second part was pragmatic and demanded social and democratic reform, a democratic constitution, and women's suffrage. It was unclear whether or not the reform path was meant to lead to the classless society implied by the first part and would thus make a revolution superfluous. Marx considered revolution necessary for the overthrow of bourgeois society, but a "revisionist" group of socialists around Eduard Bernstein disagreed. The discrepancy between the revolutionary and reformist path became the SPD's main inner conflict. The left wing considered revolution indispensable and expected the Wilhelmine state to crush the socialist movement before it became strong enough to democratize the state. The right wing believed that reforms were possible in the Wilhelmine empire and that a gradual improvement of the legal, political, and social situation of the industrial working class might result from peaceful political work. The party's electoral success and the growth of the socialist trade unions seemed to support this view. A large centrist group, dominated by party ideologue Karl Kautsky, utilized the revolutionary rhetoric to distance itself from the existing state and to enhance membership cohesion while pursuing a reformist course in its everyday activity.

The dilemma of the German socialists was not unique. In other industrializing countries, socialists also disagreed on what to make of the development of modern industrial societies. Many thought that Marx and Engels believed in inevitable immiseration of the proletariat leading automatically to revolution. After the end of the economic crisis in 1896, however, the situation of the working people grew better. In most states, including Germany, combined pressure of socialist parties and trade unions improved conditions without a revolution. Marx had claimed that this reformist path would fail because the capitalists would be unable to make the necessary concessions in the long run. Unions, so Marx, would be able to receive raises up to a certain point; then the capitalist system would turn against them and only revolution could prevent the workers from falling back into bondage. Marx's most loyal heirs feared that successful reformism would mitigate class conflicts and thus delay the desired breakdown of the capitalist system. The SPD and the socialist trade unions, however, had too much to lose to build up a radical revolutionary party like the Russian Bolsheviks, a party run in the underground and in exile by a handful of dedicated revolutionaries. The German Social Democrats got caught in the dilemma between successful reformism and revolutionary principle. Kautsky tried to square the circle by proclaiming that the SPD was a revolutionary party but not one that organizes revolutions. Although this conflict was never resolved, it did not do as much harm to the SPD as could have been expected. Until 1914 it proved to be more of an integrating than a splitting factor. The revolutionary appeal attracted frustrated workers, while the reformist program steadily and visibly increased the party's wealth and parliamentary strength and probably also its appeal beyond the working class. Many socialists, moreover, needed the revolutionary legitimation for their reformist practice. This became clear in the party debate on Bernstein's proposals for revising Marxist theory (revisionism). In opposition to Marx, Bernstein advocated a socialism that allowed for cooperation with left-wing liberals and, if feasible, for participation in government. He suggested that the SPD drop the revolutionary claim and integrate itself into the existing state, trying to democratize it from within. This was too much for the party doctrinaires, however. But after the party had (once again) officially condemned revisionism, the party secretary told Bernstein in private: "My dear Ede, ... something like that does not need a resolution or a public announcement; we just do it quietly!"[2] That the reformists did not stand up more forcefully and that they failed to win control of the party was to a large degree the effect of continuing hostility from the state and the right-to-center parties. Threats of renewed repression of the SPD never subsided, and many other parties tried to build a block against the SPD, trying to exclude it from all political influence. Only the left liberals formed alliances with the SPD for run-off elections in contested Reichstag districts, but the revolutionary thunder of SPD rhetoric could easily threaten these alliances.

The tension within the SPD became more acute in the wake of the Russian Revolution of 1905. After the Russian armed forces had lost the war with Japan, social and political tensions erupted in the Russian Empire. Bourgeois liberals together with socialists fought for a constitutional system and a national parliament, the duma. The workers went on a general strike, and the tsar, left without much armed support, made concessions, most of which he withdrew in the following two years. The outburst of revolutionary activity in Russia nevertheless inspired socialists all over the world. German socialists, in particular, thought about the general strike as a means of political struggle. But while reformists wanted to use it merely as a defensive weapon in case Wilhelm II carried out a coup d'état, the radicals on the left hoped to use the general strike as a prelude to revolution. This alienated the trade unions, which did not want to risk their achievements and funds in a dubious gamble for power. The conflict was not resolved when the First World War polarized the socialist movement further, pitting a patriotic majority against an initially small but rapidly growing pacifist and revolutionary minority.

It also remained unclear how the reformists imagined winning power in the state. A socialist Reichstag majority would not have been able to bring down the chancellor and to change the constitution – it would probably have provoked more repression. Moreover, the SPD's doctrinarianism set limits for its growth at the polls. The Social Democrats, for instance, never managed to appeal to the farmers; even their appeal to the poor rural laborers on the estates of the Junkers remained very limited. Marxist theory predicted that the agrarian sector would be mostly absorbed by the industrial sector. After the proletarian revolution, large agricultural collectives would ensure the essential supplies. This program could not appeal to farmers, who felt that the SPD threatened their property rights. Altering the program, however, would have shaken the SPD's theoretical foundation.

The growth of the SPD triggered counter-reactions both in official and unofficial quarters. The presence of an increasingly strong party committed to universal and equal suffrage in all elections threatened the power of the monarchy and the prerogatives of the conservatives, particularly in Prussia where the electoral laws gave the conservatives and National Liberals a disproportionate share of seats in the diet and kept the SPD, Prussia's largest party, out of the diet until 1908 and at miniscule strength thereafter. Much legislation was still passed at the state level and never crossed the Reichstag floor, and much power in the Reich rested on the conservative checks of the Bundesrat and the connection of Prussian and Reich government. The introduction of universal and equal suffrage in the states (even without women's suffrage, which the SPD also demanded) would therefore have amounted to a political earthquake. Wilhelm II's initial openness toward social reform, once a source of conflict between him and Bismarck, soon melted away when he realized that social reform failed to undermine the workers' loyalty to the SPD; like Bismarck, he soon began talking about a coup d'état. This seemed a risky option, however, considering that the masses of workers voting for the SPD were essential to the production process and also because of opposition in moderate political circles. Instead, Wilhelm II and his successive governments applied various strategies to isolate the SPD and to undercut its growth while constructing pro-governmental alliances among the remaining parties, albeit with only temporary success at best. Social legislation continued, however, and the generally good economic outlook from the later 1890s to 1913 made businessmen willing to accept an expansion of Bismarck's welfare state even though this policy did no more to woo the workers away from the SPD than had Bismarck's initial welfare legislation. But the German welfare system, complemented by an extensive support network of the SPD and the free trade unions, increasingly bound the workers to the state they wished to change. Contrary to Marx's famous claim, the German worker began to have a fatherland.

The growth of the SPD also triggered strong counter-movements. In the 1890s several right-wing mass organizations were founded. The most successful was the Agrarian League (*Bund der Landwirte*), founded in 1893. Although led by large east Elbian landlords and members of the conservative parties, the Agrarian League managed to present itself as the representative of all farmers in Germany. The immediate trigger for this foundation was the lowering of tariffs after Bismarck's fall, and a key demand of the Agrarian League always was protection for German products against the forces of the world market. But as the lobby of food producers, the Agrarian League was naturally in conflict with the SPD-led workers, who needed low prices for food. The ideological background of the Agrarian League also made it diametrically opposed to the SPD. Founded in large part by people close to the German Conservative Party, the Agrarian League stood for traditionalist values based on religion and the monarchy even though it also represented a popular quest for participation couched in nationalist language. Its strong anti-Semitism and racist elements indicated a deep disaffection with what was considered a modern, capitalist, and urban life form that naïve minds often associated with Jews. The Agrarian League maintained close connections to the two conservative parties and gained enormous political influence through them. In 1898, seventy-six Reichstag members (of 397) belonged to the Agrarian League, and forty-two others were closely linked to it. In the Prussian diet, a full third of the deputies belonged to it, and by 1913 it had 330,000 members.[3] The Agrarian League was the most powerful organization set up to rally the farmers, but other farmer's leagues, predominantly in Catholic regions and with ties to the Center Party, also flourished. It is therefore fair to say that the countryside was politically well organized by the 1890s – primarily around economic interest but also around conservative and partly anti-Semitic values.

Other mass organizations formed on the basis of radical nationalism and middle-class interest. In 1891, the Pan-German League united small pressure groups for colonial expansion and the rallying of all ethnic Germans in one state. The Pan-German League drew much support from professors, teachers, and administrators and became a vocal power center much more influential than its membership, which did not exceed 21,000, suggested. The Pan-German League was perhaps the most notorious element of an emerging network of nationalist pressure groups such as the League for the Eastern Marches, the Navy League, and the Colonial Society. All of these organizations brought a more racist and chauvinist tone to German politics. They claimed to support the government in its efforts to boost the position of Germans in the regions with a Polish majority (the "Eastern Marches"), colonial expansion, a powerful navy, and other causes, but they became increasingly critical of Wilhelm II and his governments. In 1912, the Pan-German League's chairman Heinrich Class published the pamphlet *If I Were the Kaiser* calling for a dictatorship, an expansionist foreign policy, and restrictions on the civil rights of Jews. His pamphlet had to appear under a pen name because it risked triggering prosecution against him because of *lèse-majesté* (insulting the emperor was a criminal offense), and it is important to note that it was highly critical of the Kaiser. An increasingly aggressive right-wing opposition to the Kaiser had formed that began urging him to do what Bismarck and Wilhelm II himself had considered doing repeatedly: to carry out a coup d'état and to roll back the democratic aspects of the constitution. Members of the nationalist leagues had connections to the conservative parties and the National Liberals, but they defied control by the parties and the government. While the SPD was growing stronger with nearly every election, the government faced an additional challenge from the right.

Clearly, Wilhelm II was confronted with a changing and often stormy political landscape. How did he try to cope with the new challenges? After Bismarck's resignation, Wilhelm II was above all determined to gain better control over the reins of government. He therefore appointed a seemingly pliant general as Bismarck's successor: Leo von Caprivi. Caprivi had fought in the Franco-German War and had worked in the Prussian War Ministry, but his most important office had been as chief of the Imperial Admiralty from 1883 to 1888 (it was still part of Prussian-German tradition that generals would play an important role in the navy). Caprivi had built up the Imperial Navy with limited resources, prioritizing coastal defense. As chancellor, Caprivi inspired much social legislation and liberalized trade. He lowered the tariffs and concluded free-trade agreements with many countries. The most enduring change occurred in foreign policy, however. Agreeing with the Kaiser's trusted advisor in the Foreign Office, Count Friedrich von Holstein, Caprivi believed that the Dual Alliance with Austria-Hungary and the Reinsurance Treaty with Russia were contradictory and that Germany had to make a choice. Hoping for closer ties with Britain, he therefore advised against renewing the Reinsurance Treaty with Russia. In Russia, the anti-German party at court promptly won the upper hand, and Russia negotiated a rapprochement with France, which was completed in a formal defensive alliance in 1894. This alliance obliged both countries to assist each other in case of a German attack. Letting the treaty with Russia expire appears as a crucial mistake in retrospect. The two most powerful nations bordering directly on Germany became allies, and Germany would now face a two-front war should its tensions with France or Russia escalate. It remains open to doubt, however, whether the German government could have prevented the Franco-Russian rapprochement for much longer. France was investing large sums in Russian industrialization and had so desperately been looking for an alliance partner that the fundamental difference of political systems between the two countries did not matter. Moreover, growing pan-Slavic and Germanic racism made the alliance of Russia and Germany increasingly unpopular in both countries. The nationalist leagues in Germany concurred with radical Pan-Slavists that a struggle between Germanic and Slavic people might be a historical necessity. Caprivi nevertheless tried to preserve Russian friendship by negotiating a trade treaty in 1894 that facilitated Russian grain exports to Germany, but this treaty failed to prevent Russia's alliance with France and provoked bitter opposition from the Agrarian League at home. Caprivi and Holstein had hoped to substitute Britain for Russia as Germany's alliance partner, but Britain refused to give up its "splendid isolation" protected by the largest battle fleet in the world. Germany's international situation had deteriorated, but it was not yet bleak; the Triple Alliance of Germany, Austria-Hungary, and Italy may have roughly balanced the Franco-Russian alliance. But diplomatic options were restricted and Germany could ill afford to make another enemy.

It was domestic policy, not foreign policy, that led to Caprivi's dismissal in October 1894. After several frustrating attempts to pass army increases through the Reichstag and after the trade treaty with Russia, Wilhelm II was ready to drop the chancellor in the face of strong conservative and agrarian opposition to his free trade policies. The breaking point was, as in the case of Bismarck's fall, legislation aiming to restrict the SPD, but this time it was Wilhelm II who advocated a hard line and his chancellor who rejected it. Wilhelm II wanted Caprivi to present a bill to the Reichstag that would have cut deeply into civil liberties and allowed for more persecution of the socialists. Caprivi, who disappointed Wilhelm's expectation that he, as a general, would simply obey his Kaiser's orders, refused to cooperate because he knew that the Reichstag would reject the bill. Wilhelm chose a pro-Prussian Bavarian aristocrat as his successor, Prince Chlodwig zu Hohenlohe-Schillingsfürst. Hohenlohe had been Bavarian minister president and German ambassador in Paris.

He was, like Caprivi, associated with the Free Conservative Party, but he had a stronger will to persecute the Social Democrats and therefore agreed to present the Kaiser's bill to the Reichstag. As Caprivi had predicted, the Reichstag majority voted against the bill. Later on, the Reichstag also rejected several milder versions of the bill.

The decisive events under Hohenlohe's chancellorship happened in foreign policy, albeit less through his initiative than through the work of two ministers appointed in 1897 whose work shaped the parameters of German foreign policy for the rest of the prewar period: Foreign Minister Bernhard von Bülow and State Secretary for the Navy Admiral Alfred Tirpitz (since 1900, when he was ennobled by the Kaiser, Alfred *von* Tirpitz). Both ministers responded to a more fundamental change in foreign policy that occurred at the end of the nineteenth century. It is hard to say when and where it happened first, but it was a European phenomenon that shaped foreign policy by 1914. First, foreign policy became more of a concern for an increasingly literate public than it had ever been before. The proliferation of a daily newspaper press and the progress in communication technique (particularly the widespread use of the telegraph) made it possible for many Europeans even in remote areas to receive a recent update on the course of world politics. At the same time, Europeans started to identify more with their nation states and considered their international prestige a matter of highest interest. Although popular opinion could not everywhere articulate itself democratically, public concern with foreign policy and national prestige put more pressure on governments. A diplomatic defeat was considered as a national humiliation and thus endangered governments more than before. Second, nationalism in most countries became more aggressive and more antagonistic to members of other nations (integrative nationalism), often blending with an arrogant racism. This racism included social Darwinist elements and imagined the world as a fighting ground of ruthless enemies, where only the fittest could survive. Competition and readiness for war seemed the only appropriate attitude between nations. A nation that became stronger was healthy; stagnation meant decline and ultimate extinction.

Although the new racism initially found most resonance among the middle classes, the workers succumbed to some of its notions, too. An unskilled English factory worker may have felt that he stood at the bottom of his own society, but integrative nationalism told him that he was far superior to a laborer – and even a prince – in India. In Germany a popular socialist pamphlet synthesized Marx and Darwin by claiming that because of selection through harsh living conditions the proletariat was the fittest class and would survive the degenerate nobility and bourgeoisie. It became one of the most popular texts read by workers.[4] To sum it up, Europeans tended to identify more strongly with their nation and its prestige and started to watch the foreign policy of their governments more critically than before. Impressed by Darwinist ideas, many came to see the situation of their nations as a crude choice between expansion or decline, hegemony or submission.

The appeal of imperialism with its claims to expand a superior civilization to allegedly grateful, less civilized people also reached Germany, and it cut across some political divides. Not only the Pan-Germans advocated colonial expansion; National Liberals and even left-leaning liberals as well as Catholics joined their voices in the imperialist chorale. A strong sense prevailed that Germany, as a pre-eminent industrial nation with a rich culture, had a role to play on the world stage on par with other European powers who had for a long time possessed colonies and exported their language and culture. The sociologist Max Weber, normally a reasonable and moderate political mind far removed from the chauvinism of the Pan-Germans, expressed this feeling in his inaugural lecture at the University of Freiburg in 1895. Weber declared that the foundation of the German Empire in 1871 should be regarded not as a terminal achievement but as a step in a continuing national history toward more glory and success. There was a growing sense, however, that Germany had lost the contest for empire. Britain and France owned huge colonial empires, and Russia had expanded southward and eastward, but Germany, since the second Congress of Berlin, owned some unconnected territories that nobody else had wanted enough to challenge the German claims to them. It was Bülow, in particular, who brought this feeling to the point by declaring that Germany ought to conduct *Weltpolitik* (world politics) and deserved a "place in the sun." The Kaiser enthusiastically approved, but what *Weltpolitik* meant was less clear. Often it was simply an emphatic claim to have a say in world matters on par with Britain and other powerful nations.

Some historians, including Hans-Ulrich Wehler, have claimed that the German government adopted *Weltpolitik* primarily for domestic reasons. After the anti-socialist laws had failed, according to Wehler, the ruling elites wanted to reconcile the rising working class with the state and its social order through integrative nationalism, passion for overseas expansion, and concern for national prestige. This should undermine the workers' loyalty to the revolutionary SPD and the trade unions and preserve Germany's backward political system. The motivation for *Weltpolitik* appears to be more complex, however. Improving communications and cheap transportation through the steamship made the globe a smaller place in which peripheral matters no longer existed. German industrialization reached the point at which the agrarian sector typically becomes so small compared to the industrial sector that a country becomes dependent upon imported food and raw materials. This alone would have forced the German government to take more interest in overseas affairs. By the late 1890s, Germany's vast overseas trade and growing dependence upon food and raw material imports made it increasingly vulnerable. The weak German battle fleet was unable to protect the influx of essential imports in case of war with the Franco-Russian alliance or Britain. What should the leaders in Berlin do? One option was to keep German sea power small but to ally with the nation that owned by far the largest navy: Britain.

Toward the end of the 1890s British diplomats themselves sounded out the chances for an alliance with Germany, but the British did not want to commit themselves as closely as the Germans wanted and did not want to recognize Germany as an equal partner in world and colonial politics. Since the British had no immediate interests on the European continent, the German diplomats had little to offer in return. They therefore feared becoming the junior partner of the British empire and being drawn into its colonial conflicts with other European powers, above all France and Russia. In Germany and Britain, moreover, a mutual alliance would have had powerful enemies as the two countries were fierce trade rivals. Conservative Germans, finally, resented the liberal political system in Britain and claimed the British national character was spoiled by commercial greed. In any case, the British diplomats were in no hurry, and the Germans were overly confident that Britain would never come to terms with its main overseas rivals, France and Russia. Britain almost went to war with France during an incident in east Africa in 1898, and it had long-standing conflicts of interest with Russia regarding the Russian desire for expansion in the Balkans, central Asia, and east Asia.

Not much, therefore, seemed to speak against strengthening the German navy. Tirpitz as naval minister proposed the buildup of a high-seas battle fleet as the means of power for *Weltpolitik*. Wilhelm II, a naval enthusiast, had repeatedly tried to increase Reichstag funding for the navy, but his proposals had always been cut down by the Reichstag because the German navy had no strategic concept for a role beyond coastal defense and because the army was considered the mainstay of German defense (the Reichstag still had yearly budgetary power over the navy; the army budget was determined only every fifth year). Tirpitz, however, offered a long-term concept. First, he wanted to prioritize one form of vessel: the heavy battleship. Coal still being the essential ship fuel, shipbuilders had two options: they could build cruisers with large coal bunkers but fewer guns and thin armament. These cruisers could travel far without having to refuel. They were fast and mobile but vulnerable in a sea battle. The other option was to concentrate on heavy battleships. With small coal bunkers but heavy armament and the most powerful guns, these vessels could destroy cruisers, but due to their limited range they had to remain near the home waters or coaling stations overseas. Tirpitz resolved that Germany, having few naval bases overseas, was best advised to concentrate battleships in the North Sea and the Baltic. This decision was crucial because it created a concentration of sea power that posed a real threat to Britain. Although Tirpitz was reluctant to admit it in public, he made it clear in private that the German battle fleet should be a lever for colonial concessions by the British empire and a deterrent against a British naval attack. To those critics who argued that Tirpitz's battle fleet could neither defend Germany's overseas commerce nor its colonies Tirpitz replied that the mere existence of a strong battle fleet indirectly shielded German colonies and trade all over the world despite the battleships' narrow range of operation.

Unlike his predecessors, Tirpitz decided to organize naval buildup by law. He thought that only a law establishing the size of the German fleet by class of vessels and the number of ships to be built within the next years would ensure continuous and consistent fleet building and avoid the need to barter the money for each ship against other requests by the parties in the Reichstag. A long-term plan, moreover, could convince the Reichstag that Wilhelm II did not simply want more ships because he was fond of them (critics spoke of the Kaiser's "luxury fleet"). An excellent manipulator of the press and of deputies, Tirpitz won a Reichstag majority for a long-term shipbuilding program that made Germany a major sea power. He assembled around him a "brain trust" for all strategic questions, and he staffed a bureau for public relations with experts who started a campaign for naval expansion (the Navy League, however, was an independent organization working for the same goal). He lured the conservative parties with the promise of high tariffs, and he appealed to the National Liberals and even to some left liberals by presenting German fleet building as a liberal idea going back to 1848, when an all-German fleet had been proposed by the liberals. Selling the idea of naval expansion to industry was not difficult, but Tirpitz also managed to get Center Party support – mostly through personal contact with its leaders in the Reichstag. Unlike most other German politicians of his time, Tirpitz took the Reichstag and the public seriously. In long discussions with Reichstag members, he impressed the deputies with his competent and rational argumentation. The first navy law passed the Reichstag against the votes of the Social Democrats and the left liberals in March 1898. It was backed by the conservative parties, the National Liberals, and the Center Party, which became increasingly important for the government in a Reichstag with a strengthening SPD.

The combination of propaganda and negotiations with Reichstag members remained successful. In 1900 Tirpitz made use of widespread anti-English feeling in Germany provoked by the Boer War to demand further naval increases. Under public pressure, the Reichstag passed a second navy bill that prescribed a doubling of the German fleet by 1907. It was the second navy law that started to worry Britain. In 1905 the British introduced a new, heavier battleship, the "Dreadnought," and adopted an ambitious fleet-building program themselves. Tirpitz reacted by convincing the Reichstag to vote for further increases of the German navy in 1906, 1908, and 1912. He limited the service of his ships to twenty years, so he could replace the older ships by the new dreadnought types. His goal was a fleet of sixty-one capital ships (battleships and large battle cruisers) to be built by 1920. Given the replacement age of twenty years, three capital ships would be built every year. The navy would thus keep up its strength and become independent of the Reichstag's budgetary rights. By building a navy through law, Tirpitz hoped to wrest control over shipbuilding away from the Reichstag and also, I have argued, to make it independent from the erratic Kaiser who took greater interest in naval matters than the experts appreciated, sometimes trying to impose his own amateurish ship designs on the admirals.

Historian Volker Berghahn has argued that building the fleet by law was an assault on parliamentary rights in general and that Tirpitz wanted to stabilize the semi-authoritarian political system against the challenge of socialists and demo-crats. Berghahn sees the Tirpitz Plan as a deliberate strategy to divert demands for democratic reform and to counteract the rise of Social Democracy. The boom of heavy industry should enable employers to satisfy trade union demands without too much disadvantage, and fleet building might create a wave of national pride that would woo at least some workers away from socialism.[5] Critics of Berghahn have argued that Tirpitz merely wanted to achieve for the navy what the army had taken for granted since Bismarck's days: relative independence from changing parliamentary constellations. Tirpitz himself would have been delighted if his fleet-building plan had strengthened the Bismarckian constitutional system, and he did hint at this possible effect when talking to conservatives, who initially disliked fleet building because it strengthened industry and drew resources away from the army. Although fleet building did nothing to stem the rise of the SPD and the socialist trade unions, Tirpitz did help to recreate the alliance of iron and rye (big industry and agrarians), which had been shaken in the Caprivi years, and he facilitated a rapprochement of the Center Party to the government. The first and second navy laws thus helped the creation of a pro-governmental bloc in the Reichstag and enhanced political stability in the short run. But for Tirpitz, this outcome was a welcome byproduct of fleet building, not his key motivation.

In the long run, however, the Tirpitz Plan was a disaster, both in domestic and foreign politics. After a few years, a threat to domestic stability arose from the cost explosion in shipbuilding. Tirpitz broke all his estimates, and fleet building could not be financed any more from tax revenues after 1902. The government resorted to loans and tolerated a disturbing increase of the deficit, particularly after Germany began to build its own dreadnoughts in 1906. The naval program therefore began to threaten the pro-governmental alliance it had helped to bring about. New taxes had to be introduced, but the tax question opened deep rifts among the parties that had supported fleet building. Industrialists did not want to augment the tax load of the workers because that measure would have boosted Social Democratic propaganda and trade union demands for higher wages. Conservatives staunchly rejected an increase in property taxes, which would have reduced their political weight in Prussia. Moreover, the conservatives and large groups within the other center to right parties began to worry that too many resources were diverted to the fleet at the expense of the army. To get a Reichstag majority for the supplementary naval bill of 1912, Tirpitz for the first time had to make substantial cuts.

In foreign policy, fleet building exacerbated an already difficult situation. When he presented his plan in 1897, Tirpitz had argued that a Germany with a powerful battle fleet would be an attractive alliance partner for one of the many rivals of the British empire or even for the British themselves. Within ten years, however, it was the British, and not the Germans, who were allied with almost every other major power. Worried about German naval buildup, Britain concluded an alliance with Japan (1902) and even ironed out its differences with its old rivals, France (1904) and

Russia (1907). For a long time, it seemed possible that the Royal Navy would simply destroy the German fleet before it was strong enough to defend itself. Such action would have represented an act of international piracy but something like a precedent for such an action existed: in a surprise coup in 1807 the British had captured the Danish fleet at Copenhagen in order to prevent the French from taking it. Denmark at the time was a neutral country but was about to be forced into the French orbit. Fears of a new "Copenhagen" were widespread among German leaders from 1904 to 1910 and added to the feverish mixture of threat and fear characteristic for German diplomacy before the First World War.[6] British and German diplomats made various attempts to stop the naval arms race, but the British were never willing to revoke their alliance with France and Russia, and the German diplomats, with Tirpitz putting his propaganda and lobbying machine into high gear, were unable to slow down naval construction enough to allay British fears. Contrary to the expectations of Tirpitz, who believed that a democratic nation would be too selfish to make the national sacrifice necessary to preserve naval hegemony, Britain built so many ships that the gap between the two navies increased after 1905. The German battle fleet, although the second strongest in the world, never worked as the diplomatic lever Tirpitz had wanted it to be and instead contributed decisively to the diplomatic isolation of Germany. When in December 1912 the German military leadership discussed launching a war at the next international crisis, Tirpitz had to admit that the fleet would not be ready for a war with Britain in the near future. Although he knew that British superiority would increase in the following years, he did not push for a start of war as soon as possible. It became clear to Helmuth von Moltke (the younger), the chief of the General Staff, that German war plans for the immediate future had to disregard the fleet, and Tirpitz lost much of his prestige within the German leadership.

Although the German naval program did not cause the First World War, it goes a long way to explaining why Germany faced such a powerful coalition when it broke out. Yet, one needs to consider that the strategic and economic situation of Germany and Britain made it impossible for either country to feel safe while the other had a powerful fleet. A crucial share of German trade passed the sea lanes around the British Isles, and a blockade by the British fleet could easily sever these vital lines. A Germany without a powerful fleet was therefore at the mercy of its largest industrial and trading rival. On the other hand, a Germany with a large fleet concentrated in home waters (and the most powerful army in the world) could not avoid representing a threat to Britain; it took only one day to steam from the German North Sea coast to the British east coast. An alliance between the two countries made perfect sense, but it was hard to negotiate not least because the British wanted to see Germany as a junior partner and because the Germans insisted on recognition as an equal. Popular currents in both countries were not friendly to each other in any case. The British press launched campaigns against German goods and accused German firms of using unfair trading methods. In Germany, "perfidious Albion" became a symbol of ruthless capitalism and arrogance. That the liberal political system of Britain deterred the Germans from an alliance is a less plausible argument, however. Wilhelm II and his advisors definitely wanted a British alliance on several occasions, and differences in political systems did not need to prevent alliances, as demonstrated by the Franco-Russian agreement of 1894.

That the buildup of the German battle fleet led to a deterioration of Anglo-German relations is impossible to deny. But this should not be confused with a moral condemnation. As historian Christopher Clark argues:

> There is a perplexing tendency of the literature on this period – and in popular present-day awareness – to see things from the Westminster point of view, to accept implicitly the notion that British colonial expansion and British perceptions of British rights constituted a 'natural order', in the light of which German objections appeared to be wanton provocations.[7]

Given Germany's rapidly growing economic weight and global trade connections, one could argue that it would have been irresponsible of a German government to neglect the military implications of these developments. Fleet building in itself did not trigger war between Britain and Germany, and there were other, perhaps more important factors that pushed Britain toward Germany's antagonists.

How did the German government cope with the problems caused or exacerbated by the Tirpitz Plan? It is important to note that the power vacuum left behind by Bismarck had still not been entirely filled. Wilhelm II's attempts to establish "personal rule" had failed. His chancellors and ministers were less pliable than he thought, and he found that he could not ignore resistance from the Reichstag. Not least, he lacked the concentration and willpower to follow up on his own political initiatives. When Hohenlohe, who was 81, resigned in October 1900, Wilhelm believed he had a successor who would implement his will with skill, charm, and loyalty: Bernhard von Bülow, foreign minister since 1897 and already a crucial political figure during the last years of Hohenlohe's chancellorship. Bülow, a supreme flatterer and wily courtier, capitalized on the Center Party's rapprochement with the government, evident during the passing of the First Navy Law, to build a Reichstag majority around the conservative parties, the National Liberals, and the Center until 1906. His domestic political priorities were the reintroduction of tariffs and the continuation of social reform. Bülow considered cooperation between big industry and agriculture important and was a practitioner of *Sammlungspolitik*, a policy of gathering these two often quite conflictual groups (the idea had been advanced earlier by Prussian Finance Minister Johannes von Miquel and was inspired by the alliance of iron and rye promoted initially by Bismarck). Bülow's tariff law of 1902 represented a compromise between agrarians and industrialists by raising tariffs on grain and iron.

Responding to the popular pressures mentioned above, Bülow hoped to rally the German people behind a successful and ambitious foreign policy. This was awkward given that Bülow at the same time had the unthankful task of seeing Germany through the "danger zone" of fleet building, the period during which the German battle fleet was most vulnerable to a British surprise attack. In terms of colonial acquisitions, only modest gains had been made: Germany had obtained a concession to the Chinese territory of Kiao-Chow with the city Qingdao in 1897 (where the Germans built beer breweries that still supply many Chinese restaurants in America), and it won land on Samoa and some Pacific islands at the expense of Spain in the late 1890s. None of these "conquests" was impressive even though each caused resentment in other countries. A more serious crisis evolved not out of Germany's own territorial designs but rather out of its attempts to foil French colonial expansion and to challenge the Franco-British alliance of 1904, the *Entente Cordiale*. Reassured by this alliance, France began establishing a protectorate over the Sultanate of Morocco, hoping to integrate Morocco into its empire. Germany, which had economic interests in Morocco, protested and called for an international conference that would secure the independence of Morocco. The German claims were legally well founded, but the threatening posture Germany adopted toward France in hopes of splitting the Franco-British alliance alienated many powers. France gave in to the German demand for an international conference, but the German threat brought France and Britain closer together. The international conference, convened in Algeciras (southern Spain) in 1906, moreover, accepted most French claims while making only minor concessions to Germany regarding the economic openness of Morocco. Except for Austria-Hungary, all powers represented at the conference, including the United States, rejected the German claims and took the side of France. Although Bülow had wooed Russia through a friendly attitude during the Russo-Japanese War and although Wilhelm II had signed a friendship agreement with Tsar Nicholas II in Björkö (Russian Finland), Russia remained committed to France (the Russian government flatly refused to ratify the Treaty of Björkö). The first Moroccan crisis thus demonstrated the degree of German isolation. It set a pattern that would be repeated several times: German attempts to break up hostile alliances only pushed its antagonists closer together while casting Germany in the role as the disturber of world peace.

After the setback over Morocco, Bülow had to fight a major battle in domestic politics. Partly through provocative government appointments by the Kaiser, who never appreciated Bülow's cordial relations with the Center Party, the specter of the *Kulturkampf* rose again and strained Bülow's alliance with the Center Party. A controversy over colonial policy in the fall of 1906 led to the break of that alliance. The background was a series of uprisings in German Southwest Africa (today's Namibia) where the German army, with the Kaiser's consent, carried out genocide against the Herero and Nama peoples in 1904–7. When the government tried to cover the cost of the military operation by submitting a request for an additional budget to the Reichstag, the Center Party, assisted by the SPD, lambasted the government's handling of the uprising and its colonial policy in general. Bülow consequently obtained a Reichstag dissolution order from the Kaiser and fought an election campaign on "national" lines, making the election a vote of confidence in the German army and its supreme commander, the Kaiser. The election results failed to weaken the Center Party, which obtained roughly the same result as in the previous election (1903). The SPD, however, lost almost half of its seats (thirty-six out of seventy-nine). This defeat was due not so much to a loss in the percentage of the vote (which declined only slightly) but to the SPD's renewed radicalism in the wake of the Russian Revolution of 1905. An upsurge in the SPD's revolutionary rhetoric and its talk about mass action on the models of the Russian Revolution alienated its left-liberal allies and therefore prevented many SPD candidates with a relative majority from winning their seat in a run-off election with liberal support. The left liberals instead supported right-wing candidates. The 1907 election gave Bülow a breathing space, allowing him to construct a new coalition of the conservative parties, the National Liberals, and the left liberals (the so-called Bülow Bloc).

The election victory of 1907 coincided with a crucial weakening of governmental authority, however. In the fall of 1906, publicist Maximilian Harden, inspired by Bülow, launched a vicious press campaign against Wilhelm's advisers at court. Harden expressed criticism of unaccountable courtiers who exercised an inordinate amount of power through backstage influence on the Kaiser, and he appealed to homophobia by revealing and attacking the homosexuality of many men in Wilhelm's entourage, above all his trusted friend and advisor Philipp zu Eulenburg-Hertefeld. The attacks provoked various libel trials, which exposed embarrassing details about the homoerotic circle around Eulenburg and its connections to the Kaiser over the following two years. Eulenburg withdrew to his estate a broken man and never saw the Kaiser again. As Wilhelm II's biographer Christopher Clark remarks, the removal of Eulenburg from the Kaiser's entourage had deplorable effects because Eulenburg had on many occasions restrained the Kaiser by giving him critical advice.[8] Bülow, who had for a long time been good friends with Eulenburg, also suffered from the scandal, not least because the Kaiser suspected that Bülow, who had come to see Eulenburg as a rival, had leaked information to the press. In any case, the foreign and domestic upheavals of 1905–7 undermined the trust of Wilhelm II in Bülow. Whereas Wilhelm had initially allowed Bülow much free rein because Bülow kept reassuring him that he was only interested in carrying out Wilhelm's wonderful ideas, Wilhelm now demanded a more direct say in the conduct of politics. Given the Kaiser's irascible and erratic character and the removal of Eulenburg as a moderating advisor, this could only complicate the exercise of power for Bülow and his state secretaries. Bülow henceforth needed to devote a large amount of his political energy to "handling the Kaiser," as he put it. The Reichstag parties did not make his job any easier, as the Bülow Bloc began to fall apart already at the end of 1907. Given the huge expenses for Tirpitz's naval program and the narrow tax base of the Reich, Bülow urged a slowdown in naval expenditure (to no avail) and demanded the introduction of new taxes. The tax issue killed his coalition, as the conservatives still fought tooth and nail against any direct taxes (taxes on property and income), whereas the National Liberals with their industrial wing rejected indirect taxes (such as sales taxes) because they hit the lower classes the hardest and induced the trade unions to claim higher wages. The conservatives and National Liberals also reacted angrily to the left liberal demand for a reform of the Prussian franchise, the foundation of conservative power in Prussia.

In this situation, Bülow badly needed some success, which he sought in foreign policy when the Austro-Hungarian annexation of Bosnia-Herzegovina in 1908 triggered an international crisis. Bosnia-Herzegovina formally belonged to the Ottoman Empire but was since 1878 under Austro-Hungarian occupation. Serbia, since 1903 under a pro-Russian dynasty, claimed Bosnia-Herzegovina as an unre-deemed Serbian territory (even though the ethnic Serb population shared the province with a large Muslim and a smaller Croatian population) and protested against the annexation. Although the Viennese diplomats had won Russian consent to the annexation in secret talks, the Russian government, reacting to the Serbian protests and to public outrage in Russia, suddenly demanded an international conference during which it wanted to articulate its own interests in the Dardanelles. Mindful of their isolation at the conference of Algeciras, Austria-Hungary and Germany rejected an international conference. A war between Austria-Hungary and Serbia, perhaps involving Russia on Serbia's side and Germany on Austria-Hungary's side, appeared possible. While Moltke was willing to support Austria-Hungary militarily if it went to war against Serbia, Bülow and the Kaiser sought to restrain their ally. The crisis was awkward for Bülow, who wanted to cultivate good relations with the Ottoman Empire for political and economic reasons (there was a large German railroad building project, the Berlin to Baghdad railway). Russia meanwhile sought support from its allies France and Britain, but both countries were lukewarm because it was no secret that Russia wanted to advance its own designs in the Balkans. In the end, Russia had to back down and publicly accept the annexation because it was unprepared for war so soon after its defeat against Japan and the Revolution of 1905. The Bosnian Annexation Crisis was a dubious success for Bülow and German diplomacy, however. Russia was embittered. Its expansion routes in Asia had been blocked by the defeat to the Japanese and the alliance with Britain, and therefore Russia saw expansion in the Balkans and free passage for its warships through the Dardanelles as its foreign policy priority. After the crisis, Russian diplomats decided to redouble their preparation for war and not to back down during the next international conflict. This determination would play an important role in the crisis of 1914. Again, as during the Moroccan crisis, the substance of German foreign policy was less of an issue than the tone. The annexation of Bosnia-Herzegovina by Austria-Hungary was no major change given that the province had already been administered by the Austrians and Hungarians for decades. The Bosnian Serb population may have resented the annexation, but the Bosnian Muslims and Croats saw Austro-Hungarian rule with far less hostility. Russia had secretly accepted the annexation. The problem was in the inflexibility, the bullying, and the readiness to go to war that Austria-Hungary and Germany displayed when the annexation provoked a hostile reaction from Serbia and Russia.

Bülow was not allowed to enjoy his dubious success. While the Bosnian crisis was still unfolding, a huge scandal broke that ultimately led to his dismissal. On 28 October 1908, the London newspaper *Daily Telegraph* published excerpts from an interview with Wilhelm II. In the interview, Wilhelm chastised British suspicions of Germany, calling the British "mad as March hares," and tried to reassure them of his most sincere friendship. He claimed to fight a heroic struggle for Britain in a country with a public opinion deeply hostile to Britain. He stated that he had supported Britain during the Boer War in South Africa (1899–1902), going so far as to send his grandmother, Queen Victoria, the successful war plan against the Boers, and he argued that he had prevented a German continental alliance with Russia and France against Britain. Whatever the truth of his assertions, the interview was a public relations disaster for him. Rather than allaying British suspicions, Wilhelm caused great concern about German hostility to Britain, and his self-serving claims came across as hypocritical and arrogant. In German and foreign newspapers as well as in the Reichstag, he unleashed a storm of criticism so powerful that he even thought of stepping down. The scandal implicated Bülow as well, although his precise role is unclear. The Kaiser had loyally submitted the interview to Bülow for comment, and various officials had urged Bülow to read the text carefully. Bülow, however, passed it on to a lower ranking official who offered little criticism. One interpretation is that Bülow simply did not bother to read the text and was therefore guilty of negligence. A second hypothesis is that he read the text and deliberately let it be published in order to humble the Kaiser so as to make him less inclined to interfere with government business. A third interpretation is that Bülow did nothing to stop the interview because he thought that it was a good move. Much indeed speaks for the third hypothesis, which would be a dismal, although hardly surprising, commentary on Bülow's diplomatic judgment. The Kaiser, however, suspected that the second hypothesis was true. Bülow tried to cover up his own responsibility for the publication of the interview while doing very little to defend the Kaiser. When Bülow in June 1909 submitted his resignation after the Reichstag rejected a tax reform bill he had submitted, Wilhelm II gladly accepted.

As Bülow's successor Wilhelm chose an able civil servant with little foreign policy experience: Theobald von Bethmann Hollweg, since 1905 Prussian interior minister and since 1907 state secretary in the Interior Ministry of the Reich. Bethmann, who had more strength of character than Bülow, was a pragmatician and is generally seen as a crisis manager for a government torn in different directions by the demands of the Kaiser, the Reichstag parties, and the extraparliamentary interest groups such as the nationalist leagues. Together with Caprivi, Bethmann belonged to the moderates among Wilhelm's chancellors. Like Caprivi, he eased restrictive policies toward Germany's Polish minority and opposed the repression of the SPD and the idea of a dictatorship. He worked toward a reform of the Prussian three-class suffrage, demanded by the left liberals, the SPD, and now even the National Liberals. In 1910, he submitted a very moderate proposal to broaden voter eligibility, but the bill did not pass the soundly conservative Prussian diet. He had more success in passing a liberal constitution for Alsace-Lorraine granting the province more autonomy and universal suffrage in local elections, but his efforts to tie the province to Germany through autonomist concessions were countermanded by actions of the army, which favored a more repressive regime in this important borderland. The Kaiser usually sided with the army in these conflicts. The most serious was the Zabern affair in the fall of 1913; a young lieutenant in the small Alsatian town Zabern had offered his recruits a prize for using their bayonets against civilians in case of conflicts. When this news leaked out, an anti-German demonstration occurred. The army then arbitrarily arrested thirty locals as alleged instigators of the demonstration. All of these actions were completely illegal and triggered a torrent of criticism in the liberal press, while fanning anti-German resentment in Alsace-Lorraine. Bethmann privately condemned the actions of the army, but he was ordered by the Kaiser to defend them. The reaction was an overwhelming vote of no confidence in Bethmann by the Reichstag (293 to 54). That, of course, had no practical consequence because the government was responsible to the Kaiser, not the Reichstag. Although Bethmann impressed on the Kaiser the need for disciplinary action against the perpetrators in the army, he in public had to defend the army and its supreme commander, the Kaiser.

Bethmann was also powerless in stemming the rise of the SPD. The failure of electoral reform in Prussia and the conflicts over taxation had thoroughly alienated the left liberals from the conservative parties, with which they had briefly collaborated in the Bülow Bloc of 1907. Meanwhile, the SPD, under pressure from the trade unions, had reined in its own radicals, whose irresponsible talk about using a mass strike to win power had isolated the SPD from the left liberals in 1906–7. For the elections of 1912, the left liberals were therefore willing to resume their earlier electoral alliances with the SPD. The outcome was a political earthquake. The SPD won 34.8 per cent of the national vote (up from 28.9 per cent in 1907) and secured 110 Reichstag seats (up from forty-three). Although the SPD was, as always, underrepresented in terms of seats, it now formed the strongest single group in the Reichstag. Together with the Center Party, which had ninety-one seats (with only 16.4 per cent of the vote), the SPD for the first time could form a majority in the Reichstag (201 of 397 seats). By comparison, the two conservative parties together won only fifty-seven seats, barely more than the left liberals (forty-two) and the National Liberals (forty-five). The election result sent a shock wave through right-wing circles. Radical rightists came to the conclusion that the Bismarckian system was doomed now that the former "enemies of the Reich" (Social Democrats, Center Party, and democratic left liberals) had a clear majority in the Reichstag. They advocated a dictatorship with a corporatist assembly representing professional groups, not a democratically elected Reichstag, as parliament. Pan-German leader Heinrich Class's pamphlet *If I Were the Kaiser* called for such a corporatist constitution – together with anti-Semitic measures and a more aggressive foreign policy. Increasingly, the men on the radical right believed that the Kaiser did not have the "guts" to carry out this desired policy, and they increasingly looked to Crown Prince Wilhelm as an alternative. Perhaps he would gently push his father aside and take over the reins of government. Wilhelm Junior, a caricature of his father whose rhetorical exploits were so obnoxious and immature that they made his father look moderate and tactful, seemed open toward a dictatorial solution.

In foreign policy, Bethmann played an unfortunate and ultimately disastrous role. Under pressure from nationalist interest groups, he helped trigger a second crisis over Morocco in the summer of 1911. Again, the German protest was legally not without justification. France had repeatedly violated the Algeciras agreement and committed outrages. In 1907, for example, the French government ignored protests by Moroccans that a French railroad construction site in Casablanca cut through a former Muslim cemetery. Locals attacked the site and killed seven workers. In response, the French navy bombarded the city, devastating entire sections of it and killing between 600 and 1,500 people. French troops then landed and committed rape, pillage, and brutal reprisals.[9] This episode was barely acknowledged in foreign capitals, however, and it would not have suited the German government to call attention to it after its own massive repression in Southwest Africa. But the fact that France had repeatedly sent troops into the interior of Morocco contradicted earlier agreements and gave the German government a legitimate cause for protest. But Bethmann and his staff were not primarily interested in Morocco; they hoped to create a huge central African empire for Germany and therefore tried to use the dispute over Morocco as a lever for winning territorial concessions from France in central Africa. The tone of German diplomacy, as during the crises of 1905 and 1908, was as threatening and alienating as it had been under Bülow. At the height of the crisis, the German navy dispatched a gunboat to the Moroccan city Agadir, thus contributing the term "gunboat diplomacy" to the political vocabulary. In the end, the French agreed to some trade concessions in Morocco in exchange for extending their rights there and ceded a strip of land to the German colony in Cameroon. Still, the outcome of the crisis was a harsh disappointment for Germany and unleashed a storm of criticism from the conservatives and the nationalist pressure groups. The Kaiser and Bethmann seemed too weak to secure a representation of Germany deserving of its industrial and economic power. Increasingly, the wisdom of diplomatic negotiations was questioned, and there was open talk of war.

The Bosnian and Moroccan crises may have lessened the willingness of several European governments to resort to peaceful mediation, but there still was no one-way road to world war at this time. Bethmann desired an understanding with Britain, and he was willing to limit German fleet building to achieve it. Such a limitation was, of course, also highly desirable from a financial point of view. But Bethmann tried to drive a hard bargain by trying to commit Britain to a promise of neutrality in case of a war between Germany and the Franco-Russian alliance, a condition Britain was never willing to accept. Bethmann also faced stiff opposition from Tirpitz regarding limitations on naval rearmament. Tirpitz still had a powerful lobby and support from the Kaiser. His navy bill of 1912 was cut down by the new Reichstag mostly for financial reasons, but he remained stubbornly committed to his program even though it was producing the wrong results in every possible sphere. Bilateral talks toward trading a limitation of German fleet building for a better understanding with Britain therefore failed in 1912. Still, Bethmann was able to negotiate a secret agreement with Britain on the distribution of the Portuguese colonies in case Portugal would prove unable to control them. In southern Africa, Portugal's colonies bordered on German and British territories. The treaty demonstrates that German and British foreign policy were not necessarily headed for war.

In the end of 1912, however, a series of proclamations and diplomatic notes caused a panic in the German leadership. In the fall of 1912, several Balkan states, including Serbia and Bulgaria, attacked and defeated the Ottoman Empire. Interestingly, Wilhelm II welcomed the victory of the Balkan states and even condoned Serbian expansion to the Adriatic Coast through the annexation of Albania, a prospect bitterly resisted by Austria-Hungary. Hoping to reassure Austria-Hungary in the wake of the Serbian victory, however, Bethmann said in the Reichstag that Germany would help defend Austria-Hungary in case it was attacked by Russia. These remarks triggered a warning from the British government that Britain would not stand aside if Germany were at war with France or Russia. The Kaiser, alarmed and outraged, convened a conference of military leaders on 8 December. This conference (often called the "War Council") plays a crucial role in the debates about the causation of the First World War, given that the Kaiser ordered some steps to be taken toward preparation for a war within one-and-a-half years and given that the chief of the German general staff, Helmuth von Moltke, argued that Germany should seize the next opportunity to go to war against France and Russia. The importance of this meeting remains controversial, however. Few of the measures for the preparation of war were actually implemented. Some historians therefore see the meeting as no more than a panic reaction to the British threat of war.

Germany certainly did nothing to trigger war during the next crisis, which broke out in June 1913 when Serbia and Greece attacked and defeated Bulgaria in fallout over the booty from the previous war against the Ottoman Empire. Serbian plans to annex most of Albania triggered massive resistance in Austria-Hungary, which wanted to stop Serbia by all means from winning an outlet to the Adriatic Sea. An international conference met in London and created an independent Albania, limiting the Serbian annexations essentially to Kosovo and Macedonia, which still meant more than a doubling of the size of Serbia. The dizzying pace of Serbian expansion alarmed even Serbia's friends – France, Britain, and Russia. But let us pause for a moment and consider the international situation and the German government's concerns at this point.

On the international level, relations were tense. German politicians felt encircled by the powerful Triple Entente (Britain, France, and Russia) and were nervous about the possibility of loosing their only reliable ally, Austria-Hungary (Italy, though nominally still a participant of the Triple Alliance with Germany and Austria-Hungary, would not have joined Germany in a war against Britain). The German general staff believed that it would have to fight France and Russia together while it was not sure what to expect of Britain. A two-front war with France and Russia was considered winnable only if Germany managed to knock out the French army quickly while Russia was still mobilizing (Russian mobilization was expected to be much slower than German and French mobilization). After the expected quick victory over France, the German army would form a defensive front against Russia in the east, and Germany would ultimately come to terms with Russia. A plan for this daring and highly time-sensitive operation had been worked out in 1905 by former Chief of the General Staff Alfred von Schlieffen. In order to deal the French army a quick knockout, however, Schlieffen stipulated that the German army had to avoid the strong French border defenses by sending the bulk of its forces through Belgium and Luxembourg (and, as was initially planned, the southernmost tip of the Netherlands) before swinging down around Paris and back to the French fortifications on the border, where the French army would be taken from behind and smashed against its own defenses. The plan may have had its military merits, but it was diplomatically foolhardy, even criminal. It demanded the violation of the neutrality of three countries and made a British declaration of war unavoidable. German war planners did not completely disregard this factor, but they believed that a quick success of the plan might present Britain with a *fait accompli* and dissuade it from taking part in the battle. A German war plan for a confrontation with Russia alone existed at first but was discarded in 1913 because German military planners became convinced that France would not stand by idly in a German-Russian war. Given that the Schlieffen Plan rested on the assumption that Russia would be slow to mobilize, German military planners looked at Russian railroad building with increasing nervousness. The completion of the Russian railroad system, built largely with French loans, would by 1917 allow rapid concentrations of Russian troops on the German border and make the Schlieffen Plan unworkable. Hence the pressure of the leading German generals for going to war earlier rather than later. They felt that by 1917 Germany would have lost even before starting to fight. The fleet would be of no help because British naval superiority was increasing rather than decreasing. Clearly, German generals were pushing for war, believing that war would break out sooner or later and that Germany's position would deteriorate with every year of peace. Hindsight, of course, makes it easy to qualify these fears. Granted, the Russian army in 1914 mobilized much faster than the German general staff expected, but it proved far less capable of fighting a modern war than had been assumed. German armies defeated numerically far superior Russian forces repeatedly in 1914–17. Nevertheless, Russia appeared as a huge threat to many Germans before the war, not least because its birthrate was much higher than Germany's. Fears of being run over by the "Russian steamroller" were widespread. Even Bethmann once commented that within a few decades Russian troops would stand in front of his landed estate outside of Berlin (he ultimately was right, although in a way that he could not have imagined in 1914).

The biggest concern of German statesmen was the growing instability of the multinational Habsburg empire (Austria-Hungary). In the face of strong unrest among the Slavic populations of the empire (particularly the Czechs, Croats, and Serbs), some Habsburg politicians favored transforming the Dual Monarchy into a triple monarchy by giving the Slavic peoples autonomy on terms similar to the deal the Hungarians had received in 1867 (the *Ausgleich*), while still maintaining a central imperial government in Vienna. This so-called trialist solution appealed to some Slavic nationalists and to Franz Ferdinand, the Habsburg heir to the throne, even though it was uncertain whether it would satisfy the Slavic groups and stabilize the empire (many ethnic Serbs in Croatia and Bosnia favored unity with Serbia under the wings of a Serb-dominated, Yugoslav state). If Austria-Hungary dissolved into states dominated by its national groups, however, Germany would loose its last great power ally and become completely isolated. Propping up the ailing Habsburg empire therefore became the highest priority of German foreign policy before 1914.

Regarding Germany's domestic situation, two opposing interpretations have crystallized, both with important implications for the outbreak of the First World War. The pessimistic approach, represented foremost by German historian Fritz Fischer and backed by Wehler, sees the Wilhelmine empire in the throes of a deadly crisis that it sought to overcome by waging a victorious war.[10] Some facts seem to support this view. The tide of democracy was rising, not only among the industrial workers but also in middle-class circles. All efforts to curb the growth of the SPD had failed, and the SPD had become the strongest Reichstag party by far in the 1912 elections. Meanwhile, the conservatives stubbornly opposed democratization and torpedoed every proposal for electoral reform in Prussia, whereas the Kaiser considered any infringement on his authority with outrage and might have considered a military coup to put socialists and democrats in their place should all other options run out. The extra-constitutional power of the army was unbroken, and the snobbish and undemocratic mindset of the officer corps had just been exposed once more by the Zabern Affair. Transforming the Wilhelmine Empire into a fully constitutional monarchy with parliamentary control over its government therefore seems unthinkable according to this interpretation – certainly during the lifetime of Wilhelm II (and we have seen what could have been expected of Crown Prince Wilhelm!). Another, more optimistic, interpretation, advanced among others by Thomas Nipperdey and Margaret Lavinia Anderson, tends to accept the notion that the Wilhelmine empire moved toward a latent democratization and does not support the argument that an internal crisis motivated the push for war in July 1914.[11] There is no doubt that the Reichstag had won much importance since Bismarck. The budget right was a powerful weapon, particularly at a time of high military expenditures. The ruling elites were increasingly aware that governing against the majority of the people would be foolhardy, considering the huge importance of the industrial working masses for the economy and for a modern war effort. The Reichstag had become more assertive and, despite the shortcomings of its electoral districting, it came close to a democratic representation of the masses. Chancellors Bülow and Bethmann took the Reichstag seriously and learned to establish fairly cooperative procedures with its majority. The attempts by Wilhelm II to establish "personal rule" had failed, although his right to make top-level appointments continued to give him significant power. Numerous scandals had damaged the Kaiser's personal authority and with it the prestige of the monarchy. Wilhelm II was hardly taken seriously any more. This is not to say that Germans in the last prewar years were keen on overthrowing him and establishing a republic. The vast majority of Germans were probably still willing to put up with him, but anybody trying to strengthen the monarch's power in Germany was swimming against the tide. For supporters of the optimistic view, the argument for an escape into war in 1914 vanishes given that they see no domestic crisis so severe that the statesmen had to escape from it by going to war, although it is still possible that German leaders may have played a decisive role in triggering the war for other reasons.

Good arguments can be found for both interpretations. Certainly, attitudes toward democratization, parliamentary responsibility of the government, and the extra-constitutional power of the army were irreconcilable. Big political fights would have awaited Germany, and progress toward democracy would at best have been very slow. But society was so dynamic and in many ways so modern that it is hard to imagine how all the political progress made since Bismarck's fall would have been turned back instead of continuing. The vast majority of the SPD was reformist in practice, and every step of the government toward letting the SPD participate in the state administration would have further strengthened the moderates in the party. A gradual democratization and increasing government responsibility to the Reichstag, which in some ways already existed, would have triggered an increasingly aggressive nationalist opposition on the right, and this might have made the government more inclined to rely on moderate circles on the left. We cannot know. But it does seem clear that the German government in the fateful summer of 1914 was not acting according to a drastic "fix it now or never" attitude toward domestic problems. German leaders had sometimes considered war as a panacea for foreign and domestic problems; war should split the alliances against Germany and unite the people in a wave of nationalism or even initiate some form of dictatorship based on the military. But this idea was balanced by the fear that war might trigger a socialist revolution. In any case, historians arguing for domestic politics as a cause for the war would have a better case when looking at the Triple Entente, where upheavals of a more dramatic kind were unfolding. In France, a huge scandal broke because a government minister's wife was implicated in a murder case, Britain was threatened by nationalist unrest in Ireland (which was still a part of the United Kingdom) and a big miners' strike, and Russia also experienced severe labor unrest.

Before the summer of 1914, in sum, Germany had an army leadership that was likely to use any crisis to press for what they considered a "preventive war" but a navy that had for all intents and purposes lost the arms race with Britain and therefore shared no interest in a general war. Bethmann and the Foreign Ministry were concerned about the weakness of Austria-Hungary, whereas the Kaiser, his frequent warmongering notwithstanding, tended to take a cautious stance when the situation became dangerous. It was a vital blow to the Austro-Hungarian Empire, caused by a terrorist act, that provided the trigger for the war. On 28 June 1914, a Bosnian Serb terrorist group launched a bomb at the Austrian heir apparent Franz Ferdinand and his wife, who were visiting Sarajevo, the capital of Bosnia-Herzegovina. The couple was not hit, but a bodyguard was injured. At the end of the day, the crown prince decided to visit the bodyguard in the local hospital, thus offering Gavrilo Princip, a student belonging to the conspiracy, another opportunity. With pistol shots, Princip killed Franz Ferdinand and his wife. Murders of princes and princesses or heads of state were not unusual; anarchist or radical socialist terrorists had murdered a French president, the Austrian queen, and several Russian tsars. But this murder gave rise to a special anger in most of Europe, perhaps because suspicions existed that the Serb government had contacts with the terrorist group responsible for the assassination. That the visit of the couple to Sarajevo was scheduled for the Serb national holiday and therefore constituted an affront to the Bosnian Serb population was not widely noticed. Why, then, did the murder in Sarajevo lead to general war?

Three main factors were at work. First, the Austro-Hungarian government, angered by continued pan-Slavic and pro-Serbian agitation within its borders, decided that it needed to react powerfully to this provocation in the interest of prestige, or else the empire might become ungovernable and fall apart. Second, the German government shared Vienna's assessment and gave green light for a punitive action from Austria-Hungary against Serbia. Some German officials explicitly encouraged such an action, making it clear that Germany would stand by Austria-Hungary even if Russia, Serbia's ally, would declare war on Austria-Hungary. Third, Serbia's ally, Russia, was determined, also for prestige reasons, to take a hard line toward Austria-Hungary and to support Serbia even if it meant a general European war. French leaders encouraged Russia to take a strong stand, whereas British leaders warned Germany and Austria-Hungary against going too far.

A punitive strike by the Austro-Hungarians would perhaps have been tolerated by other European governments had it happened right after the murder. But Austro-Hungarian diplomatic and military procedures were notoriously inefficient and time consuming. The empire had no less than three governments: an Austrian, a Hungarian, and an imperial government. The Hungarian and Austrian governments rarely agreed on anything, and the military of the Habsburg monarchy was poorly organized. The mobilization order appeared in some twenty different languages – testimony to the relative tolerance but also to the inefficiency of the empire. It took the Austro-Hungarian government four weeks to send an ultimatum to Belgrade, demanding far-reaching powers to investigate the murder and the implication of the Serb government. By that time, the outrage at the Serb terrorists had largely dissipated elsewhere, and the Austro-Hungarians now appeared as the aggressors. The Serb government accepted most clauses but rejected some, knowing well that this would mean war with Austria-Hungary. Russia had encouraged Serbia not to give in. For prestige reasons, Austria-Hungary was unwilling to consider a compromise and declared war on Serbia on 28 July. Russia now mobilized, first on its borders with Austria, but soon along its entire western border. This made the German generals extremely nervous, as the Schlieffen Plan rested on the condition that Russia would mobilize with great delay. The German government, under increasing pressure from the generals, sent an ultimatum to Sankt Petersburg, demanding that mobilization be stopped. The Russian government did not reply, and this prompted the German declaration of war to Russia on 1 August. One day later the Germans, who knew that the French would not stand by in a German-Russian war, also declared war on France. Following the Schlieffen Plan with some modifications, the German government tried to receive a permission from Belgium to march through its territory, which the Belgians refused to give. The Germans then sent an ultimatum to Belgium and invaded after Belgium rejected it. When the Germans entered Belgium, Britain demanded a German withdrawal and, when that condition was not met, declared war on Germany on 4 August. War declarations followed between Russia, France, and Britain on the one side and Austria-Hungary on the other.

Given the momentous changes and the high blood toll caused by the First World War, the question of war guilt has assumed special emotional and moral importance. In 1919, in the Treaty of Versailles, the victors of the war put the blame for the war squarely on Germany and its allies (although Germany alone had to pay). The Germans, however, reacted with indignation; up to the 1960s most Germans considered the war guilt charge an outrage. The prevailing opinions were either that the war was a logical outcome of an aggressive encirclement of Germany by the Entente or that it was an accident, as was the opinion of Edward Grey, the British Foreign Secretary, who had said: "the nations slithered over the brink into the boiling cauldron of war." Was Germany guilty of having started the First World War? In the 1960s a German historian, Fritz Fischer, argued that Germany indeed had to bear the main responsibility for the outbreak of the war. Fischer's three main theses were: first, that the German government under the Kaiser's direction deemed a European war inevitable since 1911/12, prepared for war, and decided to seize the next best opportunity to start it (Fischer points out the expansive aims of German heavy industry and the East Elbian agrarians); second, that the German government and general staff precipitated an escalation of the Austro-Serb crisis in order to launch what they considered a preventive strike against Russia and France. If war did not come about, they at least hoped to weaken the Entente and win a moral victory that would increase the prestige and stability of Germany and the Habsburg empire. Bethmann thus embraced a calculated risk of escalation; third, that a long-term continuity existed in German aims for expansion, leading right up to the Second World War: an eastern empire involving huge resettlements and predominance over Belgium and France.

Fischer's first argument lacks proof with regard to war preparations; it is true that German industrialists and leading agrarians had ideas about what Germany should annex if it came to a (victorious) war, but it has proven impossible to sustain the argument that the German government opted for war *in order* to realize these aims. Fischer's third argument makes too much of superficial similarities between German war aims in the two world wars; the racial agenda, for instance, played no predominant role in 1914–18, and the German policies in the occupied areas of Poland and Russia 1915–18 were very different from the practices in the east during the Second World War. His second argument, however, is widely accepted, although it would be wrong to exculpate Austria-Hungary and Russia. Austria-Hungary, as some historians have shown, did not need much pushing and sought rather little advice in the decisive two weeks before it submitted the ultimatum to Serbia. To their dismay, decision makers in Vienna and Budapest received conflicting and confusing signals from German officials (a blank check to go to war; advice *not* to go to war) and ultimately agreed to take action on their own. Russia, with French encouragement, also took a hard line during the crisis. Pan-Slavism and the feeling of an inevitable clash with the Germanic race played a role in making war acceptable, maybe desirable, to Sankt Petersburg. Still, the German government did share a major culpability for starting World War I. Bethmann did take a risky course in July 1914 that was designed to either achieve a major diplomatic success and stabilize Austria-Hungary or lead to general war. He accepted the thinking of the army leaders that the outbreak of war was acceptable, even desirable, in light of the perceived decline of Germany's military position in the near future. The German generals rigidly focused on a war against the Franco-Russian alliance and did not consider seriously the possibility of mobilizing against Russia alone, which might have limited the war and perhaps prevented it altogether. Ironically, the person who had become the symbol of the aggressive and brutal German abroad, the Kaiser, did nothing to exacerbate the crisis. Bethmann sent him off on his habitual summer cruise and kept him largely out of the decision-making process. When the Kaiser returned at the end of July, he even made some last-minute efforts to stop the conflagration by exchanging telegrams with Tsar Nicholas II and Emperor Franz Joseph II of Austria. But the arguments of generals, who defended the unstoppable mechanics of mobilization and war plans, prevailed. The sidelining of the Kaiser was a portent of developments in the First World War.

The war guilt question has usually focused on the leading politicians and generals, not on the peoples. This is to some extent correct given that the leaders had the best information and took the decisive steps. However, the public had become too interested in foreign affairs to be completely disregarded. How did the German public react to the prospect of war? Did it share responsibility for the outbreak of the war or at least for the risky course Bethmann adopted? A clear verdict is not possible in this question because the German public was deeply split. Large, spontaneous patriotic demonstrations took place in Berlin and other German cities throughout the crisis in support of a harsh course by the government. But even larger peace demonstrations, usually inspired by the SPD, also took place. Bethmann knew that only an immediate threat by Russia would rally the SPD to the German war effort. With its autocracy, its repressive police state, and its brutality against socialists, Russia was the *bête noire* of socialists all over the world. Officially, the SPD, as a member of the Second International, was obliged to call for a mass strike together with other socialist parties upon the outbreak of war. But previous statements by SPD leaders had made it clear that the threat of a Russian invasion would lead the SPD to renege on its promise. Bethmann therefore worked hard to make Russia appear as the aggressor. The full mobilization of Russia played into his hands because it constituted a direct threat to Germany that the SPD could not ignore and because it allowed him to represent German policy as defensive. This was a fallacy given his acceptance of the risk of escalation, but it was a successful propaganda coup leading most Germans to the passionate conviction that they were waging a defensive war – a conviction that was extremely hard to correct until the 1960s. That Bethmann risked war in order to stabilize the political system is unlikely, however. It was far from certain what the political fallout from a short, successful war would be. The conservatives and the army would have been strengthened, but the industrial workers would have demanded a prize for their national loyalty; the situation might have resembled the power dynamics that actually materialized in the last years of the war: a strengthened military leadership dealing with a powerful trade union movement and its political exponent, the SPD, and probably with a more assertive Reichstag demanding a democratization of the Prussian suffrage. Certainly Bethmann and the generals did not risk war in order to bolster the Kaiser's power. The swiftness with which the Kaiser was brushed aside in the July crisis and during the war belies this assertion.

In considering the causes of the First World War, one should not forget that barely any responsible statesman or general in July 1914 anticipated (and wanted) the war that actually came. Although there were some gloomy warnings that the next war would be long and cataclysmic, the predominant wisdom was that well-organized mobilization, massive gunpower, fast communications (telegraph), and the support of railroads would make war between industrialized nations a short affair. Since the Napoleonic period, a hundred years earlier, no war had ever affected large areas of Europe. The Franco-German war of 1870–71 had been the last violent conflict between industrially advanced nations in Europe. It had been decided within a few weeks. Other wars since 1871 had also been short, be it the Russo-Turkish War of

1877, the Russo-Japanese War of 1904–5, or the two Balkan wars (1912 and 1913). Given the interdependence of international trade, no nation in Europe seemed capable of surviving a long war. Industrialization and the concomitant population growth had made national economies so dependent upon imports and international trade that a long war – to contemporaries – could only lead to chaos, likely to be followed by a socialist revolution. Although pacifism existed as an independent movement and as a component of the socialist movement, many people in Europe and in Germany, in particular, thought that not all should be done to avert a short war. A violent but short war would, like a heavy thunderstorm, clear the air from the year-long tensions and problems. It was common among European intellectuals, particularly students, to think that their peoples had become lazy and – in a Darwinist sense – unfit, as they had enjoyed peace and unprecedented material progress for decades. What about a great opportunity to demonstrate that young Europeans were still able to endure hardship and sacrifice their lives for a higher cause?

–5–

The First World War

The war that started in 1914 was a disaster for Europe. Everything should have been done to avoid it. Not only did it extinguish close to ten million lives, mostly college-age men – it also left millions more handicapped and scarred for life. This would perhaps be less painful if the war had created a safer, more stable Europe. The opposite was true, however. Europe in June 1914 was a prospering and generally stable, livable place, but in late 1918, after the war, large parts of the continent were in chaos and turmoil. Germany experienced much domestic unrest, economic dislocation, and an unstable democracy giving way to perhaps the most brutal dictatorship in history. Even the victors among the European powers, France and Britain, did not look like victors after the war. Their economies and finances were shattered, their empires destabilized, and their overseas markets lost to new competitors who had benefited from the war. Italy, nominally also a victor, faced powerful labor unrest and great nationalist discontent with the outcome of the peace treaties; both factors favored the victory of fascism in 1922. Russia, having started on the side of the later victors, was shattered most disastrously by the war and by the following civil war, which cost more lives than the entire First World War. The radical socialist group that seized power in late 1917 established a new society and imposed a police state far more repressive and deadly than the tsarist state. The real winners of the war were the United States and some nations in South America, Asia, and Africa, together with the Australian continent, which started to make up for the absence of European imports and lessened their dependence upon European products and knowhow. It is fair to say that the First World War marked the end of European predominance over the globe, which had lasted for nearly 500 years. This was definitely not what any of the governments sending or receiving the many declarations of war in 1914 (Italy entered the war in April 1915 on the side of the Entente) expected. How did this result come about?

Let us first look at the military development of the war. The crucial fact is that the Schlieffen Plan, which should have ensured a quick decision, failed. This meant that a stalemate developed that neither side was able to break in four years. It was only the arrival of large numbers of fresh American troops in the spring and summer of 1918 that tipped the balance. But the long war of attrition that developed in the fall of 1914 had decisive consequences for the warring states; it ruined their finances, overburdened their state administrations, sowed mutual hatred through propaganda campaigns to vilify the enemy, and eroded state authority in many countries. In light of the magnitude of the sacrifices right from the start, any compromise peace returning to the status quo seemed impossible to justify. The cost of the war, both in human and material terms, was so high that governments early on decided that they could pursue nothing but complete victory. Besides, all governments firmly believed in the rightness of their cause, as did millions of soldiers.

It was not lack of effort that doomed the Schlieffen Plan. The mobilization of the regular troops went rather smoothly, and countless young Germans enlisted as war volunteers. Women cheered the soldiers and treated them with flowers and chocolate on their way to the train stations. Almost all Germans believed that they needed to defend their country. The Kaiser addressed enthusiastic crowds in Berlin, telling them that he knew no parties any more – only Germans. This feeling of national unity, although idealized and instrumentalized right from the start, was experienced by many Germans, and they later looked back to it with nostalgia. Although the older image of unanimous enthusiasm for the war has to be qualified – there was also anxiety and depression – war fever seemed to have affected millions of Germans and other Europeans as they went to war. Problems for the German war effort became obvious quite quickly, however. The Belgian army resisted the invasion. The German armies, fearing that the timetable of the Schlieffen Plan might unravel, reacted with anger and nervousness, executing over six thousand Belgian and northern French civilians suspected of illicit (*franctireur*) resistance. Meanwhile, Russian mobilization proceeded more quickly than the German generals had foreseen even in their worst nightmares. A mere three weeks after the declaration of war, two huge Russian armies were advancing deeply into East Prussia. They were still far from Berlin, but the German forces standing in their way were numerically far inferior. The German general staff panicked and deployed two army corps from the decisive right flank of its western attack to the eastern front. This was soon proven unnecessary, however, as the German troops under the command of General Paul von Hindenburg and his very capable chief of staff, Erich Ludendorff, encircled the disorganized and poorly equipped Russians and defeated them in the Battle of Tannenberg (26 to 30 August) before the reinforcements arrived. The two army corps were sorely missed in the west, however. Troops from a rapidly deployed British expedition force moved into the gap between two German armies at the extreme right wing of the German advance, and hastily formed French units counterattacked on the Marne River, just forty miles northeast of Paris. The German general staff panicked again and called off the Schlieffen Plan altogether. Chief of Staff Moltke had a nervous breakdown and was replaced by Prussian Minister of War Erich von Falkenhayn. Both sides raced to the sea, trying unsuccessfully to outflank each other, and established a line of trenches from the Swiss border to the westernmost tip of Belgium.

The failure of the Schlieffen Plan should have spelled defeat for Germany, given that nobody had planned for a long war. Germany was saved for the time being by its scientists, who managed to produce synthetic materials for explosives and rubber, crucial goods that the German war industry normally imported from overseas but could no longer obtain because the British navy had imposed a blockade. Only the Baltic Sea remained open for Swedish iron ore transports. The synthetic materials enabled Germany to hold out for the time being, but the prospects for a long war looked bleak. Even though the Ottoman Empire joined the Central Powers, as Germany and Austria-Hungary were now called, the ratio of resources and manpower favored the Entente. In almost all areas, the Entente was superior by a ratio of 5:3 even before the entry of the United States into the war. The Austro-Hungarian army, which often was not informed by the German general staff, was of little help; it suffered defeats against Russia in Galicia, required German troops to bolster its defenses, and was repeatedly beaten back by the Serbian army. In the light of these facts, the German leadership calculated that it would loose a war of attrition; therefore it repeatedly decided to force a decision through high-risk strategies and measures. None of these strategies led to a decisive success, but the Central Powers kept fighting even though their supply situation deteriorated with every year of the war, causing massive famines from the winter of 1916–17 onward.

A breakthrough in the west was highly desirable for Germany because it might finally inflict the defeat on France that the Schlieffen Plan had meant to produce in the first weeks of the campaign. But a breakthrough was extremely difficult to achieve once the armies had dug in and formed increasingly sophisticated rows of trenches, machine-gun nests, land mines, and barbed wire. The devastating consequences of an attack were demonstrated during the battle of Langemarck, a Belgian village, on 10 November 1914. Thousands of enthusiastic German recruits, most of them university students who had volunteered for service, tried to storm a hill but were mowed down by a few machine gunners at the top of the hill. Within an afternoon, over 2,000 were killed, thousands more injured. The attack became a myth of patriotic self-sacrifice and was still celebrated decades later. It demonstrated the foolishness of frontal attack against a well-defended position, but both sides refused to fully appreciate this lesson until 1918. Vast offensives on the western front took place every year with appalling casualties for attackers and defenders, but none of them led to a decisive breakthrough. It was possible to conquer a trench system after bombarding it with heavy guns for several days and nights and then launching an infantry assault, but somewhere there always were a few surviving defenders with a machine gun who would inflict severe losses on the attackers. By the time they were overwhelmed, the defending side had usually prepared new trenches farther back, so that the conquest of the first rows of trenches did not lead to a breakthrough. Worse, the defending side usually launched a counterattack on the exhausted attackers and often threw them out of the trenches they had conquered with so much blood. The exercise appeared criminally pointless but was repeated again and again, always in the hope that the decisive breakthrough would finally materialize.

On the eastern front, movement remained possible because of the vastness of the space. German armies under Hindenburg and Ludendorff inflicted another severe defeat on the Russian forces during the battle of the Masurian Lakes (8 to 15 September 1914). The apparent ease with which Russian troops, even with vastly superior numbers, could be beaten impressed Falkenhayn. He hoped to inflict a decisive defeat on the Russian army in 1915 that would make Russia willing to sue for peace and thus relieve Germany of its two-front war. Another battle in East Prussia in February 1915 inflicted huge losses on the Russian forces and expelled the last of them from German soil, but the Russians were able to build a new defensive line farther east. New offensives in the spring and summer of 1915, this time with large Austro-Hungarian forces, inflicted more defeats on the outgunned Russians, but Russia kept fighting. In September, the Russians even mounted a counterattack that was stopped by the Austro-Hungarians with some German help. By the end of 1915, the Germans had conquered most of Russian Poland, and the Austro-Hungarians had reconquered most of their territories lost in 1914, but the Russian army was still able to fight and Russia was no closer to a separate peace than it had been at the beginning of the year.

On the western front, Germany remained largely on the defensive throughout 1915, denying several big French and British attempts to break through in the Champagne. The Germans waged one major counter-attack near the Belgian city of Ypres in April and May, hoping to break through with the help of poison gas, which was a breach of the laws of war. The German army inflicted severe losses on the British army but lacked the reserves to capitalize on the initial success. Both sides used poison gas frequently from now on, albeit never with decisive success. A setback for the Central Powers was the entry of Italy into the war in April 1915. After having bargained for territorial expansion with both sides, the Italian government obtained the better deal from the Entente powers, which of course could always promise Italy more Austro-Hungarian territory than the Austro-Hungarians would concede. The Italian entry into the war was ill-considered, however. For over three years, the Italians literally fought an uphill battle against small Austro-Hungarian and German forces well entrenched on the southern slopes of the Alps. In October 1917 the Italian army was defeated during a counterattack, but the Central Powers lacked the forces to exploit their victory and withdrew to their initial positions. Italy's participation in the war did open another front for Austria-Hungary, but it was ultimately a frustrating and demoralizing experience for Italy.

Given that a breakthrough was so difficult to achieve on the western front, the Entente powers tried to increase pressure on the Central Powers in other areas. Hoping to knock the Ottoman Empire out of the war and to open the Dardanelles to aid shipments for the suffering Russian army, British and French forces landed in Gallipoli, a peninsula in the Dardanelles, in April 1915. Well-positioned Ottoman forces, however, foiled repeated assaults, while diseases took a terrible toll on the Entente forces, which included troops from Australia, New Zealand, and French West Africa. In December 1915, the Entente forces began their withdrawal from Gallipoli. Meanwhile, Bulgaria had entered the war on the side of the Central Powers (in

October). A combined Austro-Hungarian, German, and Bulgarian offensive forced the Serbian army to withdraw and allow the occupation of Serbia, Montenegro, and Albania by the Central Powers. The French and British thereupon landed in neutral Greece and evacuated the starving Serbian army to the Greek island Corfu. With the surviving Serb forces and some Italian and Russian units, they established a new front on the Greek-Serbian border in today's Macedonia, but not much movement happened there until the fall of 1918.

Naval war did not lead to a quick decision either. The expensive German battle fleet remained largely passive. In September 1914, however, a relatively new weapon raised big hopes in Germany. Within an hour, a single German submarine sank three older British warships. Although it soon became clear that submarines could destroy battleships only under unusual circumstances, they proved an effective tool against the enemy's merchant fleet. This raised legal issues, however. Naval law required that an attacking ship warn the merchant ship and ensure the evacuation of its sailors. A submerged submarine trying to warn a merchant steamer could easily be rammed and sunk by it, and submarines had no space for the crew of an enemy ship. The German naval leaders pointed out that naval law had not covered the submarine and that the British blockade was itself a violation of naval law. The former argument was debatable, but the latter was true: naval law allowed only materials essential for war production to be stopped by a blockading navy. Britain, however, cut off all goods to Germany, even food. Power considerations induced the German leadership to restrict the use of the submarines in reaction to strongly worded American protests – particularly after the sinking of the British passenger ship *Lusitania* on 7 May 1915, when 1,200 people perished, including 128 Americans. That the *Lusitania* had been carrying ammunitions and was listed as an auxiliary cruiser of the British navy made no difference. German leaders ground their teeth in the face of what they perceived as partisan American neutrality: while the US government merely protested against the unlawfulness of the British blockade, it threatened (and later declared) war on Germany for retaliating with unrestricted submarine warfare, all the while supplying the Entente with weapons and ammunitions. But German leaders were still convinced that the benefits of unrestricted submarine warfare did not justify adding the United States to the enemy coalition as a belligerent. Bethmann fought bitter battles over this issue with Tirpitz, who had not done much to advance the German submarine force before 1914 but suddenly insisted on their unrestricted use. Interestingly, the Kaiser for a long time took a cautious approach and sided with Bethmann. Tirpitz became so desperate over this that he entertained some wild schemes to have the Kaiser declared insane and to concentrate power in the hands of a few generals and himself. After a series of clashes the Kaiser had no choice but to dismiss him in March 1916, having decided once more against deploying the submarines without restrictions. Meanwhile, Germany's submarine fleet was growing and inflicting considerable damage on British shipping even while applying fairly strict rules of engagement accepted by the American government.

Still, at the beginning of 1916, Falkenhayn recognized the need to end the war as soon as possible. Germany started to feel the shortage of raw materials and food more sharply, and Russia was preparing for new offensives against the ailing Austro-Hungarian army. The failure to knock out the Russian army in 1915 induced Falkenhayn to seek the decisive victory again in the west through an attack on the cornerstone of the French frontline, the fortress of Verdun. The German attack started on 22 February 1916, and the fortress system of Verdun became the most horrific blood mill of the war, a lunar landscape of shell holes containing remains of burnt trees, shell splinters, and body parts, all ground together by successive waves of heavy artillery fire from both sides. When the desired breakthrough failed, Falkenhayn changed the strategic priority. With a chilling contempt for human lives, he now expected to "bleed dry" the French army, which would have to hold Verdun at all cost and would in the process lose so many people that it would be inclined to sue for peace. The battle raged until August 1916. It cost the Germans almost as many casualties as the French (close to half a million each), did not induce the French army to sue for peace, and left the Entente strong enough to launch a huge counterattack on the Somme in June. Until November, bitter fighting ensued in this sector of the front. At the end, the British and French had won a strip of ruined land some 25 miles long and 8 miles deep at an appalling cost: the German and British armies suffered some 500,000 casualties each, the French about 200,000. The writer Ernst Jünger (1895–1998) fought in this battle as a young officer and recorded how hundreds of men were sent to trenches under severe fire every night just to hold the line. Whereas many soldiers on both sides increasingly questioned these tactics, Jünger participated with a Nietzschean fascination, believing that he saw a new age and new man being forged in the blood mills of the western front:

> Death lay in ambush for each one in every shell-hole, merciless, and making one merciless in turn. Chivalry here took a final farewell. It had to yield to the heightened intensity of war, just as all fine and personal feeling has to yield when machinery gets the upper hand. The Europe of to-day [written in 1920] appeared here for the first time on the field of battle.[1]

On the eastern front, the Germans planned merely to hold the line in 1916, but they were drawn into unwanted battles when the Russians launched a series of powerful offensives against the Austro-Hungarians, coming close to decisive victory on several occasions. When Romania, encouraged by the Russian successes and lured by the promise of vast annexations at the expense of the Habsburg monarchy, signed an alliance with the Entente on 17 August 1916, the German military leaders concluded that the war was lost. The Romanian army had 600,000 men ready to attack the Austro-Hungarians, and there seemed to be no way to stop them from linking up with the Russians in Hungary. The Kaiser reacted to the crisis by dismissing Falkenhayn and calling Hindenburg as his successor, with Ludendorff as chief of staff. He did so only in desperation. Through their victories in the east, Hindenburg and Ludendorff had become popular heroes. Most Germans wanted them at the supreme command of the army, and many even as dictators. The Kaiser recognized that he would lose more power and prestige with such popular and independently minded giants next to him. Only the belief that defeat was imminent and the hope that the popular generals might make it more acceptable to the German public induced him to hand over the supreme command to them. Hindenburg and Ludendorff, who had always wanted to prioritize the eastern front over the western front, quickly called off the offensive against Verdun and put together a force against Romania, ironically under the command of Falkenhayn. The Romanian attack on Hungary, launched on 27 August, was initially successful but not decisive because the Russian forces aiming to link up with the Romanians advanced too slowly. Falkenhayn's army beat the Romanian army back to the border in October, and another German force under Field Marshal August von Mackensen invaded the south of Romania and conquered Bucharest on 6 December 1916. The remainders of the Romanian army withdrew toward the Russian border and kept fighting until the Romanian government agreed to sign a harsh peace treaty with the Central Powers on 7 May 1918.

In naval warfare, no progress was in sight either. On 31 May and 1 June the largest battle between the German and British fleet occurred near Jutland (Denmark), where the bulk of the fleets met without knowing the opponent's exact strength. The German fleet sunk almost twice as many ships as the British but had to withdraw in the face of the great British superiority (twenty-eight against sixteen big battleships). Although the battle was celebrated as a victory in Germany, it did nothing to alter the balance of power. Both fleets avoided another major engagement for the rest of the war, and the British blockade remained as stringent as ever. Although the German war economy had been organized efficiently under the direction of the ingenious industrialist Walther Rathenau, shortages of food became more severe, particularly in the German and Austrian cities. The urban population was forced to wait in long lines for often insufficient food rations, and farmers became more resentful at the regime of fixed prices, production quotas, and rationed deliveries. Hindenburg and Ludendorff devised an ambitious program to intensify the output of the war economy, but, as historian Gerald Feldman has shown in an insightful study, raising the output in some sectors of the economy meant creating shortages in other sectors.[2] German society was under increasing strain, and the winter of 1916–17, known as the "turnip winter" because almost everything available to urban consumers was made of cheap turnips, brought widespread famines. Given the fleet's inability to break the British blockade, the German leadership felt under increasing pressure to seek a successful end to the war at a high risk.

This was the moment when German leaders made their decisive mistake. The call for the unrestricted deployment of the submarines had swelled since Tirpitz's dismissal. Many nationalist leagues made the call for unrestricted submarine warfare their primary concern. Why should Germany blunt its most powerful weapon when its people were starving to death? The threat of an American entry into the war was dismissed, and many pamphlets pointed out that the United States was already supplying the Entente with enormous amounts of war materiel and money. Leading admirals and economists claimed that the submarines, if deployed without restrictions, would sink so much tonnage that Britain would have to sue for peace after six months, long before the United States would be able to land large numbers of troops in France. Tirpitz, who launched many intrigues for submarine warfare, made these arguments appealing even to Hindenburg and Ludendorff. Seeing no other way to bring the war to a successful end, they too began pushing for unrestricted submarine warfare. With the support of the Kaiser, Bethmann tried to postpone and perhaps avert the unrestricted submarine war by making a peace offer to the Entente in December 1916. One may doubt the sincerity of the German desire for peace, but the Entente rejected the peace offer in a rude note. American President Woodrow Wilson then asked the two sides to state their peace conditions, but it became clear that these conditions were completely incompatible and could only be imposed on either side after complete defeat. The failure of his peace initiative decisively weakened Bethmann's hand. During a conference on 8 January, he and the Kaiser had to agree to the start of unrestricted submarine warfare on 1 February. As predicted, this measure provoked a hostile American reaction. The United States, already suspicious of Germany because of a German alliance offer to Mexico (the "Zimmermann Note") in January 1917, broke off diplomatic relations with Germany and declared war on 6 April. The submarines did sink about as many ships as had been predicted in the first six months of the campaign, but the enormous industrial potential of the United States was now at the full disposal of the Entente, so that for every ship sunk by a German submarine a new ship was being built. Moreover, the Allies inflicted mounting losses on German submarines when they began organizing their merchant ships in large convoys escorted by cruisers in the most dangerous waters. By the summer of 1917 it was clear to all sober minds that unrestricted submarine warfare had failed despite the large damage it had done. This was tantamount to a disaster given that it would only be a matter of time until the United States would land a strong army in France able to break the stalemate on the western front.

Had the German leaders known in January 1917 that Russia would collapse later that year, they might well have reversed their high-risk decision for unrestricted submarine warfare. On 8 March (23 February according to the old Russian calendar), Russian workers, soldiers, and bourgeois politicians revolted against Nicholas II and began establishing the foundations of a constitutional and democratic state. Nicholas abdicated a few days later. The new Russian government decided to pursue the war effort, but the Russian army was demoralized and near disintegration. Still, the German supreme command was so disheartened by the Russian persistence that they decided to deploy a highly unusual weapon. Vladimir I. Lenin, the leader of the illegal Bolshevist Party, was living in exile in Zürich, where he was studying every day at the central library. Lenin did not have much influence on events in Russia at this time, but he was known to advocate immediate peace with Germany after the Bolshevists gained power. In April 1917, the German Supreme Command allowed Lenin to cross through Germany and to go to Russian Finland, from where he entered the Russian capital Petrograd (the old Sankt Petersburg, which was renamed at the start of the war) and began agitating for a more radical communist revolution. Unfortunately, by continuing the war, the Russian government allowed the very same erosion of state authority that had brought down the monarchy to continue. After yet more severe defeats to the German army in July 1917, Russia descended into anarchy. Power was up for grabs, and the Bolshevists, a small but well organized group, took it during a coup on 6–7 November 1917. Lenin stood by his decision to conclude peace and opened negotiations with Germany. He realized that he needed whatever peace he could get to conquer and pacify Russia, and he expected a communist revolution to take place in Germany and elsewhere, too. Any peace deal signed with the German generals might soon be discarded by a German communist government. The German negotiators, meeting the Soviet delegation in Brest-Litovsk on 3 December 1917, insisted on such severe peace conditions that the negotiations dragged on. Finally, on 3 March 1918, the Soviet delegation under the leadership of Leon Trotsky signed the treaty of Brest-Litovsk. Russia had to evacuate Finland, the Baltic states, Ukraine, and areas in the Caucasus region and to cede all claims to Russian Poland (where the Germans had established a puppet state in November 1916). The treaty was undoubtedly very harsh, but it should also be considered in the context of Entente war aims against the Habsburg and Ottoman empires, which also stipulated the dissolution of multinational empires. Many people in the areas lost by Russia had long wanted to be out of Russia. The Germans, however, planned to keep many of these areas under informal control and, at least in the short run, under military occupation. One thing is certain, however: the Treaty of Brest-Litovsk did not end the fighting in the east. German troops helped Finland expel Bolshevist units, fought against various communist uprisings in the new states separated from Russia, and intervened in some fights between Bolshevists and counter-revolutionary forces in southern Russia. Hoping (in vain) to mitigate the food shortages in Germany by exploiting Ukraine, Hindenburg and Ludendorff committed strong forces to the east at a time when they badly needed them on the western front.

In the west, the British and French launched another series of offensives in the spring of 1917, hoping to decide the war before the arrival of the Americans and therefore to have a stronger say during peace negotiations. In early April, the British attacked Arras, and the French launched a large offensive in the Champagne and Aisne regions. Having concentrated strong forces in the east for a final blow against Russia, the Germans had withdrawn their western troops to a well-prepared defensive position, the Siegfried Line, which they hoped to hold with roughly half the forces the British and French had at their disposal. The British attack, after nine days of relentless bombardment, left only a minor dent in the German positions after inflicting huge losses on both sides, and the French attacks had exactly the same outcome. This renewed senseless spilling of blood triggered a massive mutiny in the French army and led to the replacement of commander-in-chief Georges Nivelle by Philippe Pétain, the defender of Verdun in 1916. Pétain managed to stabilize the situation by executing a moderate number of rebels while improving the living conditions of the soldiers. Fortunately for the French, the Germans did not learn of the mutinies until it was too late. The failures of the spring offensives of 1917 made the French and the British army wary of launching another major offensive and more inclined to wait for the arrival of American help. The British nevertheless launched a large attack near Cambrai, where they overran weak German lines by deploying nearly 400 tanks. This success was so surprising, however, that the British failed to capitalize on it. The Germans reconquered the lost ground three days later. The battle near Cambrai demonstrated the offensive potential of tanks, but armies yet had to learn how to exploit it. The Germans, who prioritized the construction of submarines, had no resources left for tanks (they built only 20 in comparison to the Entente's 5,000) and tried to adapt their defensive lines to potential tank attacks.

The defeat of Russia relieved Germany from its two-front war although strong German forces remained committed in Eastern Europe. Hindenburg and Ludendorff now decided to wage a last massive attack on the western front, hoping to defeat France before American troops, which kept arriving in France at an increasing pace, would tip the balance. With reinforcements from Russia, the German army launched a series of attacks on the British and French positions beginning on 21 March 1918 and continuing through the middle of July. These offensives initially seemed successful; the Germans pushed back the Entente armies and repeatedly came very close to a breakthrough. For the second time (after September 1914), the front moved so close to Paris that the cannon fire could be heard there. The potentially decisive breakthrough never materialized, however. Some military experts blame Ludendorff's strategy of launching several separate attacks instead of concentrating on one single area, while others blame the useless commitment of troops in the east. In several cases, the success of the German advance became a problem because reserves could not be brought in fast enough, and sometimes the most advanced troops came under fire from their own artillery. When the quick breakthrough did not materialize, moreover, the German army suffered a creeping breakdown of morale amounting to a passive form of desertion. Thousands of soldiers with light wounds simply disappeared from their units without trying hard to reach the Red Cross stations in the rear. Many other soldiers more or less intentionally got lost on their way from the rest quarters to the now much more distant front. After a few weeks, masses of German soldiers erred around aimlessly in the poorly controlled area between the frontline and the base camps. It did not help that soldiers who had fought in Russia and often fraternized with Russian soldiers told others about the promise of a communist revolution and the senselessness of dying for big capital. By the summer, the German army was so exhausted that it could not resist a large Allied counter-offensive with strong American participation that started on 18 July. On 8 August, an attack with 450 tanks near Amiens punched a big hole into the German lines, but the German army was able to withdraw and dig in yet again. Soon it had to fall back on the Siegfried Line, which it had left in March amid hopes for imminent victory. Against an enemy with vast material superiority and far more men, any renewed offensive was unthinkable, and even holding the line proved difficult in the following months. Although they still held vast lands in eastern Europe, the Germans had for all intents and purposes lost the war. But before focusing on the end of the war, we need to consider what had meanwhile happened to German society, politics, and civilians.

More than before, the war effort depended on the support and sacrifice of entire peoples. While a large segment of the male workforce between age eighteen and fifty-five was serving in the army, women, children, and older people took over the work of men in industry and agriculture. Entire societies were working for the war, as the term "home front" implicates. The conditions of wartime work were stressful, often terrible: for many women and young people, they involved extremely long hours in dangerous workplaces, particularly in the ammunitions factories and in plants with overworked and poorly serviced machines. This was true for most countries participating in the war, but the living conditions in Germany and parts of Austria were particularly bad because of the increasing shortages of food and other consumer goods. Urban residents had to wait in long lines, often before dawn, to get the most basic items at the shops, and usually the shops were empty before everybody had been served. The lines grew longer and the store shelves emptier. Children grew up with much less attention from adults than previously. Wartime situation reports warned of thousands of youngsters employed in the war industry roaming the streets in their leisure hours without adult supervision. In addition, the losses at the front put an enormous psychological strain on the civilian population. Hardly a civilian did not loose a father, son, or brother in the war. Multiple losses within the same family were common. Over two million German soldiers were killed in the war, more than from any other nation in the First World War (although France and Serbia sustained higher losses in relation to their population). Millions more returned with handicaps, mental illness, or scarred for life by shell shock. These losses were enormously costly for the state, too, as it had to support widows and children of fallen soldiers and pay (meager) compensation for disabled soldiers. In short, the war put a heavy strain on German society and confronted the state authorities with unprecedented tasks. One of the most daunting tasks for states was the organization of the war economy. Work force and production shifted to industries that were essential for the war. If possible, factories tried to produce goods that were needed by the army. Peace goods and consumer goods became rare and thus expensive. Huge state investment went to heavy industry, particularly to the largest enterprises, as they seemed more efficient and had stronger lobbies. This created much bitterness among smaller entrepreneurs and all those businessmen and artisans who could not participate in the armaments production. Disgruntled lower middle-class people found that the state seemed to neglect them and that the workers were better off than they because the workers had large interest organizations. Many of these people tended to blame the Jews for their economic plight, blending allegedly Jewish-led socialism together with allegedly Jewish capitalism into one powerful hallucinatory target. Anti-Semitism began to find increasing resonance among these groups.

In order to give meaning to the suffering and to stabilize the home front, governments formulated war aims. The longer the war lasted, the greater the emphasis that the enemy would have to cover one's own astronomic war expenses through reparations and territorial losses. "*Le boche payera tout*" ("the boche [derogatory term for German] will pay for everything") became a mantra in France, for example. The idea to have the enemy pay was short sighted, however, because all European countries would be more or less bankrupt after the war. The theses of Fritz Fischer have made the German war aims particularly controversial. In early September 1914, while the German armies still seemed victorious, Bethmann invited interest organizations and the military to state their war aims, which resulted in a long "shopping list" of expansive goals. Industrialists, in particular, wanted to annex parts of Belgium and northern France because these regions had iron ore and therefore were an ideal complement to the coalfields and steel-producing areas of west Germany. The conservatives were more interested in eastern expansion, resulting in more land for German farmers to be settled there. They hoped to drive Russia back from the German border and to create a belt of buffer states in eastern Europe. Some conservatives also hoped to resettle Polish farmers further east in order to stop the growth of the Polish population in the Polish areas that belonged to the German Empire. To the conservatives an overwhelming victory with large annexations further promised to fan nationalism to such a degree that the existing social and political order might be stabilized. The army leaders, still in shock about the fast Russian advances into German territory in August 1914, supported some of these aims, whereas the navy was interested foremost in controlling the Belgian coast, which was an excellent location for submarine bases against Britain. Business circles, moreover, wanted to establish a European customs union reaching from France through Belgium and the Netherlands to Austria, Hungary, and the future eastern European buffer states. Eager colonialist circles in the German administration also hoped to establish a central African empire under German control. In all these plans, France should be reduced to the status of a middle power, while Russia should be pushed far back to the east. This so-called September Program remained more or less unchanged throughout most of the war.

The extreme expansionism of the September Program has led historians such as Fischer to argue that Germany went to war in order to realize it, but there is little evidence for this. It rather seems as if the German power elites came to the conclusion that the outbreak of the war had shown how vulnerable their state was and that it needed extensive territorial guaranties to avoid being faced by strong enemies on two sides ever again. In the Darwinist thinking of the period, moreover, many Germans were afraid to lose out against the huge potential of the British overseas empire and Russia's vast land empire, not to speak about the still poorly appreciated potential of the United States. Although the aggressiveness of the September Program is beyond dispute, several arguments must be considered. Since the military leaders kept information about the real situation to a minimum, those who advocated it had no realistic image of Germany's potential for winning the war. This is not an excuse for the character of the annexationist program, but it explains its lacking realism. Moreover, many Germans opposed the far-reaching war aims and preferred to end the war even if the result would not bring large expansion. The Social Democrats, the left liberals, and later in the war the Center Party challenged the aggressive war aims of the industrialists and conservatives. The government, finally, never committed itself to anything. It had compiled the September Program on the basis of an informal hearing in order to learn about the opinion of the economic and military elites. When the discussion of war aims became a threat to the domestic truce, Bethmann repressed the public discussion of war aims through stricter censorship. He also did not want to tie his hands in future peace negotiations and wanted to keep options open for a separate peace with Russia. This caused widespread irritation in right-wing circles. Pan-Germans and conservatives were not used to seeing censorship applied to them rather than to the left. From late 1914, the radical nationalists saw their prewar perception confirmed, namely that Bethmann was a weak leader who could not be trusted as an effective representative of conservative interest. Rightists repeatedly tried to induce Wilhelm II to dismiss him and appoint a more aggressive nationalist in his place (such as Tirpitz, Falkenhayn, or Ludendorff).

The German war aims should be condemned, but it would be wrong to see them in isolation. Entente war aims were not moderate either. The French did not want to back out of the war without having at least won Alsace-Lorraine and massively weakened Germany, possibly by dissolving it again. The British wanted to take away Germany's fleet and its colonies, and Russia had been promised areas in Poland, the Balkans, the Caucasus, and the right to occupy the Dardanelles. Italy wanted much territory from Austria-Hungary, some of which was not inhabited by Italian speakers. Sooner or later, Britain and France promised independence to almost all minorities of the Habsburg monarchy. After the Bolshevist revolution, they supported the establishment of a Polish state including the German territory settled by Poles and some areas settled by Germans. The British and French also aimed to dissolve the Ottoman Empire and made conflicting arrangements for Jewish and Arab autonomy in Palestine, an Ottoman province. This shows that the war aims of both sides were completely irreconcilable and could only be imposed on a thoroughly defeated enemy. The pope and President Wilson, before entering the war, suggested a peace without annexations and reparations, but neither side was willing to entertain this idea seriously, although it has to be said that a left-to-center Reichstag majority in July 1917 demanded precisely this goal. But most countries quickly lost so much in the fighting that any thought of going back to the status quo ante seemed tantamount to defeat, and most governments considered the situation before August 1914 as highly unsatisfactory, perhaps even as a cause of the war. In January 1918, President Wilson stated new peace demands in his Fourteen Points, which demanded, among other things, the return of Alsace-Lorraine to France, evacuation of Belgium and all of eastern Europe by the Germans and their allies, and a redrawing of the borders according to national majorities. These aims were considered unacceptable by the German government until it had to concede defeat in October 1918. The Fourteen Points were moderate in comparison to the aims of the British and the French, however. As French Prime Minister Georges Clémenceau said: "Wilson has fourteen points; our Lord managed with ten. We shall see ..."

Initially, Germans broadly supported the war effort. Bethmann had successfully portrayed the Russians as the aggressors, and most Germans were convinced that they were waging a defensive war brought on by a power-thirsty Russia and a jealous Britain. On 4 August 1914, the Kaiser had addressed the Berlin crowds and declared to roaring applause: "I do not know any parties any more. I know only Germans." This *Burgfrieden* (piece of the fortress) remained largely unchallenged in the first two years of the war. The Reichstag parties remained passive, and no powerful dissent arose yet from other quarters. This began to change as the problems of the food supply began to affect Germans harder. Whereas German economists organized war production effectively, although at the price of choking smaller companies and all peace industries unable to adapt to war production, it proved impossible to organize sufficient food supplies given the shortages created by the British blockade. Farmers resented the state regulations and often circumvented them by selling on the black market. Poor urban consumers, however, could not afford black market prices and suffered most directly from the shortages. In the fall and winter of 1916, food shortages reached famine proportions, and despite some relief in the summers hunger remained a constant companion of millions of Germans until the end of June 1919, when the British finally lifted the blockade. Undernourishment (and the lack of heating fuel in the winters) made people less resistant to illness. A British inquiry conducted soon after the war found out that there had been 800,000 excess deaths due to the blockade, mostly in the years 1916–19.

Maintaining order and unity became increasingly difficult under these conditions. Deputy military commanders ruled Germany under emergency legislation. They tried to be moderate and competent, but the system according to which they had to rule was antiquated. There were twenty-three generals ruling areas that were military districts and differed from administrative districts. A chaos of overlapping responsibilities was the consequence. The generals at home also had to administer censorship, which was usually mild, but often arbitrary against the left. By 1916, the police and the deputy military commanders were increasingly helpless. It was above all the industrial working class in the cities that suffered from the food shortages and began to question the war. More and more workers felt that they and their families were made to suffer for war aims that would benefit big industry and the big landlords. In the long lines outside the shops, women vented their anger at the government, and there were bread riots. Desperate urban dwellers went to the countryside at night and stole potatoes. The Independent SPD (USPD), a radical group that had broken off from the SPD because of the SPD's support for the war budgets submitted to the Reichstag, produced leaflets demanding immediate peace. There were strikes and even some mutinies in the German High Seas Fleet. As we have seen, the concern over the domestic situation played a crucial role in the Supreme Command's decision for unrestricted submarine warfare in January 1917. Meanwhile, the Reichstag parties began pressuring the government toward reform. At the very least, the government should reward the working class for its patriotic war service by reforming the Prussian suffrage. In his Easter Message of 1917, the Kaiser did promise a reform, but he left the conditions vague. In July 1917, with the failure of unrestricted submarine warfare becoming obvious to all but the admirals, a large Reichstag majority including the National Liberals was concerned enough about the change in the popular mood that they passed the so-called Peace Resolution demanding a peace without reparations and annexations. At the same time, right-wing circles became worried that the government might strike an unsatisfactory peace deal and stepped up pressure for ambitious war aims. They feared that a modest peace would allow a powerful socialist and democratic movement to take over the bankrupt, exhausted German state. A victorious peace, however, might cushion social unrest and bolster the traditional political system. These concerns led to the foundation of the Fatherland Party, a nationalist pressure group headed by Tirpitz and Wolfgang Kapp, a Prussian official who had been dismissed in 1916 after distributing a pamphlet that was extremely critical of Bethmann. The Fatherland Party professed to rally the nation together and crystallized the desperate hope for victory; behind it stood big industry, the conservatives, and the Pan-German League. The Supreme Command shared the Fatherland Party's concerns. Hindenburg and Ludendorff had therefore demanded the dismissal of Bethmann, whom they considered too soft on war aims. As Bethmann had also opposed the Reichstag's Peace Resolution, he had few friends left willing to support him, and he was dismissed in July 1917. The Kaiser appointed Georg Michaelis, a Prussian civil servant, as his successor, but Michaelis was unable to win the trust of either the Reichstag majority or the Supreme Command and was dismissed after only a few months in office.

Regional tensions also increased. Many Bavarians and other south Germans resented the sacrifices of the war and blamed the government in Berlin for needlessly prolonging it and for mishandling the war economy. Rumors circulated that Prussian troops were better fed than the south Germans and were deployed in less dangerous spots. Prussian officers, in turn, scoffed at what they considered to be "soft" south

Germans. In Bavaria, resentment against Prussia experienced the biggest revival since 1866, and there was much demand for more Bavarian autonomy within the German Empire. In order to counteract this mood and to tie the Center Party more closely to the government, Wilhelm II appointed former Bavarian Prime Minister, Georg Hertling, a member of the Center Party, as Michaelis' successor in November 1917. For a short time, the victory against Russia and the hope for grain deliveries from Ukraine softened unrest on the home front, but the Bolshevist revolution in November also inspired new visions of a world without war and exploitation. In January 1918, a huge strike wave stopped German munitions production; workers demanded peace and protested against the hard conditions offered to the Soviet Union in Brest-Litovsk. SPD leaders became so worried about worker radicalism that SPD chairman Friedrich Ebert had himself elected to a strike committee in order to stop the strikes. Ludendorff's big offensives and massive government propaganda promising imminent victory quelled the unrest for a while, but there was no doubt that German society and its political system were under extreme pressure. Whether a victory in the west would have reversed or neutralized the political momentum that had built up is doubtful. Already in the fall of 1914, Tirpitz noted in his diary in light of the sacrifices of the German people from all classes: "The traditional caste and class structure is outlived. Whether we win or lose the war, we will get a pure democracy."[3]

As we have seen, the failure of a breakthrough in the west produced unprecedented war weariness in the German army, but the Supreme Command managed to hide the seriousness of the situation for the time being. There was no panic when the Entente counterattacked in July. After the breakthrough near Amiens on 10 August, however, Ludendorff claimed to his entourage that the war was lost. Still, the generals kept reassuring the leading politicians that the western front would hold throughout the winter and that there might be new hope in a spring offensive in 1919. The German public remained relatively quiet at first. After all, Germany still controlled most of eastern Europe, and the line in the west seemed to be holding. But in September, Germany's allies began extending peace feelers to the Entente. They had held out expecting a decisive German success on the western front, but none of them was capable of carrying on the war much longer. With Bulgaria and the Ottoman Empire leaving the war and Austria-Hungary disintegrating, the Entente troops were able to march rapidly northward into Serbia. Sooner or later Germany would have had to open a new front in the southeast with no troops and no materiel to spare. At this moment, domestic politics and the course of the war suddenly became closely intertwined.

Since late 1916 the German political landscape offered a peculiar picture. On the one side it looked as if the military had established a dictatorship. Hindenburg and Ludendorff as supreme army commanders played a much more assertive role in German domestic politics than their predecessors. Their program to intensify war production gave them a pretext to interfere with many political decisions. It looked almost as if the generals were running the country altogether, and one historian has thus called the period between Hindenburg and Ludendorff's appointment and the end of war a "silent dictatorship."[4] But at the same time the Reichstag's role and authority also increased. It was decisive that the Center Party, under the influence of its ambitious leader Matthias Erzberger (who was murdered by rightist anti-democrats in 1921) realized the urgency of reform and peace. The party therefore moved away from its pro-governmental stance and informal alliance with the conservatives. Together with the left liberals and the moderate Social Democrats, the Center formed a loose alignment, called the "Reichstag Majority." Sometimes they were joined by the left wing of the National Liberal Party, as during their push for electoral reform in Prussia in early 1917. The Reichstag Majority demanded a peace without major annexations and reparations in July 1917 and managed to secure more parliamentary control over the government. After the dismissal of Michaelis, for example, the Reichstag Majority demanded to be consulted in the deliberations about the next chancellor. The dual consolidation of power in the Supreme Command under Hindenburg and Ludendorff as well as in the Reichstag had one clear loser: the Kaiser. One of his most important prerogatives was challenged when the Supreme Command demanded the dismissal of Bethmann and when the Reichstag Majority requested to be consulted in the choice of a successor for Michaelis. The Kaiser angrily bowed to the pressure although he did not allow Hindenburg and Ludendorff, who wanted Tirpitz or Bülow as chancellor, to force a chancellor on him whom he intensely disliked.

Other centers of power emerged in the trade unions and the big war-related corporations. Obviously, the smooth running of the war industries was crucial to the Supreme Command's interests, and they often found it more expedient to negotiate directly with the big industry and union bosses rather than through government intermediaries and the SPD. Repeatedly, the government merely recorded agreements made between industrialists and union leaders, mediated by the Supreme Command and implemented with the full authority of the military leadership. The union leaders, however, lost support from their rank and file. To many radicalized workers they appeared merely as bought servants of the capitalist system. Like the SPD, the unions toward the end of the war faced a powerful grass-roots challenge vaguely inspired by the Bolshevist revolution in Russia.

On 29 September 1918, Ludendorff, who was politically more active than Hindenburg (and some historians even call him the real military brain behind Hindenburg's facade), called government and party representatives to a conference. He revealed the seriousness of the military situation and demanded immediate negotiations for an armistice, which was a shock to the party leaders who had been kept in the dark. In order to ease armistice negotiations, Ludendorff proposed a "revolution from above," demanding the appointment of a government more in line with the Reichstag Majority and constitutional changes that would make the government responsible to the Reichstag. Ludendorff believed that democratization would avert a Russian-style socialist revolution in Germany by taking some wind out of the sails of the revolutionary workers' movement, and he assumed a democratic government would be more respectable in the eyes of President Wilson and might win better peace terms than the old government. In essence, however, Ludendorff wanted to saddle the Reichstag Majority with the responsibility for the defeat. This was a cynical plan: Ludendorff and other army leaders had complained for a long time that the German home front, allegedly influenced by defeatist democrats and socialists, was preventing the army from winning the war. Whether Ludendorff fully believed this is unclear. He certainly made his opinion public as often as he could and thus poured out some of the poison that later helped to kill German democracy.

Ludendorff's cynical quest for the parliamentarization of the German political system had immediate effects. Not even the most stubborn conservatives dared oppose the prestigious general. On 3 October, the Reichstag Majority accepted a liberal as new chancellor, Prince Max von Baden. The new chancellor appointed ministers from the Reichstag Majority, including – for the first time in German history – two Social Democrats. At the urging of Ludendorff, Max immediately sent a note requesting a truce to President Wilson on the basis of the Fourteen Points. By appealing to the United States, the German government hoped to revive Wilson's earlier mediation attempts and give the United States, where war passions were believed to have had a less powerful influence than in France and Britain, a moderating role on the armistice and peace conditions. Wilson answered after some hesitation, demanding that Germany withdraw from all occupied territories, from Alsace-Lorraine, and from a region in eastern Prussia that the Allies planned to open as a Polish corridor to the Baltic Sea. Max von Baden, knowing that the western front might break any day, accepted these hard conditions. In a new note, however, Wilson requested to negotiate with the "true representatives of the German people;" this was interpreted as an implicit call to overthrow the Kaiser. Wilson also demanded immediate stoppage of submarine warfare. He had been pressured by France and Britain to delay his answers and to demand more and more because the French and British hoped that Germany would break down during these negotiations and thus have no choice but to surrender unconditionally. Max von Baden stopped the submarine war but declined to change the system of government. With some justification he claimed that his government already represented the German people.

While Max was negotiating with the United States, the harsh conditions for a truce induced Ludendorff to reconsider his strategies. Although he had fully recognized the German defeat in August and September (he even suffered a nervous breakdown over it), he suddenly claimed that it was possible and necessary to go on fighting at all cost. Many Germans, including industrialist Walther Rathenau, were incensed at the prospective of being left completely at the mercy of the Entente and called for a *levée en masse*, a mobilization of the last resources against the potential invaders. This was unrealistic, however, as there were hardly any people left who could fight.

When Hindenburg received a letter from a town mayor and leading member of the Fatherland Party asking him why no *levée en masse* was taking place, he answered: "Does nobody at home know that we have been fighting to the last man for weeks already?"[5] In fact, the state of the German army was dismal. There was hardly any food and ammunition left. In *The Road Back*, the sequel to his world-famous novel *All Quiet on the Western Front*, Erich Maria Remarque describes an encounter between American soldiers and withdrawing German soldiers in Belgium right after the armistice. The well-fed Americans feel pity when they see the exhausted and severely undernourished Germans who are wrapping their wounds in packing paper for lack of bandages.[6] Without having lost a decisive battle, the German army had run out of men, weapons, and supplies. In a detrimental case of hypocrisy, Hindenburg and Ludendorff both denied this state of affairs when they stepped in front of the Reichstag in 1919 and claimed that the undefeated army had been stabbed in the back by democratic and socialist traitors at the home front.

Back in October 1918, Ludendorff envisioned continuing fighting probably more as a suicidal struggle to save the supposed "honor" of the army rather than to avert defeat. Maybe he believed that Germany would receive better conditions by showing its willingness to fight on, given that war weariness was widespread in the Entente countries, too. He did not get his way, however. After fierce confrontations, the Kaiser dismissed him on 26 October while keeping Hindenburg as supreme commander. Two days later the government, supported by the Reichstag Majority, issued several laws that realized the "revolution from above" ordered by Ludendorff in late September 1918. These so-called October Reforms transformed the Bismarckian state into a parliamentary monarchy. The Reichstag received the right to overthrow the chancellor and his government, and Reichstag members could become ministers (which had been illegal so far). The Prussian three-class suffrage was replaced by equal suffrage, and the military was put under parliamentary control. The Bundesrat, traditionally the last bastion of conservative control, lost many prerogatives to the Reichstag. The government also decided for a reform that would equalize the electoral districts. The Bismarckian constitution thus was decisively reformed, and the biggest grievances of democrats and socialists before 1914 were addressed.

But people in the streets did not believe that this turn of events was sincere and durable. The new rules seemed somewhat ambivalent as they still gave the Kaiser the right to appoint the chancellor and the ministers, and the Kaiser himself made many Germans suspicious when he left Berlin and traveled to the military headquarters in late October. Was he planning for a coup d'état with the help of the army? The October Reforms, above all, came too late. Many Germans wanted a clearer break with the old system. Social tensions now exacerbated the conflict, and the depressing expectation of defeat undermined the authority of the old regime. The October Reforms thus appeared too much as a last-minute attempt to save the old elites and to ward off more profound changes. During the feverish October, many Germans had not realized that it was the Entente that slowed down the negotiations for a truce; they had believed that their own government was continuing to prolong the war to postpone reform, and they had become increasingly impatient. Wilson's notes had made it clear that Wilhelm II was considered unacceptable as a partner in armistice negotiations. Although the Kaiser had been unusually passive and moderate throughout the war, foreign propaganda had used him as the symbol of the crude, barbarian German and declared him a top-level war criminal. The people in the Entente states now demanded his punishment. Letting him remain in power seemed impossible; his removal and legal prosecution was a war aim of the victors. Many Germans became nervous when it seemed as if Wilhelm II was the only obstacle standing between them and peace. In early November, calls for his abdication became impossible to ignore. Although some politicians including the SPD leaders suggested to save the monarchy by sacrificing Wilhelm II (through a regency for the Kaiser's oldest grandson, for example), such solutions became unrealistic as the Kaiser, under the influence of the military leaders, postponed his decision from one day to the next.

Whether all this would have been sufficient to spark a revolution is unclear. Conservative and moderate Germans abhorred the idea of revolution, particularly in a state of national emergency. The decisive spark of the revolution, however, was not the Kaiser's hesitation but the German admiralty's order to the fleet to wage a suicidal attack on the British navy. When Wilson's terms for an armistice became known, the navy decided to counteract the ongoing armistice negotiations by launching a desperate attack against the British coast in late October 1918. The German admirals had not bothered to inform the Kaiser and the chancellor of their enterprise, which was born out of a crazy military code of honor. The navy, more-over, wanted to demonstrate the value of Tirpitz's fleet building. When the admirals ordered the ships to get ready for a sortie, however, the sailors revolted. Having spent years mostly in the ports, many sailors were thoroughly disillusioned with the war. Antiwar propaganda had spread from the shipyard workers to the ships and inspired mutinies already in 1917. The sailors had no inclination to die with their admirals. They extinguished the coal in the machine rooms and marched to Kiel, the town with the biggest naval base, showing red flags and shouting socialist and pacifist slogans. According to the model of the Russian revolutions of 1917 they began to form sailors' and workers' councils (*sovety* in Russian, *Räte* in German). Although the government regained control over the situation in Kiel by sending a moderate SPD leader there who calmed down the sailors, the example of Kiel sparked rebellions in other German cities and in Austria and Hungary. In Hamburg, workers' and soldiers' councils constituted themselves, and the idea spread to Munich and Berlin. Returning soldiers often participated in upheavals and formed their own councils. So did even some farmers. In Munich, socialists under the leadership of USPD member Kurt Eisner marched on the royal castle on 7 November, and the Bavarian king abdicated and fled. Eisner became Bavarian minister president, and within two days all German princes had abdicated without attempting any resistance.

Figure 5.1 A scene near Armentières in Northern France, April 1918. (In dem gestürmten versumpften Kampfgelände von Armentières, Inv.-Nr.: 97/37, © DHM, Berlin).

To conquer and to defend these strips of mud, burned trees, shell splinters, blood, and bone, the equivalent of an entire graduating college class had to be sacrificed. As this picture was taken, Germany had defeated Russia and seemed poised to break through on the western front as well. It was high time for a decision, given that the shortages in the past two winters had been devastating for German civilians, particularly in the cities.

The Kaiser and the Supreme Command were still unsure about how to react to this massive wave of domestic unrest. The Supreme Command decided on 8 November that army units returning from the front should restore order in the name of the Kaiser, but not enough loyal troops could be found to repress what had become a mass movement all over the country. In Cologne, railroad workers blocked trains with loyal troops. The Kaiser's staying in power threatened to trigger civil war and to undermine the negotiations for an armistice. The pressure on him to abdicate increased. On 9 November Prince Max von Baden decided to take things into his own hands: he announced the Kaiser's abdication without Wilhelm's consent and appointed the moderate SPD leader Friedrich Ebert, Bebel's successor, as new chancellor. This was illegal, but it helped to mitigate tensions. The Kaiser independently decided to abdicate some hours after Max von Baden had handed power over to the SPD. Hindenburg had told Wilhelm II that no other solution remained. The following day the Kaiser crossed the border to the Netherlands, where he remained in exile until his death in 1941.

The SPD leaders were not happy about having power fall into their laps in such a dangerous and volatile situation. They had tried to effect a gradual and orderly takeover, but the competition and agitation of the more radical left forced them to spearhead the revolutionary movement in order not to lose control over it. The SPD invited the USPD to participate in the new government in order to mitigate its radicalism. The USPD agreed but demanded that the workers', soldiers', and farmers' councils be given political rights in the future. The USPD wanted the council system as the future center of power whereas the SPD feared that this would allow a minority of radical factory workers a disproportionate say in state affairs. The SPD's vision was the establishment of a parliamentary democracy along western models together with the Center Party and the left liberals. Ebert reluctantly made some concessions to the USPD but called for the election of a National Assembly that would draft a new constitution soon. On 9 November, a provisional socialist government composed to equal parts of SPD and USPD leaders took power, and Philipp Scheidemann, a leading SPD member, proclaimed the German Republic from the balcony of the Reichstag building. The SPD and USPD, however, no longer represented the entire range of attitudes on the left. An increasing number of workers wanted a transition to communism. As in Russia in 1917, they saw the establishment of a democratically founded government merely as a stage on the way to a second revolution on the Bolshevist model. While Scheidemann proclaimed the Republic from the Reichstag building, communist leader Karl Liebknecht declared the German Socialist Soviet Republic from the balcony of the abandoned imperial castle a few blocks farther east. Worried about a second, communist revolution, Ebert secured the Supreme Command's promise that the army would support the existing government against efforts to start a communist revolution.

Two days after the Kaiser's abdication, on 11 November, German delegates under the leadership of Erzberger signed the armistice in France. The Supreme Command, still trying to load the responsibility for the defeat on democratic politicians, stayed out of the negotiations, although Hindenburg in a phone call told Erzberger that he should sign whatever document he was offered. The German delegates had no chance to change the conditions of the armistice, which amounted to surrender. Germany had to withdraw all troops from the left bank of the Rhine, disband most army units, and hand over immense amounts of weapons and means of transportation (railroads, trucks). The British blockade continued until June 1919, after Germany had signed the peace treaty. But the war was over. And the Wilhelmine empire was gone. In the middle of revolutionary troubles, many Germans seemed yet unable to understand the reality and seriousness of the defeat. Germans had been promised victory for nearly four-and-a-half years, and in this hope they had endured a long, bloody struggle, hunger, and massive human loss. Hardly a family had not lost a father or son in the front lines. Ebert, for instance, had lost both his sons in the war. My own grandmother lost three brothers on the western front (a fourth one returned handicapped after having gone missing in action). It was hard to believe that all of these sacrifices now amounted to nothing and that everything was much, much worse than when the war, which was supposed to be a short, cleansing thunderstorm, had started.

–6–

Germany's First Democracy

In the wake of revolution and defeat the Germans established their first democracy, the Weimar Republic. It broke down after only fourteen years. This failure appears particularly fatal because the regime that followed committed some of the worst crimes of world history and unleashed another, much bloodier, world war. To explain the failure of the Weimar Republic to some extent has meant to explain the rise of the Nazis, a group representing a violent and hate-inspired political program. The breakdown of the Weimar Republic therefore ranks among the key issues of modern European history. One of my teachers at the University of Zürich, Professor Peter Stadler, once remarked that democracy often fails when it is introduced in a country for the first time. This was the case in France, where a democratic constitution, drafted during the revolution of 1789–94, did not survive. Only the third attempt at establishing a French democracy lasted more than a few years: the Third Republic (1870–1940). Russia was prepared to launch a first democratic experiment in 1917, which, as we have seen, was aborted by the Bolshevist revolution after a few months. Italy had developed into a fairly democratic state around the First World War, but the fascist dictatorship destroyed democracy in 1922. Similar failures of first democracies can be found in Spain, Greece, and many other nations. And yet, it would be too easy to consider the failure of Germany's first democracy inevitable. There were phases during which many voters and parties accepted the Weimar Republic. A modest economic recovery and signs of international reconciliation from 1924–9 made the Republic look relatively stable. Why did it fail then?

Explanations have stressed the beginning and the end of the Republic. Did some deficiencies of the constitution help cause the Republic's failure? Did the impact of the First World War in general and of the Treaty of Versailles in particular provide a too difficult context for the buildup of a democracy? One idea that fascinated historians for a while was that the revolution of 1918 was – as in 1848 – an incomplete revolution. It stopped halfway because the moderate revolutionaries (in this case the SPD) again aligned with the old elites to stop the radicals (in 1918/19 the USPD and the communists). The price the moderate revolutionaries had to pay was to leave strong anti-democratic pockets in the state apparatus and the army, and these anti-democratic pockets later helped to kill democracy and to bring the Nazis to power. Would German democracy have been more stable had the SPD compromised with the workers' councils movement associated with the USPD? Was such a compromise realistic at all? Are these controversies perhaps less important for the failure of democracy than the Republic's last years? Certainly the great depression of the early thirties was so harsh in Germany that any new political system would have been threatened by it. Marxist-Leninist historians, in particular, have argued that the destruction of the Republic was a scheme of big industry, which succeeded when a popular movement for dictatorship could be built up in 1930–3. We have to keep all these questions and approaches in mind as we consider the events unfolding after the revolutionary days of November 1918.

After the abdication of the Kaiser a socialist government, composed of three SPD members and three members of the more radical USPD, ruled alone. For several weeks, Germany therefore had a socialist government that was loosely controlled by a national council of workers, soldiers, and farmers councils in which the SPD had a majority. But the unity between the two socialist parties in the government was fragile. The USPD wanted institutionalized power for the councils whereas the SPD aimed at calling a National Assembly that would draft a democratic constitution and limit the power of the councils. Despite its internal differences regarding Germany's future, the government agreed to schedule general elections to a National Assembly on

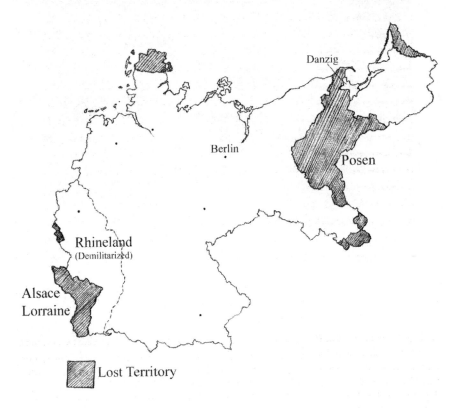

Map 2 Germany in 1919.

Figure 6.1 "Do not strangle the young freedom through fratricide and disorder! Otherwise your children will starve." Election poster of the SPD, end of 1918. ("Erwürgt nicht die junge Freiheit, Inv.-Nr.: P 57/340.1(MfDG), © DHM, Berlin).

No party during the Weimar Republic was more committed to democracy and freedom than the SPD. The poster, made from a draft by expressionist painter Max Pechstein (1881–1955), conveys the vulnerability of the newly won freedom. It probably alluded to the threat of "fratricide" from the radical left, which in these days appeared to be the biggest threat to order. Sadly, the SPD repressed radical left-wing unrest with right-wing troops who were burning to kill socialist workers and who soon became a much more serious threat.

19 January 1919. But unrest prevailed in December 1918. It is hard to imagine the chaos in Germany at that time: as the British blockade remained effective until June 1919, shortages of food and coal became more serious again as the winter approached. Many industries that had supplied the army needed to close, sending thousands of unemployed workers out to the streets. There the hungry and upset workers joined masses of returning soldiers who had no hope of employment and often could not imagine returning to civilian life. Traumatized by the war experience, they were bitter and depressed. Those workers who had employment often went on strike. Some took over their factories and tried to run them themselves. At the same time, Allied troops occupied the west of Germany, while the Polish army moved into some of the eastern territories. Bloody clashes between the Polish troops and remainders of the German army occurred. Further east, other German units fraternized with the enemies of Bolshevism and fought the Red Army shoulder-to-shoulder with counter-revolutionary armies. Although the victors asked that they be recalled, they helped to secure the independence of Finland and the Baltic states before degenerating into undisciplined marauding units. In Bavaria and other South German states separatist strivings resurfaced. In the big cities and the industrial areas shootings between restive workers and army units occurred almost daily. Right-wing paramilitary units gathered and attacked workers. In many places, the workers', soldiers', and farmers' councils could not preserve order. Authority was unclear. Determined sailors or workers occupied government buildings and the Imperial castle in Berlin whenever they wanted. Politics assumed a shrill and nervous pitch. As if that was not enough, the Dadaist movement occupied Berlin's main ballroom and proclaimed the Dadaist world revolution! Such was the scenery of the winter 1918–1919!

The tensions between the more radical socialists and the SPD soon came to a head. Many workers mistrusted the SPD and found that the SPD and trade union leaders had compromised themselves by cooperating with the old régime and the army. They believed that the capitalists had unleashed and prolonged the war for selfish reasons, and they wanted to make sure this would not happen again. State control over the industry and the nationalization of German enterprises were demands often voiced by the radical workers. In the light of later events it would have been important to keep the labor movement together. Maybe a unified left together with a moderate political center would have been able to defend Germany's democratic achievements in the long run, but the conflicts between the socialist factions escalated soon. Restive workers demanded more revolutionary actions, a constitutional basis for the councils, and guarantees for the lasting success of the revolution. They often clashed with army units that had been commissioned by the SPD for the protection of the government. Many of these units, the so-called Free Corps, were angry at the revolution and eager to shoot as many leftist rebels as possible. Since Ebert saw no possibility of building up a moderate, democratic armed force on short order he had concluded a secret agreement with the army leaders on 10 November 1918 to repress radical socialist uprisings. The SPD thus relied on Free Corps and other remainders of the old army, many of which were anti-democratic. Being attacked by right-wing armed units in the name of the SPD ministers exacerbated the suspicions of the rebellious workers. Around Christmas 1918 bloody clashes between workers and army units induced the USPD to leave the government in protest against the SPD. On 5 January 1919, after a large workers' demonstration against the government, the leadership of the newly founded Communist Party (KPD, formerly called the Spartacus League) called for an armed uprising. The leaders, Karl Liebknecht and Rosa Luxemburg, believed that they had to follow the masses toward more decisive revolutionary action. After three days of bitter fighting between radical workers and government troops, including the notorious Free Corps, the Spartacus uprising collapsed. Leaders of the Free Corps captured Liebknecht and Luxemburg, tortured them, and killed them. Luxemburg's mutilated corpse was found weeks later in a Berlin canal. The murderers were acquitted by the courts with the consent of the defense minister, an SPD member.

While Germany seemed on the verge of a second, more radical revolution, the non-socialist groups realigned and prepared for the elections. The former Progress-ives, the left-wing liberals of the Wilhelmine Empire, formed a new party called the German Democratic Party (DDP). They demanded a democratic constitution and a return to order. The Center Party was shocked by the abdication of the Kaiser and the following socialist turmoil that often assumed threateningly anti-clerical notes, but it supported the call for democratic elections to a National Assembly. The Bavarian section of the Center Party, resenting the party's more leftist course in the last months of the war, now broke away from the national party, forming the Bavarian People's Party (BVP). The right formed two parties, the German People's Party (DVP), a pro-industrialist party, and the German Nationalist People's Party (DNVP), an anti-democratic organization uniting the old conservatives and other right-wing organizations including the remainders of anti-Semitic parties.

On 19 January 1919 Germans held elections for a National Assembly charged with drafting a constitution. For the first time, women were allowed to vote (in November 1918, the SPD/USPD government had decreed women's suffrage on the same terms as men's suffrage in all elections). The result showed strong support for the parties advocating democracy – the SPD, the Democratic Party, and the Center Party – who together garnered more than 70 per cent of the vote. The SPD scored its best result ever, 37.9 per cent, the Center had 15.9 per cent and the Democratic Party 18.6 per cent. The USPD received only 7.6 per cent, and those socialists who had hoped to build a combined system of democratic parliament and councils with the support of SPD and USPD were disappointed because the two parties together had less than 50 per cent of the vote. The right-wing opponents of democracy were still weak. The DNVP received 10.3 per cent and the DVP 4.4 per cent. Given that the voting districts were redrawn so as to represent the actual population distribution, each party's share of the national vote approximately matched its share of seats in the Reichstag. An analysis of the women's vote showed that the Center Party and the

DNVP, both with a strong religious platform, benefited most from the introduction of women's suffrage.

The National Assembly was called into session on 6 February 1919 and started deliberations in Weimar, once the residence of the classical authors Wolfgang von Goethe and Friedrich Schiller. Weimar was chosen not only because Berlin was a too restive place, but also because the humanistic spirit of German classicism associated with Weimar was meant to inspire the new state with the best sides of German culture and disassociate it from defeated Prussian "militarism." The National Assembly immediately made a provisional decision about the future structure of government: a president would have strong individual powers, as in the United States, but he would leave the conduct of everyday political business to a Reich chancellor, who proposed ministers to the president. The Reichstag would be recalled, but for the time being the National Assembly assumed its role. Ebert, the leader of the SPD, was elected as president of the Republic and chose a new government with Social Democrat Philipp Scheidemann as chancellor and a cabinet on the basis of a coalition of the SPD, the Democratic Party, and the Center Party. Germany now had a government fully legitimated by democratic elections. Similar events happened in all German single states. All of them held democratic elections, and most of them elected democratic governments led by SPD members. Although disorder continued, there was a strong groundswell of support for democracy, and there were determined advocates of democracy in the Reichstag and government. They began to work on a constitution without delay.

The constitutional conferences lasted from February until July 1919. Procedures were interrupted for a while when the conditions of the Treaty of Versailles became public and led to the resignation of the government in May. Several drafts of the constitution were discussed. In July, the National Assembly voted for a definitive constitution, which became effective the following month. The structure of government stipulated by the constitution was the same as had already been in place since February. The head of state was the president, who was to be elected by popular vote every seven years. Re-election was possible. The president appointed and dismissed the Reich government and could dissolve the Reichstag. Under Article 48 he could proclaim a national state of emergency to preserve order. This article gave the president temporary dictatorial powers, which he could transmit to the defense minister or the chief of the army. It allowed the president to enact legislation without Reichstag approval, but this legislation had to be submitted to the Reichstag after six months and could then be revoked. The president also had the right to interfere with the legislation of the Reichstag and submit single laws to a plebiscite (popular vote). The Reichstag was the main legislative body. It controlled the government. If it lost confidence in a chancellor, the president was pressed to dismiss him, although the president could dissolve the Reichstag instead and try to secure the Reichstag's approval to the chancellor after new elections. The Reichstag was elected normally every fourth year by universal, equal, and secret suffrage (including women and all people older than age twenty). The seats were distributed roughly by percentage of the parties' vote. Even tiny parties could win Reichstag seats. Usually the Weimar governments were supported by coalitions of several parties, so that interparty negotiations determined the chancellor and government that the president then formally appointed. In order to limit the power of the Reichstag, the National Assembly stipulated that the signatures of one tenth of the electorate could force the government to submit a certain issue to a plebiscite (popular vote). Through the direct election of the president and through the right to a popular vote the constitution thus incorporated some plebiscitary elements. Besides the Reichstag an assembly of the single states existed, a successor to the Bundesrat. But this so-called Reich Council (Reichsrat) had mostly advisory functions; it did not have nearly as much power as the Bundesrat under the Bismarckian constitution. The workers' councils were tolerated by the constitution, but they did not receive any institutional power. Indeed they soon faded away.

The Weimar Constitution shifted the balance of power from the single states to the Reich. Taxation was increased to benefit the Reich administration and to pay off the astronomic war debt and the expected reparations. The special rights of some south German states were revoked (postal service, railroads, embassies). Prussia was still the largest and most populous single state (even though it lost most of the territory separated from Germany in the Treaty of Versailles), but it lost the institutionalized predominance it had previously enjoyed through the Bundesrat. The chancellor was not automatically Prussian minister president any more and Prussia did not receive a dominant voice in the new Reich Council. The Weimar Republic was therefore a more unitarian state than the still very federalist Bismarckian empire. This angered many people in the south German states, and separatism became a problem for the Weimar Republic during its most severe crises.

Critics of the constitution have pointed out that it gave too much power to the president, who almost figured as an ersatz Kaiser. Article 48, in particular, is often cast as a fatal flaw in the constitution because it was systematically abused after 1930. It is true that the specific articles regulating the implementation of Article 48 remained unfinished (they were to be worked out later but were never finalized), but it is often overlooked that this article was meant to safeguard democracy, not to undermine it (as was done in 1930–2). Ebert, in fact, often used this article in order to weather the many political storms that threatened to destroy the Republic in its first years. But Ebert was a democrat and used the article the way it was meant. His successor, Hindenburg, was no democrat and used the article increasingly to subvert democracy rather than to protect it. Critics have further argued that the mathematical assignment of Reichstag seats and the generous treatment of small parties gave rise to many splinter parties, which made it hard for a government to rule with clear majorities. But whatever the shortcomings of the constitution, it was a platform of compromise, and it could have been improved or corrected through constitutional channels. To blame the failure of Weimar democracy on the constitution is unfair.

With genuine will to make it work, the constitution could function well. Without democratic will, however, any constitution will have severe problems. Democratic will existed in 1919 but soon faded away outside of the SPD. A bad omen was that the radical left and the right did not approve the constitution already in 1919: the USPD, the DVP, and the DNVP all voted against it. In 1919 they still represented a small minority. But it took only one year, and those parties who opposed the democratic constitution were a majority. Many factors influenced the dramatic erosion of the broad democratic consensus manifest in the elections to the National Assembly in January 1919. None of them was more important than the Treaty of Versailles.

The Treaty of Versailles is one of the most controversial international agreements. Many observers – politicians and historians – have tended to blame the rise of the Nazis on the Treaty of Versailles, which is claimed to have had detrimental effects on the viability and domestic authority of German democracy. In general, it has seemed that the treaty was either to harsh or too mild. It was too harsh to reconcile Germany with its former war enemies and to integrate it into a lasting peaceful postwar order, and it was too mild to weaken Germany so as to make it impossible for it to ever again become a great power. The picture that emerges today after more intensive research is more complex and differentiated than that, but Versailles nevertheless remains both a highly ambivalent and crucial station in German history. The actual peace terms harshly disappointed the Germans, who felt that they contradicted the promises Wilson had made to the last wartime German government. Many Germans, for right or wrong, felt betrayed by Wilson and the United States. If we compare German expectations and the terms of Versailles, we cannot overlook sharp discrepancies. Instead of a negotiated peace, in which Germany would be a significant, if not equal, partner, the treaty gave practically no room for German input and resembled more a dictate than a real peace settlement. Instead of admitting the new democratic Germany into the community of democratic nations, the victors ostracized the vanquished nation. They even took pains to humiliate its national consciousness. Germany was – for the time being – not allowed to join the newly founded League of Nations and remained a pariah in the postwar order. Instead of a peace of reconciliation, the Germans received a peace of submission and punishment. The principle of national self-determination, instead of being respected as a general rule, was always applied if it weakened Germany and its former allies but never where it would have benefited them. Wilsonian ideology seemed to have covered traditional ruthless power politics with a moralistic glaze. How did this discrepancy come about? Were the Germans really betrayed? Should they ever have believed in a milder peace settlement?

On 8 January 1918 Wilson had presented to Congress his Fourteen Points as an outline for a moderate peace in Europe. He was prompted to do so by the critical condition of the Entente after the Russian defeat. In France and Britain war weariness was on the rise, and it seemed irresponsible to many political minds that war should be continued for aggressive French and British war aims. Wilson thus hoped to placate moderate opinion in the western countries and at the same time suggest to the Germans that they could expect a peace settlement that would not destroy their state but would give them a chance to survive as a major nation. The principles Wilson articulated were above all: economic and political equality of all nations (against satellite states, as in German-dominated eastern Europe, and for the restoration of Belgian independence). Wilson further demanded that Europe be reorganized along lines of nationality. This idea implied the German loss of Alsace-Lorraine, given that its people were mostly inclined to live in France, and Wilson also hinted at the creation of a truly independent Polish state with a corridor to the sea (this contradicted the principle of national self-determination, however, because the coast was settled by Germans). Concerning war reparations, Wilson asked that they be limited to repairing the damage done by invading troops, which applied in particular to destructions caused by the German army in Belgium and France. Furthermore, Wilson encouraged democratization. He announced that the Allies would speak seriously only to "true" representatives of the German people. (He sometimes doubted, however, that German democrats would really be the true representatives of the German people; the Kaiser's generals seemed to be quite popular.) But Wilson made it clear that Germany would be allowed to gain a place in a new, democratic world order if it was willing to respect his principles and to forego its own expansionist and hegemonic aims. The restoration of Belgium was a "must" on the American list; Alsace-Lorraine and the Polish Corridor were merely conditions that "should" be met. It was on the basis of these points that the German government had asked to open negotiations for a truce in October 1918. Wilson's answers had generally confirmed the Fourteen Points but with heavier emphasis on Alsace-Lorraine and the Polish Corridor.

One factor the Germans tended to ignore, however, was the persistence of French and British war aims. The United States was maybe the strongest member of the anti-German front, but the French had more of a stake in Europe than the United States. Georges Clémenceau, the French Prime Minister, did not take Wilson's claims seriously. In the light of French and British expectations, the German hopes for a mild peace were wishful thinking born of the desperation typical for the end of the war. A coalition war had ended; this meant that many different countries would voice their claims. Wilson could not conclude peace all alone. Moreover, the passions aroused by a world war, particularly in France and Britain, could not easily be transformed into feelings of reconciliation. For over four years, the Germans had been demonized as barbarians and "Huns" (while German propaganda had cast the western countries as uncultured and vicious tradesmen and had lambasted the French, in particular, for using "uncivilized" soldiers from their colonies). It was inconceivable that the French or British public would suddenly turn around and tolerate the former enemy as anything similar to an equal partner at the peace table.

The opening of the peace conference was a bad omen for Germany. The leading statesmen of the victorious nations chose the day of the foundation of the German

Empire, 18 January, to open the peace conference, and they later forced the German delegates to sign the treaty in the very same hall of mirrors in the castle of Versailles where the German princes had proclaimed Wilhelm I emperor of the new Germany in 1871. This was a deliberate humiliation of Germany. Negotiations were conducted mainly between the heads of state of the United States, France, Britain, and Italy, the so-called "big four." The German government was allowed to make only minor modifications at the end, when the victors had decided on the terms of the treaty. But the victors had widely differing goals. For Wilson, the priority was the establishment of a League of Nations that would mediate all future conflicts between nations and make war as a means of politics unnecessary. Wilson was prompted by fears of Bolshevism. He wanted to offer a pacifist vision to war-weary Europeans, mainly the left-wing workers. He envisioned a union of free, democratic nations, based on the principle of national self-determination, as a competing model to Lenin's call for a brotherhood of socialist societies according to Marxist ideas. Wilson wanted to weaken Germany's military potential for all times, but he had nothing against a democratic Germany becoming a major economic power again and felt strongly about leaving it unified. He feared that an excessively weak Germany might inspire France to strive for domination on the European continent. The French war aims were more far reaching with respect to Germany than the American aims. To the French, security against Germany mattered most. France wanted to change the balance of power by reducing Germany's economic and demographic weight to a point that would make it impossible for Germany to overpower France. In 1914 Germany had had about twenty-five million inhabitants more than France, and German industrial production had been much more intensive than France's. In order to reduce German superiority, to reconstruct the destroyed areas, and to cover their own war debt, the French wanted high reparations. But reparations were not sufficient because they could only temporarily bind the German economy. The French diplomats hoped further to control Germany's western industrial heartlands and – maybe – to dissolve the Reich altogether. They wanted to separate the Rhineland and the Ruhr District from Germany and to create a semi-autonomous state leaning toward France. Without its densely populated and highly industrialized West, Germany would find it impossible to threaten France again. As an additional safeguard against future German aggression, France hoped to build up an alliance network among the newly independent nationalities of the Austro-Hungarian Empire and Poland, the so-called *cordon sanitaire*. This alliance was supposed to threaten Germany with a second front again, after France's main pre-war ally in eastern Europe, the Russian Empire, had broken down. France further wanted to secure a strong position in the Middle East in territories formerly belonging to the Ottoman Empire. The British war aims were more compatible with the American aims than with the French aims. The British wanted above all to demilitarize Germany and to get hold of its battle fleet and merchant navy. They claimed their share in German reparations and demanded domination over most of Germany's African colonies. In addition to that, their interests concentrated on the Middle East (at the expense of the dissolved Ottoman Empire), where their interests clashed with French ambitions. The British believed that Germany should after a while recover as a major trading partner without ever again posing a military threat (Germany and Britain had been each other's best trading partners before 1914). Like the United States, Britain was unhappy about the prospect of French predominance on the European continent. Italy joined the conference tables to claim the lands it had been promised as a price for supporting the Entente, the South Tyrol (an Alpine region settled by Italian speakers in the south and German-speakers in the north) and the Trentino (a border area with Yugoslavia; today: Slovenia and Croatia) as well as some strips of the eastern Adriatic coast. Japan merely wanted its conquest of Germany's Chinese colony and northern Pacific islands ratified. In mostly secret negotiations over four months, the leading statesmen drafted a treaty that they submitted to the German government in early May 1919.

The main conditions of the treaty included territorial, military, financial, and judicial elements. Germany had to cede Alsace-Lorraine to France and accept an allied occupation of most of its western provinces for a number of years. The coal-rich Saar district, on the border with Luxembourg, was given to France for fifteen years. Thereafter a plebiscite would decide its future. The coal mines in the Saar district, however, were given to France, and Germany would have to buy them back if the plebiscite yielded a pro-German majority. The Rhineland and some cities on the right bank of the Rhine were to be occupied by French, British, American, and Belgian troops for five, ten, or fifteen years respectively. A small border area was annexed by Belgium (Eupen-Malmédy). In the north, a plebiscite was held to decide the fate of northern Schleswig, the province with a Danish minority. Denmark had not participated in the war, but northern Schleswig was considered an old grievance going back to the German-Danish War of 1864, which had brought that territory to Prussia. As expected, the popular vote split the province into a pro-Danish and pro-German part. In the East, Germany had to give the provinces of Western Prussia and Posen to Poland, thus offering the landlocked Polish state an outlet to the Baltic Sea (Polish Corridor). Some of Upper Silesia also went to Poland, but some areas were given the right to a plebiscite (the drawing of voting districts was arbitrary, however, giving the Poles a majority wherever possible). Danzig, a city on the Baltic Sea with a 96 per cent ethnic German majority, was promised to Poland by France, but American and British opinion prevailed and turned it into a so-called free city under the overlordship of the League of Nations. A small area in Silesia was given to Czechoslovakia, and the Memel Area, a strip of land in the North of East Prussia, was put under Allied administration and was later seized by Lithuania. The loss of the territories in the East filled most Germans with even more indignation than the loss of the western lands because the changes in the East contradicted the principle of national self-determination: Some of the new Polish territories were settled predominantly by Germans, and Danzig was a German city beyond any doubt. Moreover, a union of German Austria with Germany, although the declared wish of both peoples, was forbidden by the treaty, and several million Germans living in Bohemia (in the Sudetenland) came under Czechoslovak rule, which most of them resented. (The famous rescuer of Jews in World War II, Oskar Schindler, belonged to this German minority in Czechoslovakia.) This represented a violation of the principle of national self-determination, although it is understandable that the Entente did not want to strengthen Germany by doing what Bismarck had deliberately neglected to do: adding the ethnic Germans in the former Austro-Hungarian Empire to Germany.

The military conditions stipulated that Germany disarm almost completely and maintain only an army of 100,000 men without heavy weapons – a force useful to repress domestic unrest but not to fight a modern war. Germany had to demilitarize a fifty-kilometer zone on the right bank of the Rhine and was forbidden to own military airplanes, submarines, tanks, heavy artillery, and poison gas. The navy was limited to a few small surface ships and was forbidden to commission submarines. The existing German battle fleet had to be handed over to Britain along with all merchant ships (the British got the merchant ships, but Tirpitz's "proud" battle fleet scuttled itself outside the British bases in June 1919). An Inter-Allied Military Control Commission (IMCC) was granted considerable powers to supervise and control German disarmament. The Treaty of Versailles stated, however, that German disarmament should precede disarmament all over the world. But the victors of the world war, of course, were in no hurry to disarm themselves. This clause later provided German diplomats with a welcome lever; pointing out that the Entente powers had not disarmed fully, they could claim that the military conditions of the treaty therefore became meaningless and that Germany had the right to rearm.

Among the most controversial conditions were the financial clauses of the treaty. The Entente, in particular France, had always claimed that the Germans would have to pay not only for the damage done in the occupied regions but also for most of the Entente war expenses. To justify this demand, the victors argued that Germany and its allies had started the war and were thus responsible for all of their enemies' costs and damages. This accusation outraged most Germans, who still believed that their government had been forced into a defensive war in 1914, although some diplomatic documents published right after the war by Karl Kautsky and under Kurt Eisner indicated that the German government had pursued a risky and aggressive strategy. The reparations clauses also triggered outrage because the ultimate sum and the mode of payment were not specified because the victors could not agree on how much Germany could pay and on the way they wanted to divide reparations among themselves. Germany thus had to sign a blank check. A conference to determine a precise sum finally met in 1921, but the amount it demanded was still considered outrageous and unrealistic by most Germans. Germany also delivered vast amounts of goods as reparations, from locomotives and trainloads of coal to telephone poles and milk cows, and it had to accept trade agreements that benefited the Entente powers for a limited period.

Finally, the main judicial issue of the treaty was the demand to prosecute alleged war criminals. The Entente claimed that German leaders had conducted the war at least partly in a criminal way, mainly by opting for submarine warfare. The Kaiser, who was deemed responsible for all crimes, and about two thousand German top officers and officials including Tirpitz, Hindenburg, and Ludendorff were to be extradited and put on trial by the Entente. Many of these people were, of course, considered national heroes in Germany. Another problem was that only the losers would be prosecuted even though violations of the laws of war had happened on both sides. Strong public resistance against this demand therefore arose in Germany and even in some neutral countries. The Netherlands, for example, consistently rejected demands for the extradition of the Kaiser, and no German suspected war criminal was ever apprehended and sent to an Entente country for trial. After a few years, the victors bowed to the pressure and demanded that the German Reich court in Leipzig prosecute a much-shortened list of the most heinous war criminals. Not much happened, however. A few trials took place, during which the audience cheered the accused and the judges treated them with scandalous mildness. Unfortunately, this mood of national defiance let some people off the hook who had undoubtedly committed major war crimes, for example against French and Belgian civilians, although it was of course a problem that war crimes should be prosecuted only by one side.

The German government and people were horrified when they were informed about the peace terms. Not even the worst pessimists had expected that the treaty would be so harsh. A tremendous uproar occurred, but it seemed impossible to resist. Two German governments stepped down because they did not want to take responsibility for signing the treaty, but finally there was no choice but to sign. With the votes of the SPD and the Center Party, the Reichstag had to ratify the treaty. This was a terribly hard decision, but it was better than the alternative. Germany had no military means to oppose a threatening Entente advance onto German territory. French statesmen and generals, who found the treaty too mild, actually hoped for a German refusal because that would give their army the opportunity to dissolve Germany and to take more direct control than the treaty allowed. Many Germans, particularly on the right, advocated a desperate act of resistance even at the price of complete foreign occupation, hoping that foreign occupation would – just as under Napoleon I – produce a German uprising and unite a German people that in 1919 was bitterly divided. The majority in the Reichstag, however, resisted this fanciful alternative. But even if many Germans felt that they had no alternative to signing, there was almost universal consensus that the treaty was extremely unjust and needed to be changed at the first opportunity.

Whereas many Germans were disappointed about what they saw as Wilson's "betrayal," the Treaty of Versailles was a compromise between Wilsonian aims and French plans. In the short run, the treaty significantly weakened Germany and gave the victors economic benefits and much power mainly in the west of the country. In the long run, however, nothing spoke against a German recovery at least in the economic sphere. The trade conditions favoring the victors would elapse after five years, the occupation would have to be ended after fifteen years, and German disarmament, at least according to the letter of the treaty, was ultimately conditional upon general, worldwide disarmament. The treaty was harsher on Germany than Wilson had wanted, but he had been forced to make far-reaching concessions to his allies in order to secure a peace treaty at all and to win support for his favorite project, the League of Nations. Wilson first of all wanted to make sure that Germany would not succumb to Bolshevism; in the long run, he wished for an integration of republican Germany into a democratic community of nations. Germany could become a major economic power again, but not a military power. Wilson tried to conceal his failure to shape the treaty more according to his wishes by presenting the treaty to the American public as a just punishment for a bad criminal. To this purpose he dropped the distinction between Germany's pre-revolutionary and republican governments.

The Fourteen Points and Wilson's assurances in October 1918 had suggested a milder peace than Versailles, but the biggest problem was that the Germans still refused to acknowledge that they had lost a world war, a war that had let loose unprecedented energies and emotions and affected societies as a whole - a war, for whose outbreak the German government had to bear a large share of responsibility. The traumatic character of the defeat gave rise to illusions. Many Germans believed that Wilson had tricked them into disarming by the alleged promise of a "just" peace. As if there had been no military defeat before! It remained extremely difficult to understand for Germans how they could have lost the war without losing a decisive battle and without letting the enemy conquer German territory. That their war machine had simply run out of men and materiel and that this was decisive in a modern war was hard to understand. This trauma, the inability to understand how things had turned from seemingly imminent victory to disaster, made many Germans susceptible to distorting legends. The most perfidious of all was the stab-in-the-back myth, tirelessly propagated by Hindenburg and Ludendorff. Politicians eager for reform or revolution had, according to the generals, stabbed the undefeated German army in the back by launching a revolution at home. Even before November 1918, they claimed, the democrats had undermined the war effort by diverting popular attention from ultimate support for the war to concern about domestic gains. In other words: the socialists and democrats, those who above all represented the new Weimar Republic, were responsible for the German defeat.

Some historians see the Treaty of Versailles as just and argue that it did not look extremely harsh in the light of the German conditions imposed on defeated Russia at Brest-Litovsk.[1] Germany was not weakened enough to make it impossible for it to ever rise again as a military threat. Its structural potential for hegemony (economy, population, education) was diminished but not destroyed. On the other side, the treaty was sure to make a significant section of the German public unforgiving and eager for a revanche. In that sense it was not a "peace treaty" but, as the German writer Bertolt

Brecht once said, a truce in a European thirty-years civil war. The discourse over Versailles helped poison the political life of the Weimar Republic, as the extremely difficult adjustment period following the war was blamed not primarily on the war itself (as it should have been) but on Versailles and Weimar Germany's compliance with the peace treaty. Given the high and expansive German expectations of the war years, however, it is hard to think of a peace that would have pleased the Germans. Altogether, the statesmen of the victor nations had little latitude. The global war had created circumstances that even goodwill could not easily change. Given the intensity of emotion created by a modern war of societies – and the democratic systems that held western governments accountable to these public emotions – a generous peace deal on the lines of the Congress of Vienna over a century earlier was not possible. Germany could not be invited to the peace conference as an equal to the victors, as France had been in 1814–15, and it could not be simply reduced to its pre-war borders, as France had been. Recent historiography has also tended to vindicate Wilson's intentions. He made sure that at least some compromise between his ideological goals and the more aggressive French aims came about. The peace conference had a multitude of problems to solve: Germany was only one of them. In the following months the Entente concluded separate treaties with Austria, Hungary, Bulgaria, and Turkey. Versailles undoubtedly helped to compromise the new German democracy (although the reasons for its ultimate failure were more complex and cannot be reduced to the treaty). Perhaps the tone mattered more than the conditions. The way the conference deliberately humiliated German national sentiment cast the conditions in a more somber light than they might have deserved. The compromise character of the treaty left Germany some hope for revision, however. There was no need to accept a total and unconditional defeat, as there would be in 1945. Revision remained a distant but viable goal, and realistic German statesmen and businessmen were determined to work for it.

Meanwhile, German democracy suffered a massive assault from the left and the right. The worker unrest in the Christmas holidays of 1918 and the Spartakist uprising were only the first manifestations of a communist-inspired bid for power that was to shake Germany and many other countries in the immediate postwar period. Although the USPD had not supported the Spartakist uprising, the bloody intervention by the Free Corps, which were called and directed by an SPD minister, did irreparable damage to working-class unity. Even many moderate workers without sympathies for the Spartakists now deeply resented the SPD. As if there had not been enough trouble already, a turbulent and bloody episode seized Munich. On 21 February 1919, Bavarian Minister President Kurt Eisner was on his way to the Bavarian parliament in order to submit his resignation after his party, the USPD, had only received two percent of the vote at the Bavarian state elections. A student with radical right-wing views and a gun waited for Eisner and shot him dead. This senseless act of terror, which made the murderer a hero in right-wing circles, triggered more violence. Shootings occurred in the parliament building in Munich, and the

USPD called a general strike in Bavaria. For several months Bavaria remained unstable. On 7 April some radical socialists seized power in Munich and proclaimed a soviet republic for all of Bavaria. The regular Bavarian government, led by an SPD member, fled to another city. Journalists and writers formed an insurrectionary Bavarian government (among them the author Ernst Toller). After standing aloof for a while, the Communists entered the revolutionary government and became the dominant force, further radicalizing the Bavarian revolution. When some Free Corps and army units advanced on the city, the Communists took and murdered several hostages. In early May 1919, the counter-revolutionary forces stormed Munich and ended the Bavarian revolution with much greater brutality.

The repression of the Bavarian revolution showed how radical and violent the anti-democratic right had become. Free corps and a vast number of paramilitary units had formed – some out of remainders of the old army, others drawing younger men who had not been old enough to be drafted into the army during the war. These Free Corps were on the one hand radically anti-democratic and on the other hand passionately nationalist and opposed to every clause of the peace treaty. They secretly hoarded arms to kill Communists and fight France and Poland. Increasingly, they became a threat to the Republic. In March 1920, some Free Corps attempted a putsch. They occupied Berlin without encountering any resistance and proclaimed the rightist Wolfgang Kapp (the founder of the Fatherland Party) as new chancellor. When Germany's rump army refused to fight the putschists and declared itself "neutral," the legitimate government under SPD leadership fled to the south of Germany. The state administration in Berlin, however, did not cooperate with the putschists (because they did not believe in the success of the Kapp Putsch, not because they wanted to prevent the destruction of democracy). The working-class parties, moreover, proclaimed a general strike. This brought down the Kapp government within a few days, even though the war hero Ludendorff joined it. The putsch showed dramatically how little the German army, dominated by anti-democratic officers, cared for the Weimar Republic; it was happy to fight left-wing putschists with great brutality but decided to remain "neutral" toward right-wing putschists. The same was true for the justice system. Whereas judges meted out the most severe punishments for members of the revolutionary Bavarian government even if they had nothing to do with the hostage shootings, the Kapp putschists escaped without a scratch. The success of the general strike, proclaimed by the KPD, USPD, and SPD strengthened worker confidence in united socialist action, but the strike turned into communist uprisings in many industrialized areas and thus brought further trouble and chaos to the Republic. In the Ruhr District, for example, the army waged a brutal war on the restive workers.

When the National Assembly finally dissolved and called new elections for June 1920, a political earthquake happened at the polls. The three parties that supported democracy were crushed. The SPD lost almost half its vote and received only 21.7 per cent. The Democratic Party was punished even more severely, losing more than half of its votes; it was down to 8.3 per cent from 18.6 per cent. Even the Center Party, renowned for its stability, suffered losses and went to 13.6 per cent (down from 15.9 per cent). This meant that the three parties that had played the decisive role in drafting the constitution and had enjoyed over 70 per cent backing in January 1919 now were down to 43 per cent. Hence the phrase about the republic without republicans. Sadly, these three parties together never again exceeded 50 per cent of the vote. In short, democracy had been thoroughly discredited in Germany. A variety of reasons explains this outcome, but it was certainly important that the government coalition had to pay for the Treaty of Versailles and that the vision of German democracy on equal terms with other democracies had been harshly disappointed. After Versailles, German democracy appeared largely as an executioner of the Entente's will in the eyes of far too many Germans.

The victors of the 1920 elections were the anti-democratic parties on the left and the right. The USPD won more than 10 percent and received 17.9 per cent, not much less than the SPD (the KPD, which had not yet committed itself fully to elections, received only 2.1 per cent). Clearly, the harsh policies of the SPD against revolutionary workers and its association with the army had cost it strong support among its traditional electorate. The other big winners were on the right. The DVP under former National Liberal chairman Gustav Stresemann more than tripled its vote, receiving 13.9 per cent (up from 4.4 per cent) and the DNVP, home of many radical rightists who sympathized with the Free Corps and had supported the Kapp Putsch, grew to 15.5 per cent (up from 10.3 per cent). The election results left the SPD reluctant to take a leading role in government again and set a characteristic trend for the remainder of the Weimar Republic: government on the basis of a minority coalition and with great instability. In most governments, the Center Party took on a leading role. The Democratic Party and sometimes the Bavarian People's Party supported it, and later on, the DVP also agreed to take on governmental responsibility despite its criticism of democracy and its initial rejection of the constitution. For a short time, in 1925 and in 1927, even the monarchist, anti-Semitic, and hyper-nationalist DNVP participated in governments, but that happened under special conditions to be explained later.

There were enormous tasks to master. Erzberger as minister of finance had implemented a large-scale and much-resented tax reform in 1919, which established a broader source of revenue for the German state. Fairly generous social reforms under SPD influence had also increased spending. Despite the tax increases, the German state remained unable to pay all of its obligations, including, of course, the reparations. The latter were politically most costly, because the right blamed the centrist parties and the SPD for the Treaty of Versailles and resented having to pay at all. Under Foreign Minister Walther Rathenau, whose patriotism should have been above all suspicion, the German government adopted a so-called Policy of Fulfillment. The idea was to try sincerely to pay reparations and so show the Entente that this was simply impossible. Hopefully, the Entente would then reduce its demands. The Policy of Fulfillment, however, gave right-wing demagogues an easy target for their argument that German democracy was all about executing the Entente's will. Anti-Semitism, which had boomed on the right during the tense last war years, was an integral part of this vile resentment against everything western. The fact that Rathenau was Jewish only fanned the flames.

The times following the elections of 1920 were filled with tension. German governments were fighting on four major fronts. First, they had to deal with Entente demands for reparations and frustrating rulings about Germany's eastern border with Poland, where a small-scale war between Free Corps and Polish army units was taking place. The Policy of Fulfillment at this time did little to mollify Entente demands, and it exacerbated tensions at home. Second, a disaster loomed in the economic sphere. Although the government had altogether mastered demobilization well, albeit at the price of pushing millions of women out of their wartime jobs, the German mark suffered a drastic loss of value. The causes of the German inflation are extremely complex, but it is fair to say that the roots of inflation went back to uncontrolled state spending during the war. The war-induced pause in international trading had not made it obvious that the mark had lost its value, but the resumption of international trade in 1919 showed that the mark was worth only a tiny fraction of its prewar value. And it kept loosing value. Reparations exacerbated the problem although they were not the real cause. German governments, faced with the choice of either stabilizing the currency and paying high reparations or letting the mark slip and trying to pay reparations as much as possible in more devalued marks, all too often chose the second path. This was understandable given the domestic outrage over reparations, but it was a poor financial policy. The third problem was left-wing radicalism, which continued unabated even after the brutal smashing of the Spartakist uprising, the Munich Soviet Republic, and the mass strike in the Ruhr. On completely misguided advice from Moscow, the KPD kept preparing a violent takeover and contributed much to the instability of postwar Germany without having any real chance of taking power against the army and the Free Corps. The KPD was rapidly gaining mass support, however. In 1922, the USPD, seeing no realistic prospect for the council system any more, simply split right down the middle with one half joining the KPD and the other half returning to the SPD. Finally, the challenge from the right challenged the Republic in ever more radical and violent ways. Right-wing terrorists were hiding weapons for an overthrow of democracy and a war of liberation against France. They murdered prominent politicians and many of their own members who had revealed illegal activities to the authorities. The most famous victims, although only the tip of the iceberg, were former Finance Minister Matthias Erzberger and Foreign Minister Walther Rathenau. Erzberger was murdered by a right-wing terrorist in August 1921 for his signing the armistice and accepting the Treaty of Versailles. Rathenau was shot in June 1922 because he was Jewish and because of his Policy of Fulfillment. In both cases, hateful tirades by DNVP members had sowed much hatred against the victims. The Rathenau murder was also an act of violent anti-Semitism. At this point, however, the terror of the right was beginning to backfire. The Rathenau murder brought unexpected support for the Republic from many people on the moderate right. Among the most prominent were Gustav Stresemann, who brought his party, the DVP, into alignment with the Center Party and the Democratic Party. Another famous convert was the famous author Thomas Mann, who had been an expansionist nationalist during the war and greeted democracy with a mixture of skepticism and contempt. After the Rathenau murder, Thomas Mann became a passionate defender of democracy and advocate of civility and tolerance. Although the Weimar Republic fought harder against the radical right after the Rathenau murder, many of its moves continued to be counteracted by a lenient justice apparatus, who considered the actions of right-wing terrorists honorable, and by recalcitrant state governments.

The foremost protector of radical rightists at this time was the state government of Bavaria. During the Kapp Putsch, a right-leaning government had taken power in Munich and pushed out the SPD-led government after massive street demonstrations. Bavaria was therefore the only place where the Kapp Putsch succeeded. Thereafter, successive Bavarian governments kept harboring radical rightists, among them many sought-after terrorists who were allowed to continue their evil work under false names in Bavaria. Radical rightists built up large and well-armed organizations. The Bavarian government tolerated and even supported them because it hoped to use them to push national politics onto a more authoritarian course, to restore the Bavarian autonomy lost in 1919, and to repress a new left-wing uprising. To understand the priorities of the Bavarian governments in the early Weimar Republic, we have to consider that Bavaria's revolutionary episode in 1919 had decisively weakened it at the very time when the federalist-centralist balance of the Weimar Constitution was being negotiated. Most Bavarians felt that the constitution was far too centralist, and many of them disliked democracy and deplored the loss of their monarchy. The wartime resentment against all things Prussian mushroomed into a powerful desire for more autonomy and perhaps even separation from Germany. Bavarian particularism and German radical right-wing thinking were not always neatly separable. Ironically, the French secret service initially gave some funding to an obscure demagogue in Munich named Adolf Hitler because they believed him to be another Bavarian separatist. It was French policy at that time to support separatist movements as a step toward the breakup of Germany.

All four of these problem areas exploded in the dramatic year 1923. It began with the Franco-Belgian occupation of the Ruhr district in January. Reacting to delays in German reparation shipments of telephone poles and coal, the French government, supported by Belgium, sent the army into the Ruhr district, Germany's industrial heartland. The Ruhr occupation went ahead without support from the British and American representatives on the Reparations Commission, but it was not illegal according the Treaty of Versailles, which allowed the victors to occupy further

German territory as sanctions. France had previously occupied some cities and bridgeheads on the right bank of the Rhine on similar grounds. The Ruhr occupation was meant to control the heavy industry and coalmines in that area and thus to extract reparations directly from the source. The German government reacted with outrage and called for passive resistance including a general strike in the Ruhr district. The need to support the striking workers in the Ruhr caused the next financial disaster, however. Until November 1923, the mark lost its value with increasing rapidity, and this had severe consequences on everyday life. Whereas some speculators with access to hard (foreign) currency accumulated dizzying fortunes, the last savings of millions of Germans were wiped out. Workers received their pay by the day, and they had to hurry to spend it all after work as it would not buy them a postal stamp on the next day. The feverish haste with which money was spent boosted the entertainment industry and caused deep alarm over public morality. The world seemed to fall apart. For millions, the hyperinflation was yet another immiseration and deprivation experience after much suffering during the war and in the postwar period.

The declaration of passive resistance created a degree of unity in Germany not seen since August 1914. The ground had been prepared by a massive propaganda campaign against the French use of colonial troops in their occupation army since 1919. The black soldiers of the French army, in particular, were accused of rapes and multiple other outrages. In truth, the few blacks and the more numerous north Africans in the French army had behaved better than the white French troops and even than the German troops stationed in this area before 1914, and France had by 1922 withdrawn all black African units! But the campaign against the "Black Horror on the Rhine" had done much to delegitimize the French occupation in the United States, Britain, and Italy, and it provided a powerful background for a renewed campaign of vilification after the Ruhr occupation. Tensions rose as bloody clashes happened between French military personnel and German saboteurs in the occupied regions. The French tried to set up separatist governments in the Rhineland, but these governments lacked popularity; some separatist leaders were murdered by right-wing terrorists. Soon, however, the severity of the economic crisis and the failure of passive resistance to force a withdrawal from the Ruhr began to erode the German domestic consensus. The old divides broke open with a vengeance when Stresemann, who had the courage to take over the chancellorship in August 1923, did the only reasonable thing, namely to call off passive resistance. This step was the precondition for a stabilization of the currency, which succeeded in November, and for an international agreement that would allow Germany to benefit from the obvious differences of opinion between France and the British and Americans. But in domestic politics the pressure cooker exploded. The communists had been preparing for a revolution in the fall, hoping for a German "Red October" in commemoration of the Bolshevist revolution six years earlier. They had entered SPD-led governments in Saxony and Thuringia and begun to build up proletarian self-defense cells in these states bordering Bavaria with its radical right-wing leagues. The Bavarian government began to openly defy the Reich government in Berlin. The radical right-wing leagues that Bavaria had nurtured were armed to their teeth and thirsty for action, preferably for a march on Berlin with a stop in Saxony and Thuringia long enough to overthrow the local left-wing governments and to massacre the proletarian self-defense cells. President Ebert appreciated the seriousness of the situation and called a state of emergency, which gave him special powers according to Article 48. Ebert delegated his extraordinary powers to the chief of the army, General Hans von Seeckt. Seeckt was beleaguered by right-wing politicians, industrialists, and fellow officers who hoped he would establish a military dictatorship, arrest Ebert, and wage a war of liberation against the intruders in the west. Seeckt had no sympathies for democracy, but he had enough sense of realism to understand that a military dictatorship would lead to civil war and that a confrontation with France was foolhardy. He therefore used his powers cautiously and in consultation with Ebert and Stresemann. The biggest challenge was the development in Bavaria. Following some insulting articles against Seeckt in the Nazi newspaper *Völkischer Beobachter*, Seeckt ordered the newspaper to shut down. The Bavarian government, however, refused to comply. The crisis escalated, and General Otto von Lossow, the Bavarian army commander, decided to place the Bavarian army units under his exclusive command. This was a breach of the constitution and an outrage far more serious than the proletarian self-defense cells in Saxony and Thuringia, but Seeckt was more inclined to shoot proletarian units than fellow soldiers. With the reluctant consent of Stresemann and Ebert, Seeckt therefore ordered a military intervention in Saxony and Thuringia that led to the overthrow of the SPD-KPD governments in those states and to the dissolution of the proletarian self-defense cells. The communists tried to stage a national uprising, called Red October, but not much came of it. In Hamburg, bloody clashes between workers and police and Free Corps occurred, but communist putschism was broken for the time being. Nothing was done against Bavaria, however, whose challenge to the authority of the constitution was much more serious. To some extent, this was a power question. Bavaria had its army units and the radical right-wing leagues on its side; a confrontation with Bavaria would lead to much more fighting and bloodshed than the disarming of proletarian self-defense units in Saxony and Thuringia. But the decision to intervene in Saxony and Thuringia while leaving Bavaria unharmed also reflected on the right-wing mindset of the army and much of the state apparatus, which always considered the threat from the left much more serious and criminal than the threat from the right. The situation was still highly volatile when one of the Bavarian radical rightist leagues, the Nazi Party, decided to take drastic action. How had this party evolved?

In the revolutionary troubles of the winter 1918–19 some railway workers in Munich felt that both social change and nationalism should be the predominant goals of German workers. They founded the German Workers' Party (DAP), later called the National Socialist German Workers' Party (NSDAP or the Nazi Party). Adolf Hitler, an obscure failed artist from Austria who had fought in the German army but held no valid passport of any country, was commissioned by the political division of the local army section to watch the DAP. While doing his job, he decided to become a member of the DAP in September 1919 (his member card was not no. 7, as he claimed later, but rather no. 555). With his extraordinary rhetorical talents, his ruthlessness, and his often-theatrical behavior, Hitler turned the NSDAP into an organization tightly controlled by him personally. Supported by Bavarian general Ernst Röhm, the Nazis built up a strong and well-armed paramilitary force, the SA (*Sturmabteilung*; storm division), and became the predominant force within the fragmented Bavarian right. Hitler himself did not yet claim leadership in Germany, but he hoped to drum up mass support for a right-wing dictatorship under General Ludendorff while using Bavaria as a stepping stone for taking power in Berlin and waging a war of liberation. Ludendorff, even though he seemed mentally disturbed after the war, still had enormous authority in right-wing circles and was agitating powerfully for a national takeover.

With his venomous anti-Semitism and denunciation of Versailles and the Berlin government, Hitler whipped up mass hatred and mass support in Bavaria. He was the loudest and most obnoxious of a group of right-wing agitators. He was also one of the most radical and violent. Illegal acts by his party and the SA repeatedly brought him into contact with the Bavarian police (consider that it took very much to get the Bavarian police to step in against right-wing illegality!) but also served as propaganda for his claim to take a leading role. After the end of passive resistance, Hitler demanded with other right-wing leaders that the Bavarian government take action against the national government in Berlin. They wanted to stage a march on Berlin on the lines of Mussolini's march on Rome the previous year (which had been a fascist propaganda lie; Mussolini had been appointed prime minister legally and traveled to Rome in a sleeper car). The atmosphere in Munich became more hysterical every day. Bavarian strongman Gustav von Kahr, his army chief Lossow, and his police chief Hans von Seisser tried to keep the radicals in line by promising some action against Berlin. Right-wing busybodies including Tirpitz and Pan-German leader Heinrich Class traveled back and forth between Berlin and Munich trying to rally support for a quasi-legal putsch based on the strength of the paramilitary leagues in Bavaria and Seeckt's extraordinary powers. In the first days of November 1923, the rightist radicals felt there could be no delay any more. Currency stabilization might succeed in the near future, and political stabilization might follow in its wake. On the evening of 8 November, the SA surrounded a beer hall where Kahr, Lossow, and Seisser were giving speeches. Hitler and Ludendorff stormed into the hall and declared the outbreak of the national revolution. In backstage negotiations, they exacted a promise from the Bavarian leaders to challenge the authorities in Berlin and to launch the much-discussed march on Berlin. Kahr and his colleagues felt no commitment to a promise they had made at gunpoint, however; during the night, they took steps to repress the uprising with forces loyal to the Bavarian government. The next morning, Hitler and Ludendorff tried to save their putsch by assembling a group of Nazis and by marching to the Bavarian government center in Munich. As they left the narrow streets of the inner city and entered a broad square, horse-mounted Bavarian police awaited them. It is not clear who opened fire, but suddenly bullets were flying at the Nazis. Hitler, with the instincts of a former frontline soldier, threw himself to the ground, slightly dislocating his left shoulder. Ludendorff, believing that nobody would dare to shoot him, just continued to march upright through the hail of bullets. Neither Hitler nor Ludendorff was hit, but thirteen putschists were killed. Hitler fled but was arrested by the police at a friend's house the following day. The putsch collapsed ignominiously.

The putsch made Hitler a nationally known political figure. To many right-wing Germans, he had become a hero of sorts. He may have been pathetically mistaken in the methods he chose, but many people believed that his intentions were good and saw him as a selfless and courageous patriot who had dared to do what many others had been afraid to undertake. Hitler succeeded in deepening that impression during the trial that followed the putsch in early 1924. The judges, who shared the assessment of the putschists as well-meaning but misled heroes, allowed him much time for propagandistic speeches. Overshadowing the taciturn and deranged Ludendorff, Hitler managed to establish himself as the leading figure on the radical right. He had a rather good case, of course, because the Kahr government, trying to keep the radical right-wing leagues under its control, had repeatedly suggested that it would do precisely what Hitler and Ludendorff had done on 8 and 9 November. Kahr was immediately cast in a defensive role at the trial, and his political career was terminated. During the purge of the SA on 30 June 1934, he was murdered on Hitler's orders. For Hitler, political life also seemed to be over. He received a mild five-year sentence to be served in a luxury prison, and he was dismissed after just over a year in prison. The NSDAP and SA officially became illegal but continued to exist by blending with various other radical right-wing groups. Ludendorff was acquitted, and nothing was done to prevent him from running for election in the Bavarian elections already in April 1924 and in the German presidential elections one year later. With Kahr compromised by the putsch and the trial, nothing stood in the way of an agreement between Berlin and Munich that reintegrated the Bavarian army units into the German army (Reichswehr).

At the end of 1923, British Ambassador Lord D'Abernon could not help but admire the leading men of the Weimar Republic. They had weathered a massive storm. The Republic might very well have failed, and Germany might have disintegrated into civil war. France might have been tempted by the disorder to occupy more territory, which could have led to the disintegration of Germany altogether. Certainly, the cool head of Stresemann, and Seeckt's resistance to radical right-wing temptations, had helped to master the crisis. Much credit also belonged to Ebert, whose term as president had been prolonged repeatedly by the Reichstag because times seemed too agitated for the election of the president by the people, as stipulated by the constitution. But the Republic survived above all because the goals of its many enemies were completely incompatible. The defenders of the Republic never had to fear unity of action between the Communists and the radical right. They were able to concentrate on one opponent at a time. Still, all was not well after the big storm of 1923. Although currency stabilization did succeed, hyperinflation left deep psychological scars. Inflationary measures were a taboo from now on, and that severely limited the options of governments in the next great economic crisis only a few years later. Moreover, hyperinflation left behind millions of people who wanted their lost savings back. Many political parties made promises to them that they knew they could not keep. The institutions of the Republic, including the army and the justice apparatus, had compromised themselves again by treating right-wing insurgency, as in Bavaria, with rubber gloves while dealing most harshly with the left, as in Saxony and Thuringia. Finally, radicals on the left and the right learned from the failures of open putschism in 1923. They began building up well-organized parties – although it took the NSDAP much longer than the KPD – and devised legal, and potentially more dangerous, strategies for winning power. They were still a long way from power, however, and the years from 1924 to 1929 created conditions that, had they lasted, might well have enabled the Republic to survive.

The middle years of the Weimar Republic were characterized by international reconciliation and economic recovery. In documentaries about the Weimar Republic, the music almost inevitably changes when the narrator comes to these years, and one sees happy Germans dancing Foxtrot in beer gardens. Although Germany did experience its share of the "roaring twenties" in these years, economic conditions were still not very good. Everything just appeared to be somewhat better in relation to the war years and the postwar period. But undoubtedly the Republic stabilized and international developments suggested that Germany might, after all, be accepted as an equal by other democratic nations.

German foreign policy in these years was dominated by Gustav Stresemann, who resigned as chancellor in November 1923 but remained foreign minister to his death in October 1929. Stresemann had been such a virulent annexationist during the First World War that he gained a reputation as "Ludendorff's young man." He became leader of the National Liberal Party and transformed it into the DVP after the war. He initially was a monarchist and opposed democracy, taking an old-fashioned liberal approach that wanted elites chosen by character and merit, not mass vote, to dominate the state. The Rathenau murder, as shown, converted him into a supporter of the Weimar Republic. He was a shrewd diplomat, moreover, who recognized that the victors of the war were ultimately more interested in a stable Germany that would pay some reparations rather than in an unstable country from which they had to extract reparations at a high price. As with Rathenau's Policy of Fulfillment, this was widely misunderstood by simple minds on the radical right, and Stresemann therefore soon became an object of hatred for them. During his tenure in office he found a workable solution to the reparations issue and took important steps toward reconciliation, particularly with France.

The reparations issue was addressed by the Dawes Plan, a scheme drafted by an American banker that was meant to help restart the German economy with American loans and then extract a sum of reparations from Germany that was dependent on the degree of its economic recovery. The reparations paid to France and Britain would then enable these countries to pay back their huge war debt to the United States, which was unwilling to write off the debt, as many French and British statesmen had hoped right after the war. At a conference in London in the summer of 1924, Stresemann helped finalize the agreement. That the international atmosphere had changed since the days of Versailles became clear when the German delegation was allowed to partake in the negotiations and was treated almost as an equal. After winning domestic approval for the Dawes Plan, Stresemann worked on a treaty that would guarantee that Germany's western borders would never be changed by force. This afforded Germany some protection against earlier French designs for creating client states in the Rhineland, and it also meant that Germany freely recognized the loss of Alsace-Lorraine and Eupen-Malmédy. It was a happy coincidence that Stresemann found partners in France and Britain, Foreign Ministers Aristide Briand and Austen Chamberlain, who shared his interest in reconciliation (all three won the Nobel Prize for Peace). At a conference in Locarno (Switzerland), the powers signed an agreement to the effect that Germany's western borders could not be changed by force. It was important, however, that the Treaty of Locarno did not provide a similar guarantee for Germany's eastern borders, which were still so unacceptable to most Germans that no German foreign minister could have officially recognized them. The Treaty of Locarno also stipulated that France and Britain would support Germany's bid to join the League of Nations. Less than a year later, Germany was indeed admitted to the League of Nations, and Stresemann gave a warmly received speech at the League headquarters in Geneva. Progress in relations between Germany and western nations slowed down after this, but Stresemann's foreign policy, with the help of sympathetic foreign statesmen, had decisively undermined the Treaty of Versailles. Reparations had been cut down and were now linked to Germany's economic recovery. Through Locarno, Germany had set a precedent that it would pick and choose which parts of the Treaty of Versailles it would recognize voluntarily. This created a double standard beneficial to Germany: there were some conditions that were imposed on Germany and resented by it, and there were some conditions Germany accepted on its own free will, not under the threat of invasion and dissolution that had loomed large in 1919. Moreover, Germany was a member of the inner circle of the League of Nations, and the cordial relationship between Stresemann and Briand inspired promising ideas about European integration and specifically about Franco-German friendship. Despite remaining grievances, Germany's international position had come a long way since Versailles and the Ruhr occupation.

In domestic politics, too, the going was less rough than in the first postwar years. The Reichstag elections of May 1924 still showed late effects of the feverish year

1923. The German Völkisch Freedom Party, led by Ludendorff and some racist zealots who had left the DNVP because it was not anti-Semitic enough for their taste, did fairly well with 6.5 per cent. This party included many former NSDAP members. The KPD also did well and received 12.5 per cent of the vote (up from 2.1 per cent). The DNVP received almost 20 per cent of the vote, just a little less than the SPD. With some deputies elected on the Agrarian League ticket, the DNVP actually formed the strongest parliamentary group. The Democratic Party lost another substantial part of its electorate, getting just 5.7 per cent (minus 2.6 per cent), whereas the Center Party remained almost unchanged. Stresemann's DVP suffered losses (down to 9.2 per cent from 13.9 per cent in 1920), which mostly benefited the DNVP. An important feature was that a high share of the seats (almost 9 per cent) belonged to splinter parties. Many of these parties were constituted by groups that had suffered losses during the inflation and wanted their savings back. They formed an erratic group in the Reichstag, complicating the construction of majorities.

The Center Party and DVP, with help from the Democratic Party, formed a government under Center Party member Wilhelm Marx, who had been chancellor since November 1923. This government finalized the Dawes Plan and passed it through the Reichstag. During the final vote, the DNVP, which had attacked the Dawes Plan as a cynical exploitation scheme and accused Stresemann of treason, split right down the middle. Those deputies with strong economic interests decided in the end to support the plan because it would allow the influx of much-desired American loans. Marx and Stresemann asked Ebert to dissolve the Reichstag after the Dawes Plan vote. The new elections in December 1924 pushed back the tide of radicalism. The Völkisch Party, ineptly led and divided, lost more than half of its share of the vote. The KPD only received 9 per cent of the vote, and the SPD emerged as the strongest party again with 26 per cent. The DNVP slightly improved on its share from May 1924 while the DVP and Democratic Party recovered a small portion of their losses. The Center Party, as usual, remained almost unchanged, and the splinter parties became slightly weaker. In January 1925, the government parties invited the Bavarian People's Party and, for the first time, the DNVP to form a majority coalition under the unaffiliated finance expert Hans Luther as chancellor. The DNVP, with its pragmatic wing temporarily predominating, decided to join the government but refused to partake in a formal coalition. Opposition against the Treaty of Locarno induced the DNVP to withdraw from the government already in October 1925.

In February 1925, President Ebert died at age 54. He had been the victim of a slander campaign from the right for a long time, and his death happened because he postponed urgent appendicitis surgery so he could attend a court hearing in one of the countless libel cases that he had to launch against the vile slander in right-wing newspapers. Ebert was one of the SPD leaders who had run for election on the strike committees in January 1918, hoping to harness radical socialist activism and to end the strikes. Right-wing newspapers did not accept this motivation and lambasted him for his role in January 1918. They also accused him of high treason for allegedly having taken power illegally in November 1918; in truth he had done the only responsible thing by assuming responsibility in a very difficult moment and by calling democratic elections on short order. The deeper problem was that many conservative Germans could not reconcile themselves to the fact that the highest office of the state was occupied by a working-class man who had once been a saddle maker and was married to a woman who had once earned her living as a cleaning lady. Ebert had played a very moderate role throughout the troubled first years of the Republic and earned much respect from supporters of the Republic even outside of his party. He never had to face a popular election because the Reichstag repeatedly prolonged his term through majority vote, something it could do in politically dangerous circumstances – and there had been no lack of that in the early years. Choosing Ebert's successor was a rather difficult process, however. The election laws stated that a candidate needed to win an absolute majority of the vote (more than 50 per cent) during the first round or else a second round would take place in which the candidate with a plurality of votes would win. The first round ended inconclusively since no candidate was able to win an absolute majority. Only the DNVP and DVP agreed on a common candidate, Duisburg mayor Ernst Jarres, who received 38.8 per cent of the vote, whereas most other parties selected their own candidate who consequently drew about as many votes as his party had received in the last Reichstag elections. A big embarrassment was the radical right-wing candidate, Ludendorff, whose score was significantly lower even that his party's poor result from December 1924. For the second round, SPD, Center Party, and Democratic Party agreed on Wilhelm Marx as their common candidate, an uncharismatic but honest and experienced politician. Given the vote of these three parties, Marx was very likely to win against Jarres in the second round. Stresemann, who had worked with Marx in the government, would have accepted that state of affairs, but it was the DNVP that frantically began searching for a big-name candidate able to beat Marx. The DNVP leaders wanted Hindenburg to run, but Hindenburg begged them to leave him alone. In a revealing letter, he told them that he had virtually no political expertise, hated the Republic, and just wanted to be left alone tending to his roses. At this point, the DNVP sent Tirpitz to Hindenburg, and Tirpitz managed to secure his agreement by talking to him about his patriotic duty. Hindenburg made his approval conditional upon the consent of the Kaiser, and the Kaiser promptly sent a telegram of approval from his Dutch exile. Hindenburg therefore agreed to run for president of the Republic he so despised. He did not give a single campaign speech. He simply ran on his historical persona. And he won, albeit only by a thin margin. The decisive fact was that the Bavarian People's Party decided to support him against the candidate of its sister party, the Center. Some historians also blame the KPD, which insisted on running its own leader, Ernst Thälmann, in a pointless race. Maybe some communists would have voted for Marx had the KPD declared itself uncommitted. But KPD radicalism would have made it difficult for its members to support Marx, who looked to communists just like a less straightforward capitalist than Hindenburg.

The election of the self-professed monarchist and anti-democrat Hindenburg to the highest office of Germany's democracy had mixed repercussions. Stresemann was deeply concerned, believing that Hindenburg's success would destroy the international confidence his foreign policy had just built up. He believed that Tirpitz had launched Hindenburg as a revenge for Stresemann's own role in thwarting Tirpitz's candidacy for chancellor in April 1924. Tirpitz and other DNVP members had indeed hoped to torpedo Stresemann's course and to push the Republic onto a more radical right-wing course. Hindenburg, however, took the oath to the constitution and behaved like a loyal president. All right-wing hopes for using him as a Trojan horse in order to conquer and destroy the Republic failed – for the time being, at least. Lending a receptive ear to Stresemann and Luther rather than DNVP members, Hindenburg supported the Treaty of Locarno and Germany's entry into the League of Nations. It appeared that he made the Republic more acceptable to a large segment of moderate right-wing opinion, which had been unwilling to accept it before. This and the participation of the DNVP in government in 1925 and again in 1927 indicates that the Weimar Republic, albeit in a more conservative figuration than originally planned, did perhaps have a chance for survival. Right-wing opposition to it seemed to erode slowly as the economy picked up, fuelled by American loans encouraged by the Dawes Plan. The large industrial and agrarian organizations that had been so vehemently opposed to a Republic created by socialists and democrats seemed to make their peace with it. With Hindenburg rather than Ebert as a president, these circles could look to an ersatz Kaiser, a widely respected man and national hero.

Although the prospects for a consolidation of the Republic seemed not bad, there were some disturbing economic signs that not all was well. In the second half of the 1920s, a crisis of overproduction gripped agriculture and led to much farmer unrest. In industry, unemployment was at a surprisingly high level already in 1927; whereas nearly full employment had quickly returned after the demobilization crisis in 1918–19, a large number of workers now found it difficult to get jobs. This was not yet a major problem, however, because the social legislation of the Weimar Republic made sure that the unemployed workers received adequate support. Some economic historians blame precisely the high social expenses of the Weimar Republic for the severity of the economic crisis that followed, but it would go too far to blame that crisis on high social spending. There were some troubling economic indicators, but there is no reason to believe that they would have caused a cataclysmic crisis of the Republic on their own.

In May 1928, the Reichstag elections sent some mixed signals. The SPD gained almost 4 per cent, which brought it to just short of 30 per cent of the electorate. All the other moderate parties suffered slight losses, however. On the far right, the exhausted by its infighting between intransigent opponents of the Republic and pragmatic proponents of participation in government, lost over a quarter of its share and went down to 14.2 per cent. The KPD won marginally, whereas the NSDAP, now legal again, lost slightly and slipped to 2.6 per cent. The bad news was that the share of the splinter parties almost doubled and reached 13.9 per cent, almost as much as the DNVP, the second strongest party in the Reichstag. Obviously, some deep discontent persisted in the middle classes that was not adequately addressed by the moderate right-to-center parties or the SPD. Other discouraging news followed insofar as most of the parties who lost votes in the 1928 elections moved more to the right. This happened most dramatically in the DNVP in October 1928, when the intransigents won an internal victory and elected press magnate Alfred Hugenberg as party leader. Hugenberg, whose newspapers had been instrumental in spreading DNVP propaganda and whose financial support had enabled many a DNVP candidate to win election, was a sworn anti-democrat and former Pan-German League leader determined to destroy the Weimar Republic at whatever cost. In the Center Party and the DVP, the right wing also gained momentum after the elections. The DVP therefore became more of a force against democracy again, in spite of Stresemann's continued pragmatism. The Center Party became less committed to the Weimar Republic and more open to authoritarian alternatives. These developments happened largely in reaction to the SPD victory. Taken together, they throw a rather dubious light on the consolidation process of the Weimar Republic. In a healthy democracy, the parties that loose an election analyze what went wrong and try to do better at the next elections. The DNVP, and to a lesser extent the DVP and Center Party, behaved differently. Like a chess player with bad manners who is losing the game, the DNVP decided to overthrow the pieces and use the board to beat up the other player.

Still, under Stresemann's leadership, the DVP agreed to a pragmatic so-called Grand Coalition with the SPD, the Center Party, the Democrats, and the Bavarian People's Party. These parties together had a sound majority in the Reichstag (61 per cent), and they formed a government under SPD-member Hermann Müller. Hindenburg at first cringed at the prospect of appointing a member of the hated SPD as chancellor, but he ended up liking the moderate and cool-headed Social Democrat Müller. Stresemann as foreign minister was allowed to pursue his policy of reconciliation. The interests of the parties in the Grand Coalition contradicted each other, especially since worker (SPD) and employer (DVP) interests were both represented in government, but as long as the economic situation remained stable the parties managed to solve their conflicts by compromise. Hugenberg's radical course was alarming, but in the short run it only served to weaken the DNVP by alienating its more moderate supporters. This did not bother Hugenberg, however, who always stressed that he would rather lead a small party as a powerful ram against democracy rather than a broad "porridge" of contradictory interests. The NSDAP had been reorganizing busily after Hitler's dismissal from prison at the end of 1924. It had built up a very active nationwide party structure committed to Hitler as the supreme leader, and it was doing better in state elections in 1929 than it had done in the Reichstag elections the previous year. The Nazis appealed to disgruntled farmers in Schleswig-Holstein and increasingly also in the east Elbian regions of Prussia. Counter-factual history (imagining what could have happened under different circumstances) is particularly tempting at this point. What would have happened if the catastrophic economic crisis that began in the fall of 1929 had not occurred? It was to be expected that the NSDAP, as a well-organized protest party, would become stronger, but it was inconceivable that it once would receive over a third of the national vote (hardly anybody would have predicted that before 1930). It was clear that German democracy continued to have rather weak support. Even with the strong SPD of 1928, the original Weimar parties (SPD, Democratic Party, Center) still did not regain the absolute parliamentary majority that they had lost in 1920. The DVP's support for the Republic was fragile and increasingly dependent on the prestige and political acrobatics of Stresemann, who devoted tireless energy to keeping his considerably more right-wing party behind his course. Hindenburg seemed to cast an air of conservative respectability on the Republic, but many of his traditional friends on the right were becoming disillusioned with him. Still, there were no storm warnings in Germany at this time. The Republic had survived serious crises before. It probably would have experienced more governmental instability and at worst some authoritarian redrawing of the constitution. Governmental instability was still endemic to the French Third Republic decades after its foundation. The Weimar Republic had experienced it before and survived. An authoritarian redrawing of the constitution would have left the SPD unhappy, but it would hardly have led to a drastic change of policy. Many people in Germany and abroad doubted that democracy was really the best state form for the Germans. A more conservative Republic would not have aroused much suspicion abroad. Such a Republic would undoubtedly have pushed for more revisions of the Treaty of Versailles, aimed to rearm Germany, and played a more assertive international role, but it would hardly have caused the Second World War and the Holocaust. I believe that without the huge economic upheaval happening between the fall of 1929 and the end of 1932, the NSDAP would not have come to power, Hitler would not have become chancellor and dictator, and the Second World War would not have broken out. This does not mean that I am convinced that the Weimar Republic would have survived unchanged without the economic crisis. German democracy was not particularly strong in 1929, and it is quite likely that it would have been turned into a more authoritarian, conservative system based on the army even in the absence of the big storm. This was actually happening in many other European democracies established after the war, such as in Poland, Spain (for a while), the Baltic states, and some Balkan states as well. The Great Depression merely accelerated this process in some countries. The First World War, as Wilson envisioned it, was supposed to make the world safe for democracy, but most new democracies soon faltered in the context of sluggish economies and deep social and, in some cases, ethnic tensions.

In October 1929, Stresemann died and the American stock market crashed. Four weeks before his death, Stresemann and Briand had proposed a scheme for European economic integration at a League of Nations meeting. This was an encouraging step, foreshadowing the project of European integration after the Second World War. But Stresemann had exhausted himself in his struggle to keep his party committed to the Republic and the Grand Coalition and to ensure support for his foreign policy. His health was ruined. He suffered a stroke and died at age fifty-one. His death triggered genuine and widespread grief in Germany and abroad. After Rathenau and Ebert, the Republic had lost another one of its great representatives – probably the greatest of all. His party, however, immediately moved to the right, and the days of the Grand Coalition were clearly numbered. Maybe Stresemann would have been powerless in the face of the cataclysmic crisis of the following years, but it was fatal for the Republic that it lost its most capable defender just as the seas were beginning to get rough because of the other fatal event of October 1929, the American stock-market crash. Caused by years of unsupported borrowing and spending in the United States, the crash led to severe reactions in most industrialized countries. The United States and Britain suffered bitterly from the crisis, but nowhere was the impact as devastating as in Germany. But this was not obvious all at once. The crisis unfolded more slowly, reaching its most severe proportions in 1931 and 1932. The human suffering caused by the crisis was enormous. Unemployment rose from 1.5 million people to over six million. Hans-Ulrich Wehler even points out that this number is much too low because it reflects only registered unemployed workers; Wehler suggests that close to nine million workers were actually unemployed.[2] The generous social laws of the Weimar Republic were useless in the face of needs of such huge dimensions; the state simply could not support so many people with approximately 40 per cent of German industry being shut down. Many unemployed workers became desperately poor and lost their apartments because they could no longer pay rent. A huge crowd of homeless people was wandering along the highways of Germany, with backpacks and often without shoes. The desperation of millions was captured in the expressive works of photographer Walter Ballhause and graphic artist Karl Weinmair.

The economic crisis provided the fuel for the growth of the radical parties on the left and the right. One beneficiary was the KPD. We have seen how the KPD at the end of 1923 gave up its putschism, realizing that violent uprisings on the model of the Bolshevist takeover in Russia always triggered a brutal confrontation with the German army and Free Corps that communist workers could not win. But repression and a right-wing judiciary cemented the bonds among the radical workers. The KPD built up a larger, more disciplined apparatus and did well in the elections of 1924 and 1928. Like the Nazis, the KPD also built up a street fighter force, the Red Front Fighter's League, to protect its meetings and to intimidate political opponents. The Red Front soon engaged in bloody street battles with right-wing paramilitary units and later the Nazi SA. It distributed propaganda material and helped to organize the party's electoral campaigns. Much of the extremely aggressive and violent political rhetoric so familiar from Nazi propaganda also characterized communist propaganda. As long as economic stability prevailed, the results of communist efforts were not too impressive. With the start of the Great Depression, however, Communist votes increased and almost doubled until November 1932, when the KPD received 16.9 per cent of the national vote. The disruption of the economy and mass unemployment benefited the KPD, all the more as the crisis discredited capitalism in the eyes of many workers. The Stalinist Soviet Union was hardly affected, and most communists did not understand that this resulted more from the isolation of the Soviet economy from the world market than from the merits of socialist economics. Communist bands marching through the cities, singing aggressive songs, attracted many young, unskilled, and unemployed workers. Whereas the more skilled workers remained loyal to the trade unions (which were predominantly moderate, reformist, and thus close to the SPD), the unskilled and the young preferred the KPD to the SPD, which gained the reputation of an old men's party. The famous novel *Little Man, What Now?* (1932) by Hans Fallada casts this alignment well: the female protagonist, Bunny, has a father in the SPD and an unemployed brother in the KPD.[3] The dynamism of the KPD also attracted some intellectuals, artists, writers, and musicians. Often without joining the party, they helped its propaganda and joined its avantgarde cultural initiatives. Unlike the Nazis, the KPD embraced the new spirit of Weimar Culture. The idea of a movement that wanted to recreate society totally and rebuild traditional forms of life proved appealing to intellectuals. They spread a socialist message in films, plays, concerts, and spontaneous performances in the streets. They produced some magnificent works of art in the process. The KPD seemed young, dynamic, forceful, fascinating, and inspiring. Its appeal overshadowed the SPD's, which looked somewhat ossified, boring, and old. Usually, the intellectuals becoming fellow travelers of the KPD closed their eyes to the brutality of its street fighters and to the much more drastic brutality of Stalin's rule in the Soviet Union.

The German communists never managed to start a revolution and were brutally repressed when Hitler came to power (without the Soviet Union even protesting). Nevertheless, they helped to destabilize and bring down the Republic. Unwilling to think pragmatically, and blindly obedient to Moscow's Machiavellian machinations, they declared the SPD their main enemy. Whereas the KPD saw the Nazis as unmistakable slaves of capitalism, it claimed that the SPD was the more dangerous enemy of the working people because it looked like a socialist party. Communists thus denounced the SPD as "Social Fascists" and concentrated as much on fighting the SPD as on beating up the Nazis. Working-class unity against the right, which had helped to foil the Kapp Putsch in 1920, was anathema to the KPD in the last years of the Republic. The SPD sometimes suggested it, and a few years after the Nazi takeover even the Soviet leaders advocated it in France and Spain, where they promoted so-called "popular front" governments including communists, social democrats, and left liberals; but by then the German communist movement had long been broken up by the Nazis.

The KPD's electoral appeal was limited largely to unskilled workers and a few fellow travelers. Its electoral gains came primarily at the expense of the SPD. The NSDAP, however, had a much larger potential voter reservoir and weaker competitors than the KPD. But its meteoric rise to pre-eminence after 1929 would not have been possible without a thorough reorganization of the party in the wake of the Beer Hall Putsch. In his luxury prison, Hitler wrote his programmatic book (*Mein Kampf*), which was extremely radical and disjointed. What was more important in the short run was that Hitler in prison concluded – like the KPD leadership – that putschism, at least as a frontal assault on the Weimar Republic, did not have a chance. Every right-wing putsch had failed to win army support and antagonized many people in the administration who approved the goals of the putschists but found their methods too risky. Hitler thus decided to win power "legally" through participation in elections and propaganda. Legally requires quotation marks here because Hitler continued to foster street violence through the SA and kept bending or breaking the law when it helped him. Hitler further toned down the anti-Semitic message in his propaganda. Much as anti-Semitism was a key factor in his political motivation, he recognized that it was attracting fewer people than he wanted and alienated some potentially powerful allies on the right and in the political middle. Not that German rightists in general were philo-Semites; Jews in Germany witnessed an upsurge of anti-Semitism during and after the closing phase of the First World War, but raging against the Jews as irrationally and viciously as Hitler had done before the putsch (and as he did in his book) seemed unjustified even to many rightists. Hitler thus decided to tone down his anti-Semitism in public speeches, and this was true for the following years of his political campaigning and even for the first phases of his dictatorship.

After the Beer Hall Putsch, the NSDAP and the SA were outlawed for about one year. While Hitler was in prison, an alignment of Nazi and other racist groups joined to participate in elections under Ludendorff's leadership. They did well during the Bavarian elections of April 1924 and the Reichstag elections one month later, receiving almost 18 per cent of the vote in Bavaria. In Munich, the site of the abortive putsch, every second voter supported the NSDAP's successor organization in April 1924. In the December elections of 1924, however, the prospect of economic stability worked against radicals of all sorts and dealt Ludendorff's party a crushing defeat. His bid for the presidency a few months later was another big embarrassment. If Hitler had hoped that his own removal from politics would demonstrate that the radical right needed his leadership, he was proven right.

Before 1925 the Nazis and their associates had appeared mainly on the stage of Bavarian politics. To non-Bavarians – Germans and foreigners alike – Hitler looked like a local political matador or as a political clown escaped from the Munich Oktoberfest. This changed when Hitler left prison. Disillusioned about Bavaria as a footstep for takeover in Berlin, he started to build up a nationwide organization strictly loyal to him. The SA was rebuilt, too. Increasingly, it engaged in bloody street battles with the communist and republican paramilitary units. But like the Communists, the Nazis were unable to harvest the fruits of their organizational efforts before the Great Depression hit Germany. In the 1928 elections they received only twelve Reichstag seats (2.6 per cent of the vote); in 1930, however, their parliamentary group rose to 107 (18.3 per cent), and it more than doubled in July 1932 (230 seats; 37.4 per cent). Within four years, the NSDAP had become by far the largest party in Germany.

It was not so much those who were most directly affected by the economic crisis who voted for Hitler. The unemployed, for instance, often preferred the Communists or even the SPD. What gave the Nazis so much support was their image as a determined force of order and reconstruction at a time when all traditional structures – be they economic or social – seemed to break down. The Nazis' insistence on order was hypocritical, of course, as the NSDAP in general and the SA in particular did their utmost to exacerbate the chaos from which they promised to deliver Germany. But they managed to prove more credibly than any other party that they had the force and determination to put the country back together, and this was a powerful message for all voters who were neither affiliated with the labor parties nor with the Center or the Bavarian People's Party and felt upset about the unprecedented breakdown of economic activity. The NSDAP, and particularly Hitler, developed a dizzying dynamism during the many national and local elections in 1930–2. Hitler was the first politician to build up a sophisticated national campaign. He used an airplane and flew to dozens of towns, creating the impression that he was present everywhere. He gave speeches to the brink of physical exhaustion. Every Hitler speech was carefully rehearsed to appear spontaneous. The NSDAP had a clever set of rules for political events; the Nazis often rented a slightly too small meeting hall so that newspapers would report about excellent attendance, and the SA made sure that disturbing shouters were quickly and violently removed. The NSDAP spent fortunes on propaganda materials and used them with an uncanny effectiveness similar to successful advertising firms. Moreover, Hitler inspired his supporters far more than the leader of any other party. As a consequence, the Nazis simply did much more than the other parties in a mood of intense despair and disorientation. In a survey of party activities in Saxony, for example, historian Benjamin Lapp has shown that the Nazis organized far more rallies and special events than anybody else and that they kept up an intense activity even in periods without imminent elections.[4]

The NSDAP's appeal during the crisis years was unusually broad. Even though strongholds of the workers' movement, such as Berlin, Hamburg, Saxony, and the Ruhr proved somewhat resistant to the Nazi upsurge, as did regions in which the Center or the Bavarian People's Party had been entrenched for a while, the NSDAP did conquer the large non-socialist and predominantly Protestant German voter reservoir – people who had traditionally voted for the Democratic Party, DVP, or DNVP. The Democratic Party and the DVP were virtually wiped out in the two

Reichstag elections of 1932, receiving less than 2 per cent of the vote each, and the DNVP, trying to steal the Nazis' thunder, kept losing votes under Hugenberg, albeit at a smaller pace than the two other parties. From 20.5 per cent in December 1924, the DNVP's share of the national electorate melted to 6.2 per cent in July 1932 (although it recovered slightly in November 1932 with 8.9 per cent). Many voters left one of these three parties, which had together received between 33 per cent and 37 per cent of the national vote in all elections from 1919 to 1924, long before the greatest Nazi successes and opted for a splinter party in 1924, 1928, or 1930. But by 1932, it had become clear that the splinter parties were powerless. Like a giant vacuum cleaner, the NSDAP swept up almost all of their support. Farmers voted for Hitler, as did Protestant middle-class people. Professors and schoolteachers, who had leaned to the right already during the Wilhelmine period, supported the Nazis. The NSDAP scored its greatest successes in small and medium-size towns in predominantly Protestant regions. Although the NSDAP drew its most important backing from the Protestant middle classes, it was not predominantly a class party. It reached out to nationalist workers who had never liked the socialists (and had often voted for the DNVP, which had a worker's wing until Hugenberg's radicalism drove it out of the party), and it included large groups from all layers of German society. It even attracted a significant group of formerly socialist workers (from the SPD and KPD). In this sense, the NSDAP was a true people's party, a status the DVP or DNVP had never achieved.

But the Weimar Republic did not simply fail because of the growth of the extremist parties in general or because of the electoral successes of the NSDAP in particular. For all intents and purposes, democracy was undermined, even destroyed, earlier. Nationalist associations including veterans' leagues, farmers' leagues, and many middle-class organizations had built up mass support and become well organized already in the mid-1920s. These leagues, although claiming to represent the German people, hated the Weimar Republic because they believed that it was run by party interests and beholden to foreign influences. They envisioned a more authoritarian form of state that did not need to compromise with the left-wing workers' movement and the SPD. They articulated their claims as a common people's interest in opposition to specific class and party interests. As historian Peter Fritzsche has shown, nationalist mobilization had played a key role in securing a majority for Hindenburg in the presidential elections of 1925, but Hindenburg had disappointed most of his supporters by compromising with the parties and the Republic's elites.[5] By the end of the 1920s, former Hindenburg supporters were longing for a new charismatic strongman who would appeal to a people's community across party and class lines and promise a fundamental reform of Germany's domestic and international situation. The good showing of the SPD in the elections of 1928 and the SPD's return to the government further alienated these circles from democracy. Meanwhile, there were many people in the state administration, in Hindenburg's entourage, and in the center-to-right parties who more or less deliberately used the evolving crisis after 1929 to undermine the strength of the SPD and trade unions and to reform the political system in a more authoritarian and less democratic direction. How did this happen?

The first political victim of the Great Depression in Germany was the Grand Coalition. Even at the beginning of the crisis the preservation of unemployment insurance became a problem. Employers and the bourgeois parties wanted to cut state support for the jobless; the SPD and the trade unions felt this to be too harsh a measure at a time when more and more workers became dependent upon state support. The conflict led to the breakup of the Grand Coalition in March 1930. After this no government was ever supported by a Reichstag majority again until the Nazis entered a coalition with the DNVP following the manipulated elections of March 1933. The breakup of the Grand Coalition was not simply a matter of unbridgeable conflicts, however. There is evidence that, on the side of the bourgeois parties and the entourage of President Hindenburg, the will to compromise had strongly diminished. The Center Party, in conjunction with the other non-socialist coalition members and Hindenburg's advisors, deliberately chose a course of confrontation with the SPD in order to push the SPD out of the government and to start a phase of presidential government. They felt that time was ripe for a more authoritarian political system that would reduce democratic and social rights. The Center Party politician Heinrich Brüning, one mastermind of this intrigue, hoped to restore a more authoritarian constitution limiting parliamentary rights and keeping the socialists and trade unions out of the state. In many ways this vision aimed to recreate the political system of the Wilhelmine empire: an alliance of iron (big industry) and rye (big agriculture) holding a monopoly on political power at the top, while excluding the workers. Brüning and many of his associates vaguely thought of themselves as monarchists and ultimately hoped for monarchic restoration. Brüning's course toward a presidential government was enthusiastically supported by a DVP finally rid of Stresemann's moderating influence.

Brüning's appointment also marked a decisive step on the road from democracy to dictatorship. Hindenburg had promised Brüning that he would sign presidential emergency decrees (under Article 48) if Brüning faced opposition in the Reichstag. The government thus ceased to function democratically. Brüning usually relied on the president's emergency powers to push through the legislation he wanted. Article 48 gave the president special rights to issue emergency legislation, but the Reichstag could disapprove the president's measures later. The president, in turn, could dissolve the Reichstag and call new elections. Between the dissolution and the elections, he and his chancellor could enact laws without parliamentary control. Hindenburg's expanding role represented an abuse of the constitution's emergency powers, however. Article 48 was meant to protect the democratic functioning of the constitution, not to disrupt it. Worse, Hindenburg's failing energy (he was seventy-six when he was elected in 1925; he had already retired twice, once in 1911 and then in 1918) made him an easy prey to a group of narrow-minded rightists in his closest entourage. Hindenburg's approval of Brüning's request to dissolve the Reichstag in the summer of 1930 and again in the middle of 1932 proved disastrous. Both times the extremist parties, profiting from the economic crisis, made enormous gains, most of all the Nazis.

Brüning and Hindenburg were frightened by the rise of the extremist parties, but reducing the Reichstag's power seemed more important to them than stemming the tide of political extremism. The growth of anti-democratic parties increased the disfunctionality of the Reichstag and thus made it easier to disregard it in politics – and this was precisely what Hindenburg's right-wing advisers wanted. After the elections of September 1930 had swelled their ranks, the Nazis and Communists dealt the Reichstag's authority a final blow; they often obstructed parliamentary debates; sometimes they beat each other up in the main hall. To those who wanted to limit parliamentary rights, such as Brüning and the people in Hindenburg's entourage, the chaos in the Reichstag was a welcome "proof" that parliamentary democracy could not work. Perhaps Brüning was less cynical than it might appear, but there can be no doubt that many people in the government and the center-to-right parties were not unhappy at all about the paralysis and loss of authority of the Reichstag.

Brüning's financial and economic policy has often been criticized for unnecessarily exacerbating the economic crisis. Recent research has shown that his latitude should not be overestimated, however. It was constrained by the regulations of the Young Plan, a new agreement about the payment of reparations that was negotiated by Stresemann and implemented shortly after his death. The Young Plan made deficit spending and inflationary policies to fight the depression nearly impossible. It has often been ignored, moreover, that Germany to a large degree was obliged to follow policies of other states. Most governments fought the crisis in similar ways, and the one government that would have adopted different ones risked to slid into even greater chaos. Economists have also pointed out the shortsighted German use of the American loans in the years preceding the crisis. Short-term loans were invested in long-term projects (such as swimming pools, town halls, and other public projects). These investments created an artificial, unsound economic boom but did nothing to strengthen productivity. When the American loans were recalled, German towns often went bankrupt. Whether Brüning could have done better in fighting the crisis or not, he certainly had specific priorities that further reduced his economic latitude. His most urgent aim was not overcoming the economic crisis but further revision of the Treaty of Versailles. He wanted to stop reparations payments for good, abolish the rearmament clauses of the peace treaty, and prepare the integration of Austria into Germany (*Anschluss*) in defiance of the Treaty of Versailles. Brüning did not exacerbate the economic crisis deliberately in order to reach these goals, but he did his utmost to use the crisis in order to wring concessions from the victors. It remains unclear as to how much his prioritizing the repudiation of Versailles exacerbated the economic crisis. On one or two occasions it looked as if Brüning, following his foreign policy priorities, made decisions that ruined the German economy even more.

It has to be said, however, that Brüning, apart from his own nationalist convictions, hoped his course would win Nazi supporters over to the Center Party and the more moderate rightists.

In foreign policy, Brüning was successful. He received far-reaching concessions from the western powers. Reparations were stopped for the time being by the Hoover Moratorium, and a disarmament conference recognized Germany's right to insist on the disarmament of its former enemies, as stated by the general disarmament clause of the Treaty of Versailles. But Brüning did not keep Hindenburg's confidence long enough. When the western concessions took effect he was out of office and could no longer benefit from them. His plans for a solution of the domestic crisis had alienated the most reactionary circles in German society, those intransigent Junkers who had the strongest influence on Hindenburg. Most of all, Hindenburg became tired of Brüning's politics because Brüning failed to secure Hindenburg's reappointment without an election in the spring of 1932. This was possible only through a two-thirds majority vote in favor of Hindenburg in the Reichstag. The Nazis, the DNVP, and the KPD, however, thwarted Brüning's efforts to avoid presidential elections. When these elections took place in March 1932, Hindenburg gained almost 50 per cent of the vote, whereas Hitler received 30 per cent and Ernst Thälmann, the Communist leader, 13 per cent. In the second ballot in April, Hindenburg beat Hitler again, winning 53 per cent as to almost 37 per cent for Hitler and only 10 per cent for Thälmann. Hindenburg, however, resented that he was elected not by the right – which voted for Hitler – but by the moderate left (including the SPD) and the Center Party. Hindenburg, with his Wilhelmine mindset, felt deeply uncomfortable about having been reelected by the *Reichsfeinde*, the enemies of the state, and he blamed Brüning. At a time when a confidential contact between president and chancellor had become crucial because of the frequent use of presidential emergency decrees, Brüning could not hold out in office and was dismissed in the end of May 1932.

Brüning had not had a parliamentary majority behind him, but he was the exponent of a relatively strong party, the Center Party, and his government was temporarily tolerated by the SPD, which saw no better alternative and rightly feared the consequences of repeated Reichstag dissolutions. Franz von Papen, Brüning's successor, had hardly any parliamentary support at all. He was truly Hindenburg's man; Hindenburg liked Papen's refined manners and simplistic political ideas. Essentially, Papen wanted to accelerate the movement to a presidential dictatorship and was much more willing than Brüning to violate the constitution. On 20 July 1932 he offered an example of what he had in store: he ousted the SPD-led Prussian government and put himself at the head of this largest German state as Reich commissar. The Prussian government under Social Democrat Otto Braun was the last existing state government formed by the original Weimar coalition (SPD, Democratic Party, Center). It had lost its majority at the Prussian Landtag elections in April 1932, which brought the strong radicalization in favor of the NSDAP and KPD that was already so familiar from Reichstag elections. But since there was no majority for an alternative government, Braun kept the old cabinet in place as a caretaker government. This was entirely constitutional. Papen's intervention was not, but it was covered by Hindenburg. As a next step, Papen tried to bring the NSDAP into the government. He did so not because he liked the Nazi movement but rather because he hoped to win Nazi support for his own plans for a presidential dictatorship. He also reckoned that participation in government would undercut the NSDAP's electoral success. Hitler, however, insisted on becoming chancellor, a request that Hindenburg refused. Papen then considered a coup d'état by asking Hindenburg to suspend the Reichstag indefinitely and meanwhile redraw the constitution with a sharp authoritarian pen, but General Kurt von Schleicher, the defense minister, rejected this idea because he argued that Poland might use the ensuing chaos for an attack on Germany. When Papen met the Reichstag in November, the Reichstag passed an overwhelming vote of no confidence against him. Only the DNVP supported Papen, but its share of the national vote had plummeted to 6.2 per cent. Facing an overwhelming vote of no confidence and Hindenburg's reluctance to break the constitution all too openly, Papen resigned. Hindenburg chose Schleicher as Papen's successor. Schleicher, who had exercised strong influence on Papen, had meanwhile become apprehensive about Hitler and the NSDAP. He considered it necessary to keep Hitler out of power at all cost and sought ways to split the Nazi Party by bringing together a broad labor-based front from the trade unions to the left wing of the NSDAP.

Time was running out for Hitler. The Reichstag elections of November 1932, following the vote of no confidence against Papen, brought significant losses for the Nazis. The NSDAP received only 196 seats with 33.1 per cent of the electorate, a loss of thirty-four seats and 4.3 per cent. The election result did not mean that democracy was about to be restored, given that the KPD kept growing and that the NSDAP's losses mostly benefited Hugenberg's DNVP, but it was a clear sign that Nazi supporters were getting impatient and doubtful about Hitler's stubborn demand for the chancellorship. The NSDAP had built up a broad coalition by sending contradictory promises to different voter groups; it seemed that it may have overreached itself and that the voting public might be becoming more sober. Moreover, the Great Depression began to ease; in November 1932, most economic indicators for Germany began to reverse their evil course. Perhaps to some extent as the consequence of Brüning's austerity policy, Germany reached the bottom of the Great Depression faster than other countries. This did not bode well for a party like the NSDAP, which had thrived so much on the economic crisis. To make matters worse, the NSDAP faced internal trouble. After five major election campaigns in 1932 (two for the Reichstag, two rounds of presidential elections, and the Prussian election) the party coffers were empty, and there were strong tensions between a working-class group particularly in the SA, which was keenly awaiting the benefits of participation in government even under a non-Nazi as chancellor, and Hitler, who wanted to participate only if he became chancellor. Shortly after the November 1932 elections, the official SPD newspaper wrote with exaggerated but not entirely unjustified pride: "It will be the everlasting merit of social democracy to have kept German fascism from power until it began to decline in popular favor. The decline will hardly be less rapid than its rise has been." American historian Henry Turner therefore argues in a fascinating book that Hitler's appointment to the chancellorship on 30 January 1933 was entirely superfluous. Had Hitler been kept outside of power a few months longer, his movement might well have split and collapsed without much ado. There would have been an authoritarian and to some extent anti-Semitic Germany, and democracy would probably not have been restored on short order, but this would have been a much better scenario than what actually did happen.[6] Turner's ideas deserve much credit, although they should not lead one to dismiss the importance of Hitler's electoral victories. True, he failed to receive a majority in the presidential election in 1932; true also that he and his party never scored more than 37.4 per cent of the vote in free elections, which is perhaps not very much if compared, for example, to American presidential elections, where even the losing candidate usually receives a larger share of the vote. But the electoral success of the NSDAP was spectacular by German standards; without it, Hitler would never have come within reach of power.

Yet Hitler did not become chancellor due to elections alone. It was necessary for Hindenburg to appoint him. Hindenburg's attitude to Hitler, however, was characterized by class prejudice toward the "Bohemian corporal," as he called Hitler, and by aversion to Nazi radicalism. Hindenburg had repeatedly refused to appoint Hitler as chancellor. But powerful circles in Hindenburg's entourage worked to convince Hindenburg that appointing Hitler would do two things: first, offer a golden opportunity to smash the labor movement with the full force of the NSDAP and SA and, second, destroy the NSDAP, which would be crushed by government responsibility and, like every other party in the Weimar Republic, suffer electoral losses as a consequence of participation in government. The mastermind of this intrigue, which proceeded behind Schleicher's back, was Papen, who blamed Schleicher for his failure as chancellor and still had Hindenburg's confidence. It was of great help to Papen that Schleicher's vision of a labor-based axis from the right wing of the trade unions to the left wing of the NSDAP alarmed leading industrialists and agrarians. With the help of some prominent German industrialists and important figures in Hindenburg's entourage, Papen undermined Hindenburg's confidence in Schleicher. Without the president's emergency decrees, however, Schleicher stood no chance of success in front of an overwhelmingly hostile Reichstag. Papen had his way. On 30 January 1933 Hindenburg appointed a new cabinet with Hitler as chancellor, another Nazi as interior minister and a third Nazi, Hermann Göring, as minister without portfolio. The nine other ministers all belonged to other parties (mostly the DNVP) or did not belong to any party. Papen became vice-chancellor and Hugenberg economics minister. Given the weakness of the Nazi representation in the new cabinet, and given the fact that Hindenburg as president could dismiss Hitler, Papen was confident that it would be possible to push Hitler into the corner – until he squeaked, as Papen put it.

Papen's reasoning was profoundly flawed, however. Although it was true that voters in the Weimar Republic tended to desert parties that had the courage to participate in government in times of crisis, it was wrong for Papen to expect that the Nazis in government would act like the SPD or even the DNVP, which had both lost voters after participation in government. Having massive armies of violent street fighters without any respect for law and order, the Nazis were determined not to let power slip out of their hands once they had received access to the national government. Indeed, when the news spread that Hitler had become chancellor, the SA and huge crowds of Nazi supporters took to the streets. Tolerated and sometimes supported by the police, which was quickly put under Nazi control by the Nazi interior minister, they started a which hunt against communists and opponents of all sorts. With their massive armed street gangs, the Nazis used terror and violence to stabilize their power.

Reflecting on the failure of the Weimar Republic in 1933, we encounter two separate though connected questions. First: why did the Weimar Republic break down? Second: why did the Nazis, the most radical and violent group, succeed it? To answer the first question, we have to consider long-term, structural problems and short-term, immediate causes during the economic crisis of 1929–33. First of all, most Germans did not recognize that many difficulties of the Weimar Republic came out of the world war, which Germany had lost. Astronomic wartime spending and hidden inflation had made Germany a much poorer place after the war. As historian Richard Bessel has pointed out, the problem was that nobody acknowledged this in public and that most people remained unaware of these deep structural problems.[7] Although the old elites had started the war and lost it, leaving behind a terrible mess, the revolution of 1918 and the Weimar Republic received the blame for Germany's economic and social problems. To get rid of wartime debts, to pay reparations, and to fund a social welfare state, the Weimar governments would have had to treble the taxes of 1913 at a time when most people were much worse off. Only full awareness of the problem and a strong, united government with widespread support could have put Germany's economy and finances on a healthy standing again. This would have implied many more years of suffering and poverty, a prospective unacceptable to the German masses, who had already sacrificed so much for the war and would neither believe nor accept that all had been in vain and that they should be much worse off than before. In a nutshell: Germany was much poorer after the war than before not so much because it had *lost* the war but because it had *fought* it. Few people understood this at the time, and those who did often preferred not to publicize their views. It was easier and seemingly more plausible to blame all hardship on Versailles and the Weimar politicians who had signed the peace treaty.

The second long-term point is that conditions for the establishment of a social democracy, as envisioned by the original Weimar coalition, were not good at all. The SPD and later the democratic middle parties received power at a time when nobody else wanted it and when circumstances for the buildup of a social welfare state, the goal of the SPD, could hardly have been worse. Ludendorff's shrewd plan worked: the SPD and the German democrats had to share the blame for the mess the old elites had left behind in 1918. Some historians have criticized the SPD for not having imposed more socialist control over the political system (for instance by upgrading the workers' councils), but more socialism would more likely have led to civil war than stabilized democracy. As chaotic as Germany seemed in the winter of 1918–19, the countryside remained orderly and conservative. It would have risen against the socialists had they imposed more far-reaching reforms.

The third long-term problem of the Weimar Republic was the widespread anti-democratic feeling on the left and, most of all, on the right. To the radical left the Weimar Republic was a capitalist state based on a conservative and reactionary military, an aggressive industrialist group, and wrongheaded socialists who had betrayed their cause by allying with reactionary circles. The social achievements of the October Reforms in 1918, the eight-hour working day, for example, were withdrawn in the course of the Republic's history. Young, unskilled workers did not consider their interests compatible with the institutions of Weimar democracy and usually voted for the Communists. To rightists, the Republic was unacceptable. They saw the revolution of 1918 as a cut through the sacred thread of German history and never forgave the socialists and democrats for having consented to the overthrow of the monarchies. The stab-in-the-back legend served conveniently to put the blame for the defeat and the following peace treaty on the democrats and socialists. To the right, Weimar and Versailles formed a unity, with the Weimar governments being the willing executioners of foreign interests. Rightists further argued that parties and parliaments had far too much power. They believed that parties part and undermine the true interests of the state.

Apart from these long-term problems we have to consider short-term causes of the Republic's breakdown and the rise of the Nazis. The first step toward this was the establishment of a presidential cabinet under Brüning in March 1930. Obviously the right, the industrialists, and the conservative middle no longer wanted to work within the democratic framework of the constitution. They conspired in late 1929 to overthrow the Grand Coalition, exclude the SPD from power, and start a gradual transformation of German democracy into an authoritarian system. What exactly brought about this change is still not entirely clear. It seems as if big business circles reasoned that the beginning depression would make the removal of the SPD from power not only desirable but also possible. Trade unions and the parties associated with them often lose members at times of high unemployment and economic trouble. A crackdown against the SPD thus appeared possible, and it implied also an assault on democracy in general, since the SPD was the most outspokenly democratic party. Brüning and Hindenburg, with his stubborn industrial and agrarian entourage, became the gravediggers of the Republic. From March 1930 on the governments no longer worked fully within the framework of the constitution. Even though Hindenburg's emergency powers conformed to the constitution, they were used in an unconstitutional way because they aimed to undermine democracy, not to protect it (as Ebert had used them). The destruction of democracy from 1930 to 1932 did not lead to a stable authoritarian system but gave the Nazis unprecedented opportunities for expanding their power and ultimately for taking over a weakened state.

This is the next important point in explaining the failure of Weimar. Although Hitler did not come to power by election, he would never have done so without the overwhelming electoral successes of his party from 1930 on. We thus have to try to explain the sudden and rapid rise of the Nazis. Some historians stress that it was sudden in appearance only. The anti-democratic and anti-socialist attitudes from which the Nazis drew existed already before 1930. The traditional supporters of these views, the DVP and the DNVP, had compromised themselves by 1930 and allowed strong Nazi inroads into their electorate. The NSDAP could capitalize on the older resentments against the Republic and the socialists and become the most credible alternative to the more moderate parties. But the Nazi message went beyond traditional anti-republican feeling. The Nazi idea of *Volksgemeinschaft*, for example, gave a vision of social unity and coherence to a society that was being torn apart by political and social antagonisms. The *Volksgemeinschaft* idea was a powerful propagandistic motive mainly among the young. The Nazis also managed to gather splintered older groups and infuse them with a spirit of unity. The very vagueness of the Nazi program proved more of an advantage than a drawback. The Nazis could promise many things to many people; contradictions did not bother them. The NSDAP's appeal embraced simultaneously anti-elitist, anti-capitalist, as well as fiercely anti-socialist and elitist notions. The party showed Janus faces on many sides: it appeared as reactionary and revolutionary, anti-modernist and dynamic-modern, agrarian-romantic and technologically enthusiastic. The Nazis made promises to everybody and expected that all internal contradictions would be resolved in a "pure" *Volksgemeinschaft*.

But what was the specific content of the Nazi ticket in election campaigns and what were its most successful elements? Abolition of Versailles came first, then law and order, restoration of a functioning economy, work, jobs, and anti-Semitism (in this priority). The Nazis received so many votes not primarily because of their anti-Semitism (and often in spite of it). (And even voting for an anti-Semitic candidate did not automatically mean condoning the Holocaust and the Second World War.) The Nazis were elected first of all because they made the most convincing point about abolishing Versailles, reconstructing the country, restoring jobs and national wealth, and leading Germany to new glory. Brüning still hoped to obtain foreign concessions by trying to fulfill the Treaty of Versailles in order to show that this was impossible; this was nothing else but Rathenau's policy, only that Brüning practiced it more ruthlessly. Hitler, however, preached unconditional rejection of the treaty. And few people doubted that he was serious about what he was saying. Whereas the reform programs of the presidential cabinets remained half-hearted and doomed because they lacked popular support, the Nazis' revolutionary rhetoric and their impressive, nationwide organization convinced many voters that only the Nazis could restore order and prosperity. Their violence was obvious, and it bothered even some of their supporters, but it failed to deter many voters because Germans had grown accustomed to political violence since the revolution of 1918. Particularly in the cities, political violence had never ceased even in the Republic's quiet years. Many Nazi voters even felt reassured by Nazi violence because they believed that the Nazis would restore order with an iron broom and repress the feared communists once they gained power.

The responsibility for the Nazis' rise to power also lies with the Nazis themselves, with the millions of Germans who voted for them, with the industrialist and agrarian circles who did everything to undermine Weimar democracy (particularly from 1930 on), and with the opportunistic, anti-democratic, and anti-socialist attitudes of the center-to-right parties. The Communists must share the blame for having undermined the Weimar system. It has been argued that the Social Democrats were also responsible for the breakdown of Weimar because they did not rise energetically against the anti-democratic forces, but the problem is that the chances for resistance were slim. The SPD, greatly weakened by the Great Depression, pursued a policy of responsibility when it tolerated Brüning and voted for Hindenburg in 1932 as a lesser evil in order to keep the system from falling into Nazi hands much earlier.

It is difficult to see what could have been done to avoid Hitler's appointment. After all, Hitler was the leader of the strongest party in parliament. Although the German constitution did not force the president to appoint the chairman of the strongest party chancellor, this would not have been an unheard of procedure. In Britain, for example, the leader of the strongest party always has the first opportunity to form a government. On the other hand, to give Hitler power meant to surrender the state to a band of radicals intending to revolutionize Germany's society and political system. In historical hindsight, everything should have been done to keep Hitler out of government. But options were scarce. To govern with the Reichstag had become impossible after Nazis and Communists had won an obstructing majority in it. Had Schleicher tried to get approval from the Reichstag he would have been defeated. There was no other way than to dissolve the Reichstag again or to adjourn it indefinitely, which would have violated the constitution. Hindenburg, after having strained the constitution beyond its limits before, should maybe have gone further in early 1933. Schleicher and Hindenburg should have declared that a temporary dictatorship was necessary to overcome the economic crisis. They should have held new elections only after the situation had improved. Schleicher and Hindenburg would have had to use their influence on the army in order to get its support for a dictatorial government. Such a temporary presidential dictatorship would have turned the tables on the Nazis. If they had reacted by starting an uprising they would have split their movement, since even many SA hotheads would not have risked an encounter with the army. Open insurrection, moreover, would have alienated the Nazis from their supporters in industry and the administration. On the other hand, if

Figure 6.2 A line of unemployed people waiting to register at the Employment Office in Hannover. Photography of Walter Ballhause, early 1930s. (Arbeitslosenschlange, Inv.-Nr.: Ph 92/104, Walter Ballhause © DHM, Berlin).

Somebody wrote "Elect Hitler" on the barrack in the background. Although it is likely that more people in the line voted for the Communists than for Hitler, mass unemployment helped to radicalize even those Germans who were not directly in danger of losing their jobs. For many, the Great Depression represented the third big immiseration experience in a generation (after the First World War and the inflation). It confirmed their sense that democracy was not working in the interest of the people and that fundamental change was necessary.

the Nazis had remained passive, they would most likely have lost support. Hitler had an excellent instinct for these situations. He knew that it was urgent for him to gain power in January 1933. He had experienced a similar situation in early November 1923, when he had felt that the tide of radicalism was receding and that his promises were starting to work against him. Back then, he had started a putsch at the last moment and run into disaster. In late 1932 Hitler again became nervous and felt that things began to slip out of his hands; he even spoke of suicide.

The full presidential dictatorship that might have defeated the Nazis did not come into being, and it would have been a risky venture, though a risk that would have deserved to have been taken in light of the disastrous consequences of the Nazi dictatorship. Schleicher had toyed with this idea for a while but rejected it because of the threat of a Polish invasion, whose plausibility seems more than doubtful. It would have been difficult to convince the army leaders to repress the SA if necessary, as the army hoped to incorporate the SA troops at some point and did not see the Nazis as the main danger, but rather the foreign powers and the Communists. This is a crucial point: to the reactionary agrarians and industrialists in Hindenburg's entourage, to the leaders of the center-to-right parties, to the military, and to many administrators, the Nazis were not such a terrible alternative after all. All of these conservative circles in Germany shared much more with the Nazis than with the Communists or even the Social Democrats. The Nazis were intensely nationalist and wanted Germany to rise as a great power again; that was what the conservatives wanted, too. The Nazis were anti-democratic and anti-socialist. So were the conservatives. The Nazis seemed to have the power to repress communism. Well, was that not what most conservatives had hoped for since 1919? In a nutshell: the circles around Hindenburg had few options left in early 1933 because they had contributed to demolishing the democratic political system. But they could have done more to keep Hitler from coming to power. Just imagine that the Communists had been as powerful as the Nazis were at the time: the old elites would have exhausted every single possibility to keep the Communists from power. The point is that the old elites and the center-to-right parties agreed with many Nazi goals even though they had misgivings about the NSDAP's violence and radicalism or felt some snobbish disgust for its "plebeian" character. That there were only few options to hold the Nazis off in 1933 was partly an effect of the destruction of the Weimar system but partly also a result of the electoral success of the Nazis.

–7–

Nazi Germany, 1933–9

By some standards, Hitler's first years in government were stunningly successful. During the incessant campaigning of 1932 and early 1933 he had promised to bring Germany out of the Great Depression and to restore its international standing. Nobody could deny by the end of 1938 that he had fulfilled his campaign promises. Unemployment had declined so rapidly that Germany began to experience a severe labor shortage in 1937. Although the Nazi regime had destroyed the trade unions and the socialist parties, it displayed a strong commitment to social solidarity and to help for the poor through its Winter Aid Program and many other initiatives. In international policy, Hitler had fulfilled two of the boldest German dreams: unification with Austria and annexation of the Sudetenland, the region of Czechoslovakia bordering on Germany and Austria and settled predominantly by ethnic Germans. Germany had become a major power again, and the Versailles peace order was shaken down to its foundations. Although Hitler had employed bullying tactics and the threat of war, he seemed to have refuted those critics who had argued before 1933 that Nazism automatically meant war, and this was a very good thing given that war was not a popular option in Germany even after years of Nazi propaganda. True, Hitler had built up a dictatorship, democracy was gone, and so was much of the elite of German culture and science. True, there had been massive repression, but it was concentrated in the first months after the Nazi takeover and had become less noticeable thereafter. In any case, democracy at the time of the Great Depression seemed to be an increasingly rare form of state. Most democracies founded after 1918 had failed twenty years later. Even in countries with stable democracies, many observers were willing to concede that authoritarian state systems seemed to fit some countries better than democracy. If Hitler had died in October 1938, for example, his historical persona would appear in a different light. Historians who argue that all his successes were only meant to build a powerful base for a shockingly criminal and reckless expansion, although being objectively right, would have a hard time proving their case. Although evidence for Hitler's real aims did surface before October 1938, some historians would argue – in unison with many contemporaries – that he did not mean everything he said and might well have moderated his stance in the face of power political realities had he lived longer. It is important to understand that Hitler's regime was in the eyes of many Germans (and not only Germans) unbelievably successful in its first years. Hitler was able to win over a large segment

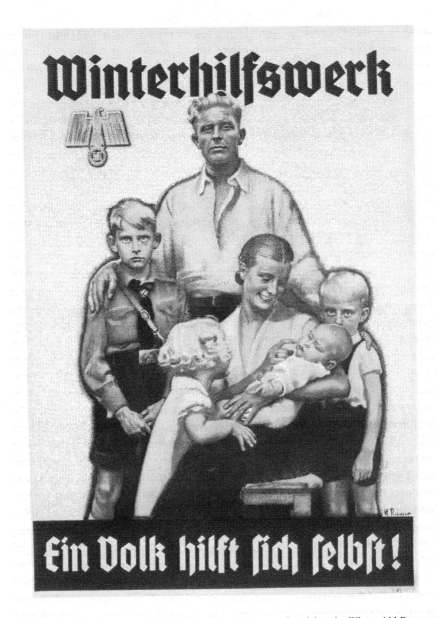

Figure 7.1 "A people helps itself," Nazi propaganda poster advertising the Winter Aid Program (approximately 1933). ("Winterhilfswerk / Ein Volk hilft sich selbst!", Inv.-Nr.: P 99/25, © DHM, Berlin)

This extensive collection and aid program initially benefited the mass of unemployed and homeless people. It represented perhaps the most popular and effective Nazi claim: that the German people could help itself through social solidarity. It also reaffirmed traditional gender roles and expressed the regime's desire to reverse the decline of the birth rate in Germany. The oldest boy is wearing his Hitler Youth uniform.

of the majority of Germans who had *not* voted for the NSDAP in 1932 and again in the already quite unfree elections of March 1933. He personally became enormously popular and accumulated a political capital that he was able to use for many years to come. How did this come about?

In the short run, Hitler sought to reassure the moderates who had brought him to power and whose support he needed for some time. He at first stressed continuity over revolutionary change. On the surface, not many things seemed to have changed in the German government. Only three out of twelve ministers in the new cabinet belonged to the NSDAP. Most of the other ministers had already been members of the Brüning, Papen, and Schleicher cabinets. If anything, it looked as if a return to regular legislative procedures based on the Reichstag might become possible again, given that the new cabinet had more support in the Reichstag than most of its predecessors (the combined share of seats of the NSDAP and DNVP amounted to 40 per cent). Hitler, however, secured an important concession from his conservative allies right before Hindenburg appointed him: the right to call new elections. This seemed quite unnecessary because the Reichstag had just been reelected in November 1932, but Hitler hoped to win an absolute majority in a new election campaign in which he would be able to use the power of the state in support of his party. With his usual good sense for power, Hitler had ensured that his party colleague, Hermann Göring, would become Prussian interior minister (Prussia was effectively controlled by the Reich government since Papen's coup in July 1932). This was crucial: the appointment of Göring placed Prussia's strong police apparatus under Nazi control and therefore allowed the Nazis to purge a force that, until 1932 under SPD leadership, had often sought to rein in illegal Nazi activities. A Nazi, Wilhelm Frick, also became interior minister of the Reich, giving the NSDAP power over the police in all of Germany. On 1 February, the Reichstag was dissolved and Hitler called new elections to take place on 5 March 1933. The election campaign was by no means democratic and free: SA gangs terrorized the streets and political meeting halls. Frick and Göring made sure that the police did not interfere, as it had during previous campaigns. In Prussia, Göring even hired 50,000 auxiliary policemen, mostly SA members, allegedly "to keep order" during the campaign. The purged police forces with this Nazi "help" persecuted the opponents of the regime. Many Communists and Social Democrats were intimidated, beaten up, and shot. Göring went so far as to implore his police officers to make eager use of their guns. The first "wild" concentration camps were opened as detention and torture centers for the political opposition. Meanwhile, the Nazis started to purge the state administration. People who disagreed with their views were dismissed, as were Jews.

The decisive opportunity for Hitler to expand his power came on 27 February 1933. The Reichstag burnt down after young Dutch communist Marinus van der Lubbe had put fire to it. The Reichstag fire offered the Nazis such an excellent opportunity to conjure up fears of a communist uprising that some historians suggest that it was a Nazi plot. However, van der Lubbe seems to have acted alone, and the Nazi leaders were as surprised by the event as everybody else. Nevertheless, they took immediate action to exploit this excellent opportunity. The Communists, who shared the conservatives' view that the Nazi government would quickly ruin itself, had made no preparations for an uprising, but their earlier putschism and the general anti-communist hysteria lent credibility to the Nazi allegations that a Communist uprising was imminent. The Nazis were able to apply their terror even more ruthlessly while declaring it a campaign for law and order. With the support of the centrist parties, the NSDAP passed an emergency decree, the so-called "Decree for the Protection of the People and the State" (28 February 1933), which legalized the Nazi terror that had already been practiced for several weeks and allowed even more flagrant violations of basic rights.

Although the elections of 5 March were heavily manipulated by the NSDAP, the Nazis – to their dismay – did not receive the absolute majority of the votes. Their share of the vote increased from 33 per cent to almost 44 per cent, certainly an impressive rise, but short of the hoped-for absolute majority. The KPD, with most of its leaders already in concentration camps, lost less than expected and fell from 16 per cent to 12 per cent. The elected Communist deputies were all arrested before the new Reichstag even met. The SPD, also under severe terror, fell only slightly from 20 per cent to 18 per cent due to higher voter turnout but received almost as many votes as in November 1932. Through their monopoly on propaganda, the Nazis managed to win over many new voters but failed to make many converts among those people who had voted for another party before. With his strengthened parliamentary group, Hitler could have agreed to a coalition with the DNVP and governed with parliamentary support in accordance with the Weimar constitution. NSDAP and DNVP together held a majority of the seats. This would have made Hitler independent of presidential emergency decrees and of the intrigues of his conservative watchdogs in the government and in Hindenburg's entourage. Instead, Hitler decided to suspend the Reichstag. To this end he needed the consent of a two-thirds majority in the Reichstag. This meant that he needed to woo the center-to-right parties, particularly the Center Party, the BVP, and the DNVP.

To show the German conservatives that he felt committed to a common Prusso-German nationalist heritage, Hitler staged an emotional reunion with President Hindenburg in Potsdam, the traditional residence of the Prussian kings. This move was deftly planned by the new Nazi minister for propaganda, Joseph Goebbels. Right after the political theater at Potsdam, Hitler submitted a bill to the Reichstag that intended to give his government the right to decree laws without any parliamentary control for the following four years (the Enabling Act). The center-to-right parties had misgivings about this bill, but they hoped that they would gain more power over the Nazis by cooperating with them than by opposing them. For reasons difficult to understand in retrospect, they believed that the Nazis would respect laws in the future. By approving the bill, the center-to-right deputies hoped to save their own parties and organizations and to exercise a mitigating effect on the Nazi dictatorship.

In reality they became the gravediggers of the last remainders of German democracy – and also of their own parties. On 23 March they passed the bill with the necessary two-thirds majority. Only the SPD deputies voted against it although they knew that they might pay for this by being sent to a concentration camp. Surrounded by SA guards and swastika flags, the SPD deputies remained loyal to their democratic ideals, and their leader, Otto Wels, held a courageous speech arguing that the Nazis had power on their side but not justice. Wels was perfectly right. The rule of law, which the center-to-right parties mysteriously hoped to preserve by complying with Hitler, had been suspended immediately after 30 January 1933. The SA was let loose to settle accounts with old enemies – not only without being held accountable for its crimes but even with full police support. The Enabling Act gave the regime free rein to pursue its politics through terror and compulsion. Since the terror was directed mostly at the leadership of the left-wing parties, the majority of Germans probably felt little discomfort. Many middle-class Germans on the contrary felt that it was right to "punish" Social Democrats and Communists and were all too willing to forgive what they saw as understandable excesses that would likely be reined in later, once the Nazi regime had stabilized.

In this context, the Nazis felt safe enough to launch a first nationwide act of terror against Jews. The SA, whose lower-class resentment against capitalism and big business had always had an anti-Semitic flavor, had been pressing for measures against the Jews since Hitler's appointment. On 1 April 1933 a boycott of Jewish stores was decreed. The SA took up positions in front of Jewish-owned stores and harassed people entering them. Some violence against Jews occurred. But the April boycott was not a success for the regime. It unleashed a storm of criticism in the American press and alienated many Germans, who did not want to let their government tell them where to shop and sometimes even felt sorry for the Jewish shop owners. In a pattern that would be repeated later, the Nazi regime reacted to the dubious outcome of an illegal action by stepping up legal, or "cold," persecution. A few days after the April boycott, the government enacted laws banning Jews and anti-Nazis from jobs in the state sector. This "Aryan Paragraph" was soon extended to other professional groups, aiming to create an apartheid system where Jews were no longer considered Germans and would be forced to emigrate or live in a separate, strictly confined, society.

The regime also used its new powers to destroy and repress almost all independent institutions. Arguing that Germany needed only one party, the NSDAP, the new regime destroyed all other parties – first those of its enemies and then those of its friends. The KPD was banned right after the Reichstag fire (although its candidates were still allowed to run in the elections of 5 March), and the dissolution of the SPD followed a few weeks later. By July 1933, all parties except the NSDAP, even the DNVP, had been outlawed. Often the party leaders themselves, seeing no purpose for their parties any more, took the first steps in dissolving them. On 1 May, the regime arrested the leaders of the free trade unions, took all the assets of the unions, and forced their members into a Nazi-controlled organization, the German Labor Front (DAF). The Enabling Act also gave the regime power over the governments of the single states. During the spring of 1933 Hitler ordered the remaining non-Nazi governments to step down. They were replaced by Nazi governors (*Gauleiter*). The predominant party in Bavaria, the BVP, tried to resist but to no avail. In similar ways, the Nazis took over almost every organization and leisure club in the entire country (a process called *Gleichschaltung*). Usually they formed parallel associations to existing ones; a Nazi league of professors next to the older professor's league, a Nazi women's league next to older women's organizations, and so on. Sooner or later, the Nazi group took over its rival. Sometimes this takeover required some bullying, but all too often leaders of the non-Nazi organizations, seized by a contagious mood of hope and renewal, were eager to demonstrate their loyalty to the new regime by leading their organizations into the corresponding Nazi league. In the intellectual and artistic realm, Nazi terror destroyed many aspects of the rich Weimar culture. On 10 May, Goebbels staged a public burning of books by democratic, socialist, and Jewish authors in Berlin. Goebbels conjured up the image of a Germany poisoned by destructive and divisive ideas and art works and of the Nazis as the strong-willed, healthy Germans cleaning up a vast cultural mess. Thousands of intellectuals, artists, and academics, including many luminaries of Weimar culture and science, emigrated. Most of them sooner or later came to the United States, some after exile in Czechoslovakia, the Netherlands, or France.

Only two institutions remained largely exempt from *Gleichschaltung*: the churches and the army. To neutralize the Catholics, Hitler concluded a Concordat with the Vatican in July 1933. He promised to leave the Catholic Church and its organizations unharmed if the Catholics abstained from political activity outside the NSDAP. The Vatican and the German Catholic leadership agreed, and Hitler's guarantee (which, of course, was merely tactical) reconciled many German Catholics with the regime for the time being. The Lutheran Church, the predominant Protestant denomination in Germany, was in a more complicated situation because of its traditionally closer connections with the state. A pro-Nazi Church group, the "German Christians," advocated the adaptation of the Protestant church to the Nazi state by purging Christianity of "Jewish" influences and making it look more like Nazism. The "German Christians" made big gains in Church elections, and Hitler for a while used their help in an effort to control and consolidate the Lutheran Church, which was still organized along the state boundaries effective until the war of 1866. A strong minority within the Lutheran Church, however, aimed to keep the Church and its theology independent of the Nazi state. This opposition formed its own platform, the *Bekennende Kirche* (Confessing Church) with Pastor Martin Niemöller as its leader. At first, the Confessing Church merely wanted to exempt the Lutheran Church from *Gleichschaltung* and to stress its autonomy, but some of its members, including Niemöller, gradually rejected more aspects of the Nazi regime and later on formed part of the anti-Nazi resistance. The struggle for the Lutheran Church continued until

1934, when Hitler lost interest in Church questions. Grass-roots Nazis and local party leaders repeatedly increased pressure on the churches in the second half of the 1930s, but the Church question remained in limbo. After 1939, the Nazi leaders seem to have resigned themselves to "solving" the Church question once and for all after final victory in the Second World War. The second group remaining exempt from institutional *Gleichschaltung* was the army. There were leading Nazis, however, who advocated the integration of the army into the existing Nazi paramilitary force, the SA. With a membership of four million people, the SA under General Ernst Röhm hoped to become a popular militia replacing or integrating the army. To Röhm, this would have followed the logic of *Gleichschaltung* – the integration of non-Nazi organizations into a corresponding Nazi organization. The elitist army leaders, however, balked at the thought of being placed under the command of street fighters who were much more experienced in beating up political opponents than in carrying out military maneuvers. The army's refusal to submit itself to SA command did not imply any opposition to the Nazi regime, however. There were strong expressions of support for the Nazi state from all ranks of the army that were not only motivated by the desire to stave off SA claims. Most army leaders were genuinely pleased because the Nazis had eliminated the Communist threat and promised to intensify rearmament. The conflict between the SA and the army remained unresolved for the time being.

By the second half of 1933 almost all groups in German society were either repressed or more-or-less satisfied. The economy had started to recover already in late 1932, and the smashing of the free trade unions may have made it easier for industrialists to make profits again – at the expense of the workers, to be sure. Unemployment declined and terror became less conspicuous and widespread after the outbursts in the first half of 1933. Most of the German middle and upper classes, thoroughly disappointed by democracy and afraid of socialism, were happy that the regime had repressed the left, the largest threat these groups had been able to see before 1933. Those Germans who were neither Jewish nor socialist could live largely the same way as they had before, and often slightly better, since order had returned (a questionable and superficial order, of course) and since the economy had started to recover. Although the Nazis claimed the credit for the economic recovery, it came less from their policies than from an international trend that had started already in the second half of 1932. To some extent, the speedy recovery also was an outcome of the harsh measures taken by the Brüning government. Regardless, the Germans who had voted for the NSDAP because they wanted law and order and economic recovery felt that they had made the right choice. As far as one can tell in a dictatorship, the regime was popular in Germany. Observers in the West had watched Hitler's takeover with dismay, and the terror in the months following his appointment had disturbed them further. But when the initial wave of terror died down, foreign observers began to consider Hitler's Nazism as a German variant of Mussolini's fascism and maybe as a good state form for the Germans – a message powerfully reinforced by Nazi propaganda for example during the Berlin Olympics of 1936.

Hitler, however, was faced with the dilemma of most leaders of revolutionary movements after taking power. In order to stabilize his rule and make his government work he had to cooperate with the state administration, the economic elites, and broad circles of the population who were not members of his party. This meant cultivating a moderate, restrained, and legal stance – at least after the initial wave of terror. On the other side, the zealots in the NSDAP demanded more radical action and watched the accommodation of the regime with the elites with suspicion. This dilemma was most pronounced in the SA. With their daily violence and massive propaganda campaigns, SA troops had made the Nazi rise to power possible and had helped in the consolidation of power. After terror subsided in the late spring of 1933 no new role was available to the SA. The police was firmly in Nazi hands, so the SA was not needed for "keeping order" any more. Plans to incorporate the SA into the army hurt the pride of many SA members. They had fought for a new society, and many of them had more radical visions of Germany than Hitler seemed willing to realize for the time being. Many SA members expressed vague ideas of a national *socialism*, including the socialization of the industry, but these ideas worried the industrialists and big businessmen, people the regime could ill afford to alienate at a time of recovery after the worst economic crisis in modern Germany. Most SA members also wanted to step up terror against the Jews, but the regime was reluctant to allow this because the public – in Germany and abroad – tended to be shocked by anti-Semitic violence, as the reactions to the April boycott had shown.

In 1934 the conflicts between the army and the SA came to a head. Röhm kept arguing that the German army should be infused with Nazi spirit and be merged with the SA, with the SA receiving the leading role. The army leaders, with their strong esprit de corps, cringed at the thought of merging the army with "plebeian" street fighters under partly homosexual leaders. Hitler had to make a choice. Given that he was committed to preparing for war, he reasoned that he needed the professional expertise of the army leaders. He therefore decided to ally with the army and sacrifice the SA leadership. To this end he used another paramilitary formation that had been built up alongside the SA in the late 1920s: the Schutzstaffel (SS). The SS under the leadership of Heinrich Himmler and Reinhard Heydrich originally fulfilled functions comparable to the first mission of the SA: it protected Nazi meetings and leaders. But the SS slowly became a more powerful elite force, which incorporated Hitler's racist ideology to its extremes. On Hitler's orders, SS units murdered the leaders of the SA during a gathering in Munich on 30 June 1934. To justify this murder, Hitler claimed that there had been an attempted "Röhm Putsch." This was a fabricated lie. Röhm and the SA had become restive and worried, particularly when signs multiplied that the SA leadership had lost Hitler's favor, but they had no plan and no intention to start a putsch. The SS troops, moreover, did not limit themselves to killing SA leaders; under the cover of the so-called Röhm Putsch they settled accounts with

Hitler's older enemies and rivals. They shot Gustav von Kahr, the Bavarian dictator of 1923 who had thwarted Hitler's Beer Hall Putsch; they killed former chancellor Schleicher and his wife, and they murdered a whole group of Vice-Chancellor Franz von Papen's advisers – people who had criticized Nazi repression in the preceding months. Papen himself was spineless enough to continue working for the regime. He was dismissed as vice-chancellor and became German ambassador to Vienna, later to Ankara. In popular parlance, the murders of 30 June 1934 became known as the "night of the long knives." Even though many observers in Germany and abroad felt repelled by the violence, few people outside the SA could feel sorry about the SA leaders, who had been murderers themselves. The SA remained in existence, but it was diminished and partly absorbed by the army. The elimination of the SA leaders, which remained Hitler's only major purge, was the last step in his consolidation of power. Paradoxically, it increased his popularity because it made many Germans believe that the Nazi Party had decided to return to law, not only to order, by curbing a notoriously unruly and violent group within its own ranks. The German army leaders, grateful to Hitler for having sided with them, hastened to reaffirm their loyalty to the regime. They introduced an oath of allegiance to Hitler personally that every German soldier from now on had to swear.

The last step toward a full dictatorship occurred right after the death of President Hindenburg on 2 August 1934, when Hitler with a stroke of the pen made himself president and chancellor of the German Reich in personal union. Hitler from now on called himself "Führer (leader) and Reich chancellor of the German people," and he consolidated the office staff and the powers of chancellor and president. Needless to say, no popular elections would be held any more for the presidency. Potentially, Hindenburg could still have dismissed Hitler after 30 January 1933. The Weimar Constitution had remained in place even though all of its democratic elements and basic rights had been suspended or perverted, and according to the constitution, the president could appoint and dismiss the chancellor. But Hindenburg, who had never coveted political office, increasingly withdrew from active politics after Hitler's appointment. He occasionally intervened, such as when he requested that Jews who had served in the First World War be exempt from the mass firings in 1933. Hitler took care not to offend Hindenburg's conservative allies too much as long as the "old man" was still alive, but it is hard to see how Hindenburg could have made much of a difference had he cared to interfere more. After the Enabling Act and the dissolution of all non-Nazi parties, control by the Nazis was nearly complete. The Reichstag and all the state diets included only Nazis; the police was under total Nazi control, and the army, though still independent, was eager to be on good terms with the regime. But Hindenburg did not die a worried man. In spite of his earlier misgivings about appointing Hitler, he felt that he had done the right thing.

What role did terror and repression play in stabilizing and maintaining the regime's hold on power? Undoubtedly, terror was crucial in the destruction of all organizations hostile to the Nazi regime. After that was accomplished, terror took a less central position, but it is important to consider that resistance against the Nazi regime was nearly impossible. Already in the spring of 1933 the SS built up an efficient political police force, the Gestapo (acronym for Secret State Police). Given the lack of any legal guarantees to individual citizens (such as the right to a defense lawyer, privacy, a fair trial), the Gestapo had free rein to persecute critics and to punish them harshly enough to deter the rest of the population. In its concentration camps, enemies of the regime were tortured and forced to work. But the secret police was so terribly efficient in part also because of the regime's overwhelming popularity. Many people readily denounced everybody whom they suspected of subversive activities, and it was hard for those who were arrested once to escape the pincers of the Gestapo. Terror, which was most pronounced at the beginning and at the end of the Nazi dictatorship, helped to uphold solidarity with the regime, but it was for the most part not essential to maintaining the regime in power. Resistance was hopeless, no convincing alternative to Nazism seemed to exist (democracy and communism were thoroughly discredited), and – last but not least – Hitler was highly popular.

How did Nazi policies evolve after the consolidation of power? In the economic realm the Nazis initially did little beyond the containment of the trade unions and the dismissal of the Jews. Many farmers had voted for Hitler and readily agreed to put their interest organizations under united Nazi leadership. The small business owners and artisans did not resist when they were forced into similar Nazi organizations. Heavy industry and big business were left unharmed except for the dismissal of Jewish managers. Hitler even gave leading industrialists positions of power in his government and in the administration. Most industrialists at this time were grateful to the Nazis for having destroyed the socialist parties and tamed the trade unions, and they were eager to capitalize on the opportunities offered by the economic recovery. Businessmen who had watched the "socialist" element in the SA with concern felt reassured after the taming of the SA during the "night of the long knives." Rearmament projects, highway building, and state support for the automotive industry further fuelled the economic recovery. After 1936, however, rearmament took an economically irresponsible pace, and state control over the economy intensified. The government drafted a four-year plan that should prepare Germany for war by 1940, although neither the industrialists nor the public were informed that the priority of the plan was to ensure readiness for war. The plan's insistence on autarky and rapid rearmament sometimes contradicted industrialist interest and raised concerns about the future of the economy. Economics Minister Hjalmar Schacht resigned as a consequence. Despite occasional tensions, however, business relations to the government remained good, and the Nazis always tried to placate business concerns.

The extent to which the regime won over the industrial workers is less clear. Undoubtedly, the Nazis made inroads into this group, which had been the most anti-Nazi sector of the German population before 1933. With party-directed educational and leisure programs (*Kraft durch Freude*, or KdF, meaning Strength through Joy), the regime gave the workers a sense of entitlement to what used to be privileges of the upper classes such as paid holidays, vacation trips, musical and theater performances, and a car. The *Volkswagen* ("people's car"), also called *KdF-Wagen*, was supposed to cost only 999 marks and be available to every worker. In the long run, the Nazi regime also hoped to replace the big working-class apartment complexes by individual houses with a small piece of land for each family. These houses looked like a combination of suburban home and family farm, all done in old German style. This was an attempt to decentralize the workers and to bring them into closer contact with the "soil." The Nazis believed that exposure to agricultural work would wean the workers of all remaining socialist strivings. This decentralized rural housing, of course, made commuting necessary, and the Nazis considered cars all the more important in this respect; individual commuting would prevent the potentially seditious meeting of workers in the public trains and buses. In addition to these material perks, which remained largely on the drawing board because the intense rearmament and then the war imposed other priorities, a stream of propaganda sought to reassure the workers that they were of good racial stock and deserved a prominent place in the *Volksgemeinschaft*, the community of the people. Nazi catch phrases such as "nobility of work" and workplace embellishment programs ("beauty of labor") were meant to flatter the workers. Although few workers ever received the opportunity to sail to the Norwegian fjords or the Spanish Atlantic islands on a shiny KdF cruise ship, the regime's wooing of the industrial workers was not fruitless. The reports smuggled from Germany to the exiled headquarters of the SPD mirror increasing complacency of many formerly socialist workers. Yet, grumbling never stopped. Many workers did not appreciate the tight regulation and surveillance on KdF trips, complained about their low wages and long hours, and devoted much cynical commentary to Nazi propaganda. Probably the most important fact in the lives of most industrial workers was simply that they had work. Given the recent memory of the Great Depression, low wages and long hours seemed preferable to unemployment.

The regime also wooed the farmers, telling them that they would occupy a central place in the future Aryan state. Nazi ideology insisted that agricultural work was racially healthy and would be the way of the future. Although most Nazi leaders were fascinated with modern technology, some of them also mused about creating a predominantly agricultural state, focusing on the imagined bond of "blood and soil." The plan for winning *Lebensraum* (living space) in Eastern Europe was predicated on the sick notion of settling a racial "elite" on the conquered land and let them farm in those areas, using the slave labor of the local population. In the short run, the regime wanted to protect the German farmer from speculation and therefore passed a law that forbade the selling of family farms. This law was rather unpopular, however, given that some farmers badly wanted to sell unprofitable family farms. The regime's priority on autarky, motivated by war preparation and the need to earmark sparse foreign exchange for buying raw materials necessary for rearmament, did not benefit most farmers either. Farmers experienced much state interference from production quotas to price controls, and these measures were highly unpopular. The regime also alienated many farmers, particularly in Catholic regions, because some local Nazi firebrands insisted on increasing repression of the churches. Ironically, the farmers were one of the least satisfied groups in German society as early as 1934, and things did not get much better when the regime intensified rearmament with the Four-year Plan in 1936.

Nazi policies toward women carried contradictions as well. In ideology, Nazis wanted women to stay home and breed as many children as possible, but after a few years this approach clashed with the priorities of an economy that was running red hot because of intensified rearmament. In the beginning, the regime aimed to push women out of the labor market in order to make room for unemployed men. The gains derived from this policy were largely fictional, however, because many married women had already been dismissed during the period 1930–2 and because it often made no economic sense to dismiss a woman in order to hire a more highly paid man. To encourage women to leave jobs and to raise Germany's birthrate, marriage loans of 1,000 marks were offered to newly wed couples, who were allowed to keep one quarter of their loan for every child they had. Mothers of four children or more even received medals and were honored in ways similar to soldiers and veterans. The Nazis told women that their role as breeders of children of a higher race was essential, and they seem to have instilled many of them with a sense of pride in motherhood. Nazi organizations for girls and women, though not as comprehensive as their counterparts for boys and men, organized German girls and women in mostly traditional roles. They seem to have been rather popular and gave many women a sense of mission and importance they had missed before 1933. But some women scoffed at the pro-natalist Nazi policies; in popular parlance, for example, the motherhood medal was called the "rabbit medal" in allusion to the rapid breeding habits of rabbits. The birth rate in Germany did increase after 1933, but it is questionable whether this was an outcome of Nazi policies. Many couples had delayed marriage during the Great Depression; the economic recovery, probably more than the Nazi family policies, gave them the confidence that they could marry and have children. At the same time, education and skilled jobs for women became harder to obtain. Yet, these reactionary policies soon conflicted with the demands of a rearmament economy. Around 1937 there was a severe lack of workers in Germany, and women were encouraged to join the work force. In 1939 almost half of all working-age women were employed. The war massively increased the need for labor, and the regime repeatedly considered schemes for a labor draft for women. This was a pet project of Propaganda Minister Joseph Goebbels, but Hitler, true to the Nazi ideological stance, always thwarted such initiatives. The racism of Nazi ideology in some ways also empowered women and ascribed primary importance to them: as mothers, they were responsible for choosing a racially valuable mate and for breeding genetically healthy offspring. This and the extension of female employment (which was higher in 1939 than in West Germany until the 1980s) instilled many women with a sense of independence and importance that made them less concerned about lacking freedom. Although women remained legally subordinate to men, faced discrimination in all upper-level jobs, and received lower pay than men, the opportunities for female employment under the Nazis were greater than in the Weimar Republic and in postwar West Germany. But this was largely due to economic circumstances and happened in contradiction to official ideology.

In their invocation of the *Volksgemeinschaft*, the Nazis appealed to social equality, sharing, and support for the poor. The overall goal of their policies toward workers, farmers, and women was the consolidation of a united, tight-knit community that would not crack under the pressures of a new war. Behind this goal, however, lurked a much more radical vision. In essence, the Nazi regime planned to enact a giant genetic engineering project that would create a supposedly pure and superior human stock of so-called Aryans. This project involved a multitude of policies from compulsory sterilization and forced abortion to euthanasia and genocide. The outlines of this project were only slightly visible before the war, but the irony is that the Nazi promise of social harmony and equality among Germans was window dressing. Racial theorists and eugenicists had argued that there were at least six major racial types among the Germans, with the tall, blond, and blue-eyed "Nordic" type being the most precious. In the long run, Nazi policies would likely have channeled state services toward members of the "higher" types and discouraged the "lower" types from procreating. In the long-term Nazi plan, German did not equal German at all. It is mind-boggling that this project was launched without any reliable genetic science and largely based on an amalgam of previous eugenic research, much of it already discredited, and common prejudices. Criminals, prostitutes, pimps, and all sorts of "asocial" people were targeted for sterilization, forced abortion, or confinement because they were considered of lower genetic stock. A series of laws passed in 1933 to 1935 allowed the state to sterilize a range of people believed to have hereditary illnesses, including alcoholics and some criminals. Given that the Nazis believed that people of low racial stock always have the highest birth rate and that "bad" genes spread like an epidemic over several generations, they also sterilized some groups that seemed particularly dangerous to the racial stock such as the children of German women and French African occupation soldiers from the Rhineland.

Purifying the "German race" by improving the racial stock of Germans was one thing. The other side of the medal was "purging" the German population of people who did not in Nazi thinking deserve a place within the *Volksgemeinschaft*. Already the program of the NSDAP, formulated in 1920, argued that no Jew could be a German and that Jews had to be stripped of German citizenship. Believing in the pernicious influence of Jews in government and public life, the Nazi regime had quickly expelled most Jews from government offices and leading positions in public life in 1933. In 1935, partly in response to grass-roots Nazi anti-Semitism and partly in order to present a major legislative breakthrough at the annual party rally in Nürnberg, Hitler ordered the formulation of new laws regulating German citizenship and the status of Jews. A committee of party hacks, doctors, eugenicists, and judicial experts feverishly tried to define who was Jewish and who was not. This was a frustrating task for this committee because, as they had to admit, nobody had yet found chemical evidence of "Jewish blood" or another foolproof method to distinguish between Jew and non-Jew. Physical categories such as appearance did not provide clear markers because committee members admitted that it was sometimes impossible to tell a Jew from a non-Jew on the basis of appearance and because there had been some mixing between Jews and non-Jews. Behavioral categories also did not help because Nazi ideology stipulated that Jews, with their cunning, were able to pose as pure Aryans. In the end, the committee settled for a complex formula ultimately based on the membership of a person's grandparents in the Jewish religious community. The Nürnberg Laws, passed by the token Nazi Reichstag present at the Nürnberg rally, made marriage between a Jew and a non-Jew illegal, took German citizenship away from Jews and forbade them from flying the German flag. Less stringent provisions were introduced for people with partial Jewish ancestry, so-called *Mischlinge*.

The Nürnberg Laws still represented a policy of restriction and segregation, not genocide. Jews could still be tolerated in Germany if they lived their lives apart from non-Jewish Germans. Some German Jews even saw the Nürnberg Laws as a reassuring sign because the regime seemed to have reined in illegal and violent anti-Semitism and spelled out the rules under which Jews could live in Germany. After approximately one-quarter of German Jews had emigrated in 1933 and 1934, some German Jews came back at the time of the Nürnberg Laws believing that Jews could live in Germany in relative safety, albeit as a discriminated group, until the Nazi regime might break down. However, the Nürnberg Laws by no means put an end to persecution. Depriving Jews of German citizenship made it easier to confiscate their property and to exclude them from a range of rights and privileges. Jewish survivors who experienced the 1930s in Nazi Germany remember how almost every week a new law was promulgated that further restricted the rights of Jews. Jews were not allowed to sit down on park benches, to use swimming pools, to go shopping except during certain hours, and much more. Life became progressively difficult for Germany's Jews. Jews were encouraged to emigrate but not forced to do so. The Nazi regime set up Jewish committees that prepared Jews for emigration to Palestine, but the British authorities ruling Palestine, mindful of escalating Arab resentment against Jewish immigration, were unwilling to admit a large number of German Jews. Prospects to obtain a visa to another country were not much better because many countries still suffered from the effects of the Great Depression and were unwilling to admit Jews. It took much patience, money, and (often) foreign connections to emigrate. Those Jews who did manage to leave sometimes became the target of anti-German resentment in their host countries. The policies of exclusion of unwanted "racial" groups and the efforts to "purify" the German race drastically escalated during the war, but, except for the discrimination against Jews, they were not yet prominent to a degree that would have made many Germans feel threatened by the regime before the war. The persecution of the Jews met with some approval, much indifference, and some mumbled disapproval.

The most successful aspect of the Nazi regime, aside from overcoming the Great Depression, was its foreign policy. Within five years, Hitler and his aides managed to rearm Germany, to dismantle almost all of the remaining legacy of the Treaty of Versailles, and to turn Germany into a strong, even hegemonic, power in Central Europe. This seemed like a spectacular success, and it made Hitler more popular than ever before in Germany. His ultimate foreign policy aims, however, went far beyond these successes; they included above all the conquest of a giant *Lebensraum* (living space) in Eastern Europe, which would be the principal geographical realm in which the Nazi genetic engineering project was to take shape, entailing the deportation, enslavement, and murder of millions. This was a far more aggressive and radical program than anything Hitler's conservative allies – and indeed most Germans – wanted. They still saw revision of Versailles as the top priority. They wanted to return to the German borders of 1914, mostly in the East at the expense of Poland, and they expected at some point to realize the *Anschluss* of Austria and to annex those territories of Czechoslovakia that were settled predominantly by Germans (the Sudetenland). For a while, Hitler's radical aims overlapped with the more limited revisionism of his conservative allies. As a first step, Hitler wanted to rearm massively and to strengthen Germany's position through the revisionist program of the conservatives. To strengthen Germany's position for the ultimate struggle against the Soviet Union, which always was his top priority, Hitler hoped to win Britain as an ally. He thought that the British, given their concern about the increasing strength of Japan and the United States, would let him expand in Eastern Europe, as long as he would not threaten Britain and its empire directly. Whether Hitler envisaged world dominion to be achieved during his lifetime is not clear. But much evidence suggests that the conquest of living space in the East and the "removal" of the Jews did not constitute the end in his vision. The violent creation of an Aryan elite in continental Europe should probably have led to a final struggle for world dominance between an Aryan-dominated Germany and the United States. (Breeding a supposedly "pure" Aryan elite, of course, would have taken several generations.)

Although Hitler had presented the general outlines of his foreign policy program in *Mein Kampf*, he wisely chose not to propagate his ultimate goals right away. To the public, he declared that he had only peaceful aims. Those who watch Leni Riefenstahl's film *The Triumph of the Will*, which focuses on the Nürnberg party rally of 1934, will note the repeated stress of peace, work, and unity. That the commitment to peace was always expressed in the most aggressive tone and mimicry, however, should have raised some eyebrows already then. Hitler indeed started preparations for rearmament almost immediately after taking power. As soon as the economy recovered a little, he increased military expenditure. Already in 1933 he announced German withdrawal from the League of Nations because he did not want to violate openly the League's disarmament clauses. Hitler's foreign policy until 1938 accepted significant risks, but it was not yet foolhardy. As Tirpitz's fleet-building plan had passed a danger zone during which a surprise attack on Germany could have destroyed everything, Hitler feared that German rearmament might trigger an attack by France and its eastern allies, Poland and Czechoslovakia, before Germany was ready. Hitler also looked out for allies and tried to remain on friendly terms with some of Germany's potential enemies.

First he sounded out the chances for an alliance with Italy, just as he had conceived it in *Mein Kampf.* But although fascist Italy under dictator Benito Mussolini seemed to have much in common with Nazi Germany, Mussolini initially turned a deaf ear to Hitler's advances. When Austrian Nazis staged a putsch in Vienna in July 1934 and demanded unification with Germany, Mussolini even sent tanks to the Austrian border. This demonstration of armed might impressed Hitler and saved Austrian independence for the time being. French and British diplomats remained suspicious of Hitler's peaceful declarations and watched German rearmament with unease, but they did not consider the situation serious enough to justify an attack on Germany. They were aware that Nazi Germany was breaking the disarmament clauses of the Treaty of Versailles, but in a sense they were standing on hollow ground in this matter: In one of its more idealistic clauses, the Treaty of Versailles demanded that German disarmament be followed by disarmament in France and Britain, too, but that had not happened on a larger scale. Hitler, moreover, secured a surprising success in chipping a hole into the anti-German alliance network set up after 1918. In January 1934 Poland concluded a non-aggression pact with Germany. This was a radical departure from the pro-Soviet and anti-Polish policies of the Weimar governments and the German military elite. So far, Germany had cooperated with the Soviet Union in order to ward off a Polish attack and, ultimately, to win back the territories lost to Poland after 1918. Hitler's non-aggression pact with Poland angered some of Hitler's conservative allies, but it was a pragmatic, cynical move. As Poland was the key power in French plans to contain Germany, this pact took the bite out of France's eastern European alliance system, the *cordon sanitaire*. If Poland did not help France in a war against Germany, France would have a difficult time forming a second front in the back of the German troops.

Poland's decision to sign a non-aggression pact with Germany indirectly resulted from some French decisions. After the First World War, France had been the main guarantor of the Versailles system. In the second half of the 1920s, however, French politicians concluded that their initial aim after the war, namely to weaken Germany's economic and military potential in the long run, was failing. The German economy recovered and looked prosperous from 1924 to 1929, and even during the Great Depression it was obvious that at some point the Germans would again be able to build up a powerful industry and military. France itself was not seriously affected by the Great Depression before 1933, but economically and demographically it was still weaker than Germany. With its low birthrate and high war casualties, France was likely to fall behind even further. In the mid-1930s a severe shortage of recruits had to be expected. In this period the children born during the First World War would come of age, and the boys would join the army. The birth cohorts of 1914–1918, however, were so small that France's army would for several years suffer a severe lack of men (these recruitment years were therefore called the "hollow years"). To make matters worse, France could not rely on strong foreign help to keep Germany unarmed and powerless for all times. The United States was not much interested in European affairs. Britain also seemed less interested in Europe than in overseas problems. Italy, although initially determined to deny German claims on Austria, had never been happy with the postwar order. The only reliable allies of France, Poland and Czechoslovakia, seemed too weak in the long run to help France subdue a newly self-assertive Germany. France therefore decided to prioritize its own defense and to build a defensive wall on the German border, the Maginot Line, an elaborate system of interconnected fortresses and bunkers. The First World War had taught that it took far fewer people to defend a well-prepared defensive position than to storm it. Since France had a shortage of men, it seemed reasonable to build the best possible fortress system.

As reasonable as it looked from a French perspective, however, the Maginot Line had two serious flaws. First, France's prioritization of defense sent troubling signals to its eastern European allies because it weakened the credibility of a potential French military strike against Germany. The Maginot Line could not be used to punish Germany if it violated the Treaty of Versailles or attacked one of France's allies in eastern Europe. Poland's dictator, Marshal Josef Pilsudski, concluded that an agreement with one of his hostile neighbors, the Soviet Union and Germany, was necessary. He therefore agreed to the non-aggression pact with Hitler. The second flaw of the Maginot Line was its geographic limitation. It covered only the border between Germany and France. Both the German-Belgian frontier and the Franco-Belgian frontier (where the Germans had attacked in 1914) were left unprotected. The north of France had sandy ground on which building fortresses posed difficulties. A protective wall on the Belgian-German border was more feasible, but it was never built because Belgium feared to lose its independence by agreeing to the full extent of military cooperation with France that would have been necessary to extend the Maginot Line along the Belgian-German border. Hindsight, of course, makes critique easy. The Maginot Line offered France time for mobilization in case of a war with Germany, but France would probably have fared better by expanding and modernizing its offensive and mechanized weapons. To make matters worse, the Great Depression hit France with some delay in 1933–36 – exactly at a time when Germany was bouncing out of it with great force. At the time when a preventive strike against Germany would have been possible, France faced economic difficulties – not as severe as those affecting the more industrialized economies of Germany or

Britain but bad enough to intensify a widespread war weariness caused by the heavy losses of the First World War. Hitler, moreover, made foreign countries believe that his foreign policy was no more than the traditional revisionism of the Weimar governments – not least by leaving Schleicher's foreign minister, Konstantin von Neurath, in office until early 1938. When French leaders finally became alarmed about German rearmament, it was too late for them to stop it.

One success that had more to do with the legacy of the peace treaty than with Hitler's foreign policy was the return of the Saar district to Germany. The Treaty of Versailles had separated it from Germany for fifteen years. A popular vote should then decide its future. The population of the Saar district, having never consented to French rule, voted overwhelmingly for return to Germany in January 1935. This both reflected and increased Hitler's popularity among Germans. In March 1935 Hitler felt safe enough to reintroduce general conscription. This blatant violation of the peace treaty did not provoke a punitive French attack, but it prompted France and Britain to form a closer alignment with each other and with Italy. At a conference in the Italian town Stresa in April, the three powers condemned Germany's step and emphasized that treaties were sacrosanct. This so-called Stresa Front was too little to impress Hitler, however, much as Mussolini's alignment with France and Britain displeased him. A real alliance evolving from the Stresa conference could have embarrassed him, especially since France also concluded a treaty of mutual assistance with the Soviet Union, which, for tactical reasons, had started to cooperate more closely with the western powers in an effort to contain Hitler's Germany. Already in June 1935, however, Britain undercut the Stresa Front by signing a bilateral treaty with Germany, in which Germany agreed to limit its future naval buildup to 35 per cent of the Royal Navy's strength and promised not to build more than 45 per cent of the U-boats the British owned. The Anglo-German Naval Treaty reassured Britain that German rearmament would not repeat the prewar naval arms race, and it seemed to bind Germany without giving it anything in return. In the context of the pre-1914 naval arms race, this would have been a highly desirable treaty for Britain. In the context of 1935, however, it was a success for Hitler because it undermined the Stresa Front, which had just emphasized respect for existing treaties. The Anglo-German Naval Treaty, however, blatantly contradicted the Treaty of Versailles, which had fixed the size of the German fleet at a much lower level and forbidden submarines altogether. Hitler, who was not ready for a naval arms race with Britain anyway, gave away nothing important. In *Mein Kampf*, he had argued that Bülow and Bethmann had made a great mistake by challenging Europe's land powers and Britain simultaneously, and he was for the time being determined to avoid Tirpitz's footsteps.

Whether the Stresa Front could have become a stable framework for containing Nazi Germany is debatable, but it would have deserved more commitment and effort. The Anglo-German Naval Treaty encouraged Mussolini to launch an action that soon destroyed the Stresa Front completely: He ordered troops from the Italian colonies of Eritrea and Somalia to invade Ethiopia, an independent African state and a member of the League of Nations. This put Britain and France into a difficult position. As the leading powers of the League of Nations, they had to punish Italy, impose sanctions, or even go to war until Italy withdrew its troops and restored Ethiopia's sovereignty. As European powers concerned with German rearmament, however, they could not afford alienating Mussolini because they needed him in their effort to contain Germany. Instead of making a decision, France and Britain adopted the worst possible policy by imposing half-hearted economic sanctions on Italy. Their obvious reluctance to punish Italy destroyed all confidence in the League of Nations, while their sanctions, though harmless, alienated Italy enough to push Mussolini into Hitler's arms. Hitler meanwhile played a double game. He secretly provided the Ethiopian resistance with weapons so as to prolong the military conflict and deepen the rift between Mussolini and the western powers. At the same time he gave Mussolini diplomatic support. Hitler's policy succeeded and gave him another opportunity to make a bold move. In March 1936, with the Stresa Front in shatters, Hitler risked the next big violation of the Treaty of Versailles by sending troops into the demilitarized zone in the Rhineland. Many in his entourage considered this too risky a step, and Hitler himself was afraid of a French and British declaration of war. But nothing happened. France was absorbed by a domestic crisis, and Britain concluded that the Rhineland was German territory after all. This new success again boosted Hitler's domestic popularity. The remilitarization of the Rhineland also had strategic importance. If Hitler wanted to attack the Soviet Union, he needed to put his own troops to the French border in order to protect Germany and in particular its industrial sector in the Rhineland and the Ruhr against an attack by France, the Soviet Union's ally. And he was now increasingly committed to realizing his true foreign policy aims.

In 1936 Hitler adopted a more vociferous anti-communist foreign policy. He hoped to convince the British to finally conclude an alliance with Germany – as a bulwark against communism. To underpin his anti-communist orientation, he also decided to intervene in the Spanish Civil War. Spain had been a democratic republic from 1931 on but suffered from strong social tensions between socialist workers and anarchists on the one side and the feudal aristocrats, the Catholic Church, and the army on the other side. In 1936, left-wing liberals, socialists, and communists won the elections and formed a Popular Front government similar to the government that had just taken power in France. In reaction, General Francisco Franco, the head of fascist militias organized after the Italian model, launched a putsch. Neither side could at first prevail. A bloody civil war started that ended in 1939 with a fascist victory. The republicans received support from the Soviet Union, France, and an international brigade of socialists and republicans from other countries. Britain provided naval assistance. The Spanish fascists received much military support from Italy as well as some support from Germany and Portugal. Hitler wanted to prevent Spain from joining the Franco-Russian alliance against Germany. He also hoped to bind Mussolini more closely to Germany by launching a common "fascist" initiative. Hitler's plan again worked out. In November 1936 Mussolini formally committed himself to Nazi Germany. The alliance of Berlin and Rome was called the Axis, which was meant to suggest an axis of anti-communist resistance in Europe. Only one month later, Japan, worried about Soviet power in East Asia, signed an alliance with Germany, the so-called Anti-Comintern Pact, and Italy joined the pact in the following year. Reassured by these alliances, Hitler started to intensify war preparations against the Soviet Union by implementing the so-called Four-Year Plan. Within four years, Hitler told his closest confidants, Germany had to be ready for war. In public, Hitler concealed the Four-Year Plan's military implications and stressed that it was merely meant to create full employment.

After the quick succession of events in 1935 and 1936, an outwardly quiet year followed in European politics. But important decisions happened either elsewhere or in secret. After six years of warlike conflict, Japan invaded China in July 1937, alarming Britain and the United States, which both had economic and political interests in East Asia. Even more than before, Britain was now willing to grant Germany some eastward expansion in Europe if that might preserve European peace. To this end, the British government adopted the controversial policy of appeasement. It signaled to Hitler that Britain would make concessions regarding the status of Danzig, the city under League of Nations control, Austria, and the Sudetenland. In return, the British hoped to commit Hitler to international treaties that would limit German expansion and integrate Nazi Germany into a more stable international order than Versailles had provided. Appeasement has received a very bad reputation because it is usually misconstrued as a spineless submission to a corrupt and aggressive dictator. In reality, it had clear limits and conditions. A moderate revision of the Treaty of Versailles, which was widely considered too harsh in Britain and the United States, seemed to be a matter of justice and reason that might serve British interests by creating a stable situation in Europe. Germany would check the influence of the Soviet Union, about whose extensive industrialization and rearmament the British worried as much as about Japan's expansion in the Far East. At no point, however, did British diplomats plan to give Hitler a blank check for eastward expansion. If he proved impossible to restrain, appeasement would at least buy Britain and France some time for rearmament. In retrospect, one can argue that it was naïve to assume that Hitler could be appeased, but at the time it was not that obvious what Hitler wanted and whether he was even completely in charge at all. It was no secret to the British government that leading German generals and even some high-ranking Nazis were increasingly worried about the risks of Hitler's foreign policy. In any case, most statesmen felt that everything had to be attempted in order to prevent another big bloodletting on the lines of the Great War, which was still very much alive in people's memories. Hitler did not always understand the limitations of appeasement, however. Projecting his own crude Darwinism and craving of racial expansion on the British, he believed it would be in the best British interest to win Germany as an ally against the Soviet Union and as a power that the British could ultimately use in an alliance against the remaining world power, the United States.

Sooner or later the differences between what the British and French were willing to grant and what Hitler really wanted had to clash. In early 1938 Hitler readied himself for a more aggressive foreign policy. Although he still hoped for an alliance with Britain, he made preparations to realize his aims against British resistance if necessary. But first he had to overcome some difficulties in his own state apparatus and in the military. The foreign ministry, the economic leaders, and the highest generals had grown restive and critical of Hitler because they considered his foreign policy dangerous and precipitated. Even a military coup against Hitler was discussed. Hitler reacted by appointing some blind followers to the top of the economy and the military. He also dismissed the conservative Foreign Minister Neurath and appointed a Nazi, Joachim von Ribbentrop, in his place. Thus prepared, he increased pressure on a reluctant Austrian government to let the Austrian Nazis participate in government. This would have been the first step toward *Anschluss,* the unification of Austria with Germany. When Mussolini told Hitler that he would not oppose *Anschluss* any more and when the Austrian government continued to reject cooperation with the Austrian Nazis, Hitler ordered German troops to invade Austria on 12 March 1938. Initially he wanted to leave Austria some independence, but when he witnessed the enthusiasm with which many Austrians welcomed the German troops he found it safe enough to absorb Austria completely. Britain protested at first but recognized the *Anschluss* only two weeks later.

This success encouraged Hitler to begin bullying Czechoslovakia. The German minority in the border areas, the Sudetenland, had become restive and claimed to be repressed by Czechoslovakia. The Nazi press intonated a drumbeat of supportive propaganda. Yet the Sudetenland was not really Hitler's priority. He did not believe in any case that he would be allowed to annex it without triggering a war. What he really wanted now was to destroy Czechoslovakia immediately and to start war against the Soviet Union soon thereafter. He believed that he did not have much time to realize his program of expansion and that the sooner he acted, the better. He secretly ordered the German army to get ready for war by 1 October 1938. In public, Hitler declared that he had peaceful intentions and promised that the Sudetenland was Germany's last territorial claim in Europe. His impatient policy triggered a major domestic and international crisis in September 1938. Most of Germany's conservative elites, particularly the generals and some former high state officials, were deeply concerned about Hitler's increasingly risky course. Secretly they warned British Prime Minister Neville Chamberlain of Hitler's more far-reaching intentions and asked him to remain tough. They hoped that Hitler would back down if he encountered resistance from Britain and France, which he did not expect. Backing down would weaken him at home. There even was some talk of a putsch by the generals to replace a weakened Hitler with a more careful leader. Chamberlain, however, did not take these proposals seriously and preferred a gentleman's agreement with "Herr Hitler." To that end, he visited him in his private home in the Bavarian Alps in the middle of September. Chamberlain agreed to pressure Czechoslovakia to hold a plebiscite in the regions inhabited predominantly by Germans. Given the public mood in the Sudetenland, this essentially meant handing the territory over to Germany. Hitler was surprised by this generosity, which threatened his plans for war. Initially, he agreed to Chamberlain's proposal, which offered him a great public success while frustrating his desire for war. A few days after Chamberlain's return to London, however, Hitler demanded immediate annexation of the Sudetenland without a plebiscite. This was a reckless policy that pushed Europe to the brink of war. Hitler's critics feared that a German attack on Czechoslovakia might trigger war with France, Britain, and the Soviet Union, whereas Hitler was confident that Britain and France would stay out of the conflict. At the last minute, Chamberlain asked Mussolini for mediation. Mussolini, who had no interest in war yet, agreed with Hermann Göring, at this time one of the more cautious Nazi officials, to set up an international conference in Munich. On 29 and 30 September the leaders of Britain, France, and Italy met with Hitler – excluding the Czechoslovak government and also the Soviet Union. They agreed on a compromise plan that originated from the conservative circles in the German foreign office and counteracted Hitler's wishes. Britain, France, and Italy granted Germany control over the Sudetenland without a plebiscite. They also offered some Czechoslovak territories to Hungary, which had been treated rather badly during the redrawing of the borders in 1919–20, and Poland, which coveted a small area of Czechoslovakia. In return, Germany – with all other conference powers – had to guarantee the inviolability of the remaining territory of Czechoslovakia. In addition, Germany and Britain also concluded a non-aggression pact. A triumphant Chamberlain flew home and declared that he had saved peace in Europe. Since non-aggression pacts were so popular and easy to obtain, Hitler concluded another one with France in the end of 1938. He made it clear to the French, however, that he wanted a free hand in eastern Europe.

The irony of the Munich conference was that it drove Hitler's popularity in Germany to its highest levels despite the fact that Hitler had secretly desired a radically different outcome. Going to war was no more popular in Germany than in France and Britain, and it appeared to the German public that Hitler had made some of the most important German dreams come true without resorting to war. Only a few people understood that Hitler was less than happy with the Munich Conference because he had hoped to go to war and to redraw the map of eastern Europe without any foreign interference. Hitler's exuberant gratitude to Mussolini after the *Anschluss* turned into outrage because Mussolini's mediation had spoiled the planned war. Hitler's rage also targeted Göring, who had supported Mussolini. Hitler was particularly upset because the people of Munich had enthusiastically applauded Chamberlain and French Prime Minister Edouard Daladier for their commitment to peace. On the international level, the Munich Conference also had major repercussions. France and Britain had sided with Germany and forced an unwelcome border correction down the throat of the allied Czechoslovak government. They had also made Czechoslovakia powerless. With the Sudetenland, the Czechoslovak army lost its best defenses. Moreover, the Munich Conference led to a reorientation of Soviet foreign policy. As an ally of France and Czechoslovakia, the Soviet Union should have been invited to the Munich Conference. Chamberlain, however, had done everything to keep Soviet dictator Josef Stalin away from the conference table. Britain wanted to be the main mediator of European affairs, and Stalin would probably not have agreed to a settlement pleasing Hitler. Understandably, Stalin drew his own conclusions. Although he had considered Nazi Germany as the predominant threat to the Soviet Union, he now suspected that the Western powers were playing Germany off against the Soviet Union. He was terrified at the thought of the capitalist powers standing united against the Soviet Union and began thinking about ways to reach an arrangement with Hitler that might deflect German aggression away from the Soviet Union and toward the West. Finally, the Munich Conference also prepared the ground for a reorientation of western foreign policy. Chamberlain, his public exuberance notwithstanding, became highly skeptical of appeasement and intensified British rearmament efforts. Daladier, who had never quite believed in appeasement, drew the same conclusions.

Still, to most Germans, Hitler's foreign policy until 1938 appeared extremely successful and inspired widespread enthusiasm and adulation. In reality, Hitler's successes did not reflect his real aim and were made possible by the fact that those powers that had imposed the Treaty of Versailles on Germany had become critical of the treaty and willing to accommodate Germany within the limit of some of the principles enshrined at Versailles, in particular national self-determination. It made no sense for the British and the French to risk another war to keep ethnic Germans out of Germany. It was fatal, of course, that their generosity benefited Hitler and not Stresemann and that it strengthened the Nazi dictatorship and not the democratic Weimar Republic. But the generosity displayed by Chamberlain and Daladier in their understandable, perhaps laudable, desire to avoid another major war in the late 1930s would have been unacceptable to the French and British public in the 1920s, when the hatred and resentment triggered by the war were still fresh. In the perspective of the 1930s, the legacy of the First World War for France and Britain appeared highly questionable. Both countries were nominally among the victors, and yet they were in some ways much worse off after the war than they had been before. No victory would have left a good taste after a generation of young Frenchmen had been wiped out, but the frustration was compounded by severe economic problems and political divisions throughout much of the 1920s and 1930s. Britain had suffered less directly from the war than France, but it also faced major economic problems after the war and lost its leading financial position to the United States. The British empire, larger than ever after the acquisition of some former German colonies and

Ottoman provinces, was becoming increasingly unstable. If *winning* a world war left these countries so weakened, who can blame their politicians and voters for wanting to prevent a new world war at almost any cost?

Hitler also profited from a temporarily advantageous geo-political situation. Britain, as the most powerful European state, was so concerned with Japanese expansion in East Asia that it was willing to grant Hitler concessions in Europe hoping to preserve peace there. The Japanese threat also reduced American interest in Europe, which had never been great after the war. As long as Germany and the Soviet Union neutralized each other in Eastern Europe, Britain did not feel threatened much by either power. In retrospect, of course, appeasement appears as a serious mistake. But it has to be interpreted in the context of the 1930s. The British and French leaders sincerely wanted to preserve peace. They did try to contain Hitler with the help of Italy and the Soviet Union in 1935. They could have done more to ensure the success of these containment efforts, but Italy and the Soviet Union, not least because of their own expansive goals, were dubious allies in the long run. After giving up containment, the British and French leaders allowed Hitler to remedy some German grievances that seemed justified on the grounds of national self-determination. As soon as it became clear to them that their generosity did not appease Hitler, they abandoned appeasement and intensified rearmament. But first they had to make a good-faith effort to find a *modus vivendi* with Germany and to preserve peace. Nothing less would have justified a policy of confrontation to a domestic public that had learned that even winning a world war did not pay. Neither the western leaders nor most Germans were fully aware of Hitler's radical long-term goals, particularly his racial utopia and the conquest of living space in the East. Even to those who knew about them, these goals seemed too fanciful and unrealistic to be taken seriously. Foreigners and most Germans alike saw Hitler as a revisionist politician, more radical and aggressive than Stresemann or Brüning but essentially concerned about the same limited and predictable goals. That Hitler's vision was radically different from either Stresemann's or Brüning's goals emerged only gradually after 1938.

There were still some questions in eastern Europe that Hitler could hope to settle peacefully to Germany's advantage: the "international" status of Danzig, populated predominantly by Germans, violated the principle of national self-determination, and so did the fact that many territories mostly settled by Germans belonged to Poland. Like the Sudeten Germans, the German minorities in Poland frequently complained about repression, and even the French and British admitted that the drawing of the German-Polish border in 1918–21 had consistently favored Poland over Germany. Had Hitler wanted, he could perhaps have joined Danzig to Germany, redrawn the Polish-German border to Germany's advantage and linked East Prussia, since 1918 an exclave, with the German mainland – all without going to war. The Munich Conference had set a precedent, and a Polish government trying to save the integrity of its country would hardly have found more support from France and Britain than the Czechoslovak government. Such a policy would have been overwhelmingly popular in Germany. But Hitler's foreign policy already carried the seeds of disaster. His irrational and aggressive demeanor in the Sudeten crisis had exhausted the willingness of Britain and France to make concessions to him. Italy, lured into an alliance with Germany, was not the strong ally that Hitler, who tended to overrate Mussolini, expected. Moreover, the German-British alliance that Hitler desired never materialized, and it became clear to him that the British did not want to give him the free hand that he desired in eastern Europe. On the domestic front, finally, dissatisfaction mounted as the strain of rapid rearmament and the striving for autarchy, geared toward war, produced many shortages in the consumer sector. After 1936, the irresponsible pace of rearmament might have triggered an economic downturn had not the acquisition of Austria and the Sudetenland with their assets provided fresh fuel to an overheating economy.

In the months after the Munich Conference pressure from below combined with the reckless desires of an increasingly self-confident and pushy dictator to make Nazi policies significantly more radical on the domestic and international stage. Many rank-and-file Nazis had long wanted to step up persecution of the Jews. This was likely to trigger negative foreign reactions, but the regime seemed to care less and less about that. In fact, any foreign outcry about the plight of the German Jews might serve to confirm the crazy Nazi conspiracy theories that "international Jewry" was threatening Germany from without and from within. Hitler himself was more than ever determined to launch his war in the East in the near future. After Munich, he felt reassured that he had a high degree of control within Germany and that Britain and France, though perhaps unwilling to condone his claims as they had just done in Munich, would at least not go to war to prevent his reorganization of eastern Europe. Many leading German officers, diplomats, and other elites still felt apprehensive about Hitler's war plans, but they became increasingly insecure. Hitler's bullying had worked on so many occasions already. In a pattern that was to repeat itself several times until 1940, Hitler always seemed to prove his more cautious advisors wrong. His diplomacy was reckless, but it seemed to work. It was hard for the skeptics to argue with success.

Persecution of the Jews reached a shameful new peak when SA street fighters attacked Jews and put fire to synagogues and Jewish cultural institutions all over Germany on 9 November 1938. Goebbels sought to depict the pogrom as a spontaneous expression of outrage after a Polish Jew had shot a German diplomat in Paris the day before as a sign of protest against the persecution of the Jews in Germany. In reality, the pogrom, which received the euphemistic term *Reichskristallnacht*, translated as Crystal Night or Night of Broken Glass, was anything but spontaneous. With Hitler's approval, Goebbels called SA sections and other Nazi organizations to action just as their fanaticism was stirred by the anniversary of the German Revolution of 1918 and the repression of the Hitler Putsch in 1923. Police and firefighters were instructed not to interfere unless the fires threatened non-Jewish property. Ninety-one Jews were killed during the pogrom, and approximately 26,000 Jewish men were arrested and detained in concentration camps without any legal grounds. The pogrom was meant to give grass-roots Nazi activists, particularly in the SA, a chance to vent their frustration, which had been building up in the face of a perceived inactivity of the regime in its Jewish policies. The popular response to the pogrom, as reported by police spies, was rather cold, however. The seemingly senseless destruction of valuable property drew much criticism from bystanders, some of whom also condemned the inhumanity of the action. Sensing the negative popular response, Hitler immediately distanced himself from the pogrom. Nevertheless, Crystal Night ushered in a wave of punitive regulations and laws that made life for Jews in Germany almost impossible and, together with the violence during the pogrom, demonstrated to German Jews that they were no longer safe. In a show of utter cynicism, a meeting of Nazi officials under Göring's leadership three days after the pogrom blamed the violence on the Jews themselves and decreed that they would have to pay for the damage. This led to a wave of expropriations of Jewish property – acts of legalized robbery. Crystal Night triggered extremely negative responses in the democratic countries including the United States, but it did not markedly increase their willingness to welcome Jewish refugees. In July 1938, after the ruthless expulsion of many Jews from annexed Austria, United States President Franklin Roosevelt had already called a conference on Jewish emigration in the French lake resort Evian, but neither Evian nor the increased persecution after Crystal Night opened up many new opportunities for Jews to leave Germany. Whereas some German Jews had believed in the early years that Nazism would pass quickly or that the Nürnberg Laws had marked the extent to which Nazi persecution would go, most German Jews were now fully aware that they could not safely stay in their home country. But emigration was a hard decision even for those lucky enough to get the necessary papers. It usually meant leaving some family members behind and abandoning them to an uncertain fate.

Crystal Night did not enhance the popularity of the Nazi regime but, sadly, it also did not do much damage to Nazi popularity because most Germans, after years of apartheid and Nazi propaganda, had become so estranged from Jews that they did not care. The Nazi regime was firmly in place; open opposition appeared impossible and pointless. True, the regime had its drawbacks. The high pace of rearmament was causing shortages in the consumer sector; people worked long hours for low wages; the *Gauleiter* were almost without exception incompetent, corrupt, and obnoxious, and the same could be overheard in conversations about some Nazi ministers; Nazi functionaries at the local level could be mean and repressive toward the churches; the state of law had largely been suspended, and the regime was ruthless against its real and perceived enemies. But Hitler seemed to rest above all these problems. He was believed to represent only good intentions and to be endowed with highly unusual powers; if something seemed troubling in Nazi Germany, many Germans would just say: "if only the *Führer* knew." Of course, often the Führer in reality did not only know but even was responsible for the problem. But there were undeniable successes of the regime. Even many non-Nazis gave Hitler credit for having overcome the Great Depression and made the country strong and proud again. Life in Nazi Germany seemed better for most Germans. The Nazis provided much popular entertainment and a sense of security and stability that had been woefully lacking during most of the Weimar years.

–8–

Germany in the Second World War

There is no war guilt question for the Second World War, as there is for 1914. In the course of the spring of 1939, Hitler committed himself to going to war within a few months. He felt that his regime was stable enough for war and that he was riding an unstoppable momentum. His increasing impatience for war had various sources. First, he recognized that the high pace of German war preparation would buy only a temporary advantage because other countries were also beginning to intensify rearmament. The annexation of Austria and the Sudetenland had improved Germany's military situation (and that was most important to Hitler – not the righteousness of these claims on the basis of national self-determination), but if he decided to strike too late, his weapons would be obsolete and his opponents strong enough to take on the risks of containing Nazi Germany. Second, situation reports indicated that the economic situation in Germany remained tenuous and that the hardships of war preparation on workers and farmers led to increasing grumbling and dissatisfaction. Hitler was convinced that war would be the panacea for these problems. Conquest would resolve the economic problems and, at the very least, take off the minds of Germans from problems that seemed petty in Hitler's view. Finally, Hitler became increasingly obsessed with his own mortality. From the beginnings of his political career in the early 1920s, he had assembled unquestioning and admiring followers around himself, first in the party, and then in the state. This entourage incessantly flattered his narcissism and swelled it to delusional proportions. It is no exaggeration to say that by 1939 Hitler considered himself a genius who appears to a people at best once in a millennium. But he remained aware that he was mortal, and he was terrified that one day he might be assassinated and that the German people, bereft of his ingenious leadership, would fall. Hitler's blind faith in his once-in-a-millennium qualities made him increasingly eager to realize all he could envision for Germany within his lifetime. Even without suffering from any acute illness, Hitler became obsessed with his mortality and felt increasingly pressed to act quickly.

The first major act of foreign policy after Munich was the invasion of the rest of Czechoslovakia on 14 and 15 March 1939. The sinister manipulation of Czechoslovak President Emil Hácha, then on a visit to Berlin, and the encouragement to Slovak autonomists to declare independence from Czechoslovakia could not cloud the fact that this was a ruthless act of aggression against the state whose boundaries Hitler had just promised to respect in Munich. Hungary was allowed to annex still more

Slovak land. The Czech part of the country was made into the German protectorate Bohemia and Moravia, and Slovakia, minus the territories taken by Hungary, became essentially a German vassal state under the leadership of the Catholic Slovak cleric Jozef Tiso. Neither France nor Britain was prepared to intervene militarily. But appeasement was now definitely dead. After Crystal Night the public mood in Britain and France had already become more critical, and the German invasion of Czechoslovakia was the last nail in the coffin of appeasement. Hitler, however, was triumphant. To his secretaries, he boasted: "I will go down as the greatest German in history."[1] But public opinion reports indicated that the German public was less enthusiastic. Whereas the annexation of Austria and the Sudetenland had triggered overwhelming, often hysterical approval, the destruction of Czechoslovakia was not seen as a justified move and heightened fears of war. A week after the invasion of Czechoslovakia, Hitler therefore followed up with a cheap propaganda success by annexing the Memelland, a small region with a German and Lithuanian population on the northern border of East Prussia. Lithuania had occupied this formerly German territory after the First World War and annexed it illegally in 1923. Its German population had become increasingly receptive to Nazi propaganda.

Map 3 Germany in 1940.

The recklessness of Hitler's foreign policy at this point made it unlikely that he would win major concessions from Poland and the western democracies, although the Polish government was not opposed to negotiations. But who could trust Hitler with a new agreement, after he had just broken the Munich Treaty by invading Czechoslovakia? Britain and France issued a guarantee for Poland and sought to reassure the Polish government of their support. The Soviet Union was still holding talks with Britain and France about an alliance to contain Nazi Germany, but its demand to allow its troops to march into southeastern Poland in case of war met with Polish resistance (the Poles suspected that these troops would never leave again). While Hitler tried to deceive the public that he was interested in keeping the peace and wanted no more than a revision of the border, he had decided on the destruction of Poland as an independent state. He did have to consider the widespread German aversion to a large war, however. At the very least, he needed to make sure that his attack on Poland would not lead to a declaration of war by Britain and France, which many Germans feared. In the end, a surprising agreement with Stalin made Hitler confident that he would be able to localize a war with Poland. Stalin, distrustful of British and French diplomacy after Munich, had secretly extended feelers to Hitler since the spring of 1939. Hitler himself was so fixated upon his desired destruction of the Soviet Union and initially confident that the British and French would not interfere with his plans in eastern Europe that he paid no attention. But Foreign Minister Ribbentrop, who sincerely desired to form an alliance with the Soviet Union (and Japan) against Britain, which he hated, kept the contacts alive. In August, as Hitler was committed to an attack on Poland, he recognized that these contacts suited his interests and authorized Ribbentrop to fly to Moscow on 22 August. The following day, Ribbentrop and Soviet foreign minister Vjatcheslav Molotov signed a non-aggression pact in Stalin's presence. A secret additional protocol divided Eastern Europe into German and Soviet spheres of interest. The news of the Hitler-Stalin Pact hit like a bomb. The French foreign ministry thought that Poland now ought to compromise with Germany, although France and Britain after some further thought reaffirmed their guarantee for Poland. Japan, Germany's ally, was bewildered. The Japanese government had signed the pact with Germany and Italy because it saw the Soviet Union as its primary antagonist in East Asia. In fact, Japan and the Soviet Union had been at the brink of war earlier in 1939, when some of their troops on the Sino-Russian border had opened fire on each other. The Hitler-Stalin Pact led to a reorientation of Japanese policy toward southward expansion, a policy that was likely to lead to a confrontation with Britain and the United States, not with the Soviet Union. The German public was equally surprised, but many Germans reacted with relief because the pact seemed to make the dreaded two-front war less likely. The military and much of the public had long harbored strong anti-Polish feelings and had seen the Soviet Union more as a potential ally than as the satanic antagonist portrayed by Nazi propaganda. Some avid Nazis, however, felt betrayed after decades of propaganda. The garden of the party headquarters in

Munich was littered with discarded party badges on the day after the announcement of the pact.

On 1 September, Germany attacked Poland without any declaration of war. In order to disguise this act of blatant aggression, the SS staged an attack on a German radio station by concentration camp inmates forced to wear Polish army uniforms (the SS conveniently shot the prisoners after the event so as to leave no witnesses). Even though Nazi propaganda against Poland had gone into overdrive during the preceding weeks, Hitler was highly nervous when he told the Nazi Reichstag that German troops were since early morning "shooting back." Indeed, the German populace reacted with apprehension to the outbreak of war. There were no jubilant crowds as there had been in August 1914. The mood darkened when Britain and France submitted an ultimatum and, after Germany failed to withdraw its troops from Poland, declared war on 3 September. The Soviet Union, as expected, stood by as the German army in a lightning (*Blitz*) campaign defeated the courageous but poorly equipped Polish army. After three weeks of fighting, the Soviet army moved into the eastern territories of Poland promised to Stalin by the secret additional protocol of the Hitler-Stalin Pact. German and Soviet soldiers fraternized on the demarcation line, while the German army launched a last, fierce assault on Warsaw. In early October, Polish resistance ceased. The Polish government fled to Romania and then to Britain. Germany annexed major territories of Poland and established essentially a colony under a German governor in the central area around Warsaw (the *Generalgouvernement*). SS units following the army killed thousands of Polish teachers, intellectuals, and clergymen – people the Germans considered to be the backbone of Polish nationalism (the Soviet Union soon applied similar policies in its own territories of Poland, including the murder of over 25,000 Polish army officers). The SS also murdered Jews and pushed many of them east into the Soviet zone.

Although Hitler had been wrong about the British and French declaration of war, he did localize the war in the short run. France and Britain mobilized, but they did not take any major initiative. The French army moved into the Maginot Line and into positions along the unprotected border with Belgium, and the British sent some troops to northern France. The bulk of the German army was concentrated in Poland in September, and the western borders were guarded by weak forces. A young French general staff officer who suggested that France take advantage of this situation by attacking and seizing the German industrial heartland in the Ruhr district provoked a humiliating reprimand by the older officers who reminded him of the lessons of the First World War. The French army was poorly prepared for an offensive in 1939; its predominant thinking was focused on defense. Britain and France expected that a blockade would, as in the First World War, sap German strength. This might take a long time, but Britain and France could better afford to wait than Germany. Should the German army foolishly try to attack, it would meet defeat while running against the Maginot Line or, if it chose to invade Belgium, while meeting a concentration of the best French and British troops. Europe was at war, but in the months following

Poland's defeat not much seemed to go on. Italy rejected Hitler's invitation to enter the war. Finland withstood a Soviet attack in a fierce but limited winter war. On the Franco-German border, the opposing armies did little harm to each other. The French nicknamed this phase the "drôle de guerre" ("phony war" in English); the Germans spoke of *Sitzkrieg*, meaning "sitting war" – in contrast to the *Blitzkrieg* (lightning war) practiced in Poland.

Hitler, however, was committed to strike in the West as early as possible. Against the advice of his more cautious generals, who wanted him to seek a peace agreement with the western powers, he ordered an attack for the middle of November. Bad weather, however, led to repeated postponements in the following months. The German air force needed a longer period of clear weather for its planned raids with bombers and dive bombers against enemy positions, which had proven highly effective in Poland. On 10 January 1940, the Belgians made a surprising discovery that looked like a huge benefit for France and Britain but turned out to be a fatal misunderstanding. A German plane carrying a staff officer with the war plan against the western powers had to make an emergency landing near the Belgian city Mechelen; the officer tried to destroy the documents, but the Belgians recovered enough to gain a clear understanding of German intentions. The German war plan, which the Belgians leaked to France and Britain, was highly unoriginal. The German army was to invade the Netherlands and Belgium with massive tank forces and rush to the North Sea. This plan vaguely resembled the Schlieffen Plan, although it did not imply a move into northern France designed to surround the allied armies. What was so fatal about the Mechelen incident was that the British and French felt confirmed in their expectation of a massive German offensive into the heart of Belgium, while the German High Command, unbeknownst to the Allies, abandoned the plan for a very different scheme developed by General Erich von Manstein and implemented with Hitler's backing.

Before the phony war in the West ended, however, Scandinavia briefly became the focus of the war. During the winter of 1939–40, the British and the French had considered supporting Finland against the Soviet attack by sending troops to Finland via Norway and Sweden. The French, in particular, were interested in stationing bombers in Finland and in bombing the Soviet oil fields in the Caspian Sea region. The Soviet Union was supplying Germany with huge amounts of goods, including oil, steel, coal, and food. An Allied move into northern Scandinavia would also have cut the Swedish iron ore shipments to Germany, which were important for German war industry. Stalin, however, decided to make peace with Finland in March 1940, just as the Red Army was winning the upper hand after a series of embarrassing setbacks. The Soviet Union, perhaps in fear of the discussed Allied intervention, was satisfied with annexing several Finnish provinces and with receiving some military concessions. Still, northern Europe remained of crucial interest to the Allies and Germany. British naval forces were beginning to lay mines in Norwegian waters, and British forces had been formed to land in northern Norway to cut the iron ore shipments from Sweden and, potentially, to beat the Germans to the place. The Germans, worried about Allied moves and hoping for a better position for their navy, arrived slightly earlier, however. On 9 April they invaded Denmark and Norway, claiming to protect these countries from an Allied invasion. Whereas Denmark was occupied without resistance, Norway fought the German invasion – with French and British help. By early May, however, the Norwegian and Allied forces were beaten in most places except in the vicinity of Narvik, a city in the North where the fighting continued until a final Allied defeat in June. For the Germans, the occupation of Denmark and Norway followed primarily from naval strategic priorities. Controlling the Norwegian coast meant safeguarding one of the sea lanes on which the Swedish iron ore was transported to Germany. Moreover, this coast offered the German navy better bases for its war against Britain and made it harder for the Royal Navy to maintain the blockade. Ultimately, however, the invasion of Norway cost the German navy dearly. Some ships were lost, and many others sustained significant damage, making them unusable for many months. Most of these damaged ships were not combat-ready for a planned invasion of Britain in the fall of 1940.

Then the long-awaited storm in the West broke loose. The Allies had received ample warnings from the German resistance and from their own intelligence, but they had become numbed because the attack had been postponed many times due to bad weather. On 10 May 1940, the Germans finally attacked all along the border to Luxembourg, Belgium, and the Netherlands. The best French and British forces moved into central Belgium, trying to establish a defensive front with the retreating Belgian and Dutch armies and hoping to defeat the bulk of the German forces in that area. Manstein's plan, however, created an entirely unexpected situation. Seven of Germany's ten tank divisions rushed through the Ardennes forest in the southernmost tip of Belgium, established some bridgeheads across the Meuse River within three days, and broke through the weak French defenses in this sector just to the northwest of the Maginot Line. By 15 May, the German forces were fanning out and turning toward the sea. Within five days, they had reached the British Channel and cut off the strong British and French forces in Belgium. Meanwhile, the German advance into the Netherlands also made much headway with the help of paratroopers and soldiers from glider planes. On 14 May, German bombers destroyed the Dutch city Rotterdam, not aware that negotiations for the surrender of the Dutch army had already started. The next day, the Dutch army capitulated, and the Dutch queen went into exile in London. The situation for the Allies was bleak. Attacks on the exposed German pincer in northern France did not succeed, and the Allied forces in Belgium suffered heavy losses. By the end of May, the British decided to evacuate their troops out of the port of Dunkirk. After heavy fighting, the evacuation of most of the British Expeditionary Force and some French troops succeeded, but all heavy weapons and equipment had to be left behind. The Belgian army now also surrendered. The Dunkirk evacuation was celebrated as a victory in Britain, but Prime Minister Winston Churchill, who had replaced Chamberlain on the day of the German attack, cautioned in private that wars are not won by evacuations. On the German side, it was believed for a long time that Hitler had deliberately allowed the British army to escape in an attempt to win British friendship. This is a myth, however. Hitler had become nervous after the unexpectedly rapid advance of his armies and therefore ordered a halt in the end of May, trusting air force marshal Göring's (hollow) promise that the air force alone would be able to prevent an Allied evacuation by bombing the harbor and the ships. Some German tank commanders had also cautioned that their tanks needed to be serviced after long days of an extremely rapid advance.

Despite Dunkirk, the defeat in Belgium was a disaster for the Allies. Although the French command, with the help of some Allied troops evacuated from Dunkirk, improvised a new defensive line from the Somme River to the Maginot Line, the Germans were now numerically superior. On 5 June, they launched a second offensive, broke through the French lines near Amiens and then beat the French army back from river to river. A stream of civilian refugees made any counter-attack impossible. On 10 June, Italy, assured of the success of the German breakthrough, declared war on France and Britain. The Italian army attacked French positions in the Alps but made no headway. On the German front, however, there was no holding any more. The French government left Paris on 10 June; four days later the Germans marched into the city. On 17 June, Marshall Pétain, the hero of Verdun, took control of the French government and asked for an armistice, while German troops were advancing increasingly unopposed into the southern central regions of France. On 22 June, the armistice was signed in the presence of Hitler, who had insisted on using the same railroad car in which German delegates had signed the armistice ending the First World War. The armistice took effect in the morning hours of 25 June.

The defeat of the Allies – and it was an Allied, not only a French, defeat – was a huge surprise. Why did Nazi Germany's army succeed in a few weeks where the Kaiser's armies had failed in more than four years? It was not a question of numerical superiority. The German and Allied forces were evenly matched on 10 May. The German air force did have numerical superiority on the battlefield because the British held back a significant part of their air force for home defense, a move bitterly resented by many Frenchmen after the defeat, but the German forces were numerically inferior in other categories. It was not a question of the quality of materiel either. The French and British armies had some excellent tanks that were superior to most German models, and they had airplanes that matched the best German designs. The French artillery, still largely based on the 75 mm gun from the First World War, was better than the German artillery in some respects. Several factors appear crucial, however: the German war plan, the greater strategic and tactical flexibility of the German officers, and the fighting spirit of the German forces. Manstein's plan of sending the bulk of the German tank force through the Ardennes was risky because it exposed the tanks to air attack on long, narrow, winding roads. But the plan was a complete surprise for the Allies. They realized what was happening only after the

Germans had crossed the main rivers in their way. The breakthrough was difficult to contain because the Allies could not be sure at first where the German forces would go next: south into the back of the Maginot Line, west toward Paris, or northwest toward the Channel? After the initial breakthrough, the Manstein Plan forced the Allies to fight a very different war from what they had expected, and neither the British nor the French forces were able to adapt quickly. The Allies had no reserves, and their tanks were largely dispersed along the entire front line, not concentrated in large mobile units as they were in the German army. Second, German strategy and tactics were more flexible and creative. Thanks to the Treaty of Versailles, Germany had had to disarm, but this proved to be less of a disadvantage than expected. The rebuilding of the army under the Nazis allowed many comparatively young and innovative officers to rise to top positions. There were still some of the old-school officers whose thinking revolved around the experiences of the First World War, but there was more room for new approaches than in the French or British army. The German officers, foremost among them Erwin Rommel, were highly creative, flexible, and independent. Riding in the frontlines with their troops, they did not wait for headquarters' instructions to fix a critical situation. Finally, the German troops fighting in the West seemed more dedicated and spirited. Contrary to the popular image, the British and the French fought well except for some of the French units posted in the crucial sector near the Ardennes – but these units were posted there precisely because they were not expected to see major fighting. Some French elite units from mainland France, North Africa, and West Africa even fought extremely well. But the Germans always persisted and broke through. War diaries from the best French units often note with perplexity the fighting spirit, creativity, and persistence of the Germans, who seemed to fight with a vengeance.

The consequences of the Allied defeat in the West were enormous. To Hitler and to many other Europeans, it seemed as if the Second World War had ended. This was it. True, Britain was still free and, to Hitler's surprise, unwilling to settle peacefully with Germany; but what could Britain do with a small army that had lost most of its heavy weapons? Churchill tried to boost morale by stressing three avenues to victory: continued naval blockade, aerial bombing, and encouragement of resistance in continental Europe. The first strategy was not effective as long as Stalin kept providing raw materials and food to Nazi Germany. The second rested on exaggerated hopes; in the short run, it was Britain that had to fend off German aerial bombing. The third strategy did not look encouraging either. Resistance on a larger scale started only a year later, when the German attack on the Soviet Union released the communists from self-imposed passivity. Even later, one can hardly say that the blockade, bombing, and the resistance were crucial for victory despite the damage they undoubtedly inflicted on the German war effort. Most Europeans probably shared Hitler's assessment in June 1940, namely that the war was won and that Europe west of the Soviet Union would be reconstituted as a German-dominated European union. That is why Mussolini hastened to declare war on the

Allies on 10 June; that is why the Pétain government opted for collaboration with Germany after the armistice; that is why Stalin occupied the three Baltic states and pressured Romania for territorial concessions in June 1940, and that is why millions of Germans cheered in the streets during the endless victory parades in late June and early July. In the light of the First World War, this impression is understandable. In the First World War, the western front had been the decisive theater of the war. The Germans failed to win there, and when the Allies gained the upper hand, they won the war. The Germans had defeated vastly superior Russian forces in the First World War, but this had not been decisive. In 1940, most observers expected a swift German victory again, should either Hitler or Stalin break the mutual non-aggression pact. True, the Soviet Union under Stalin had industrialized at a rapid pace, but there still was much doubt about Soviet war-making capacity. Stalin had ruthlessly purged the Soviet officer corps, and the Soviet army had handled the Finnish war of 1939–40 with appalling incompetence. The victory against France was crucial for Hitler because it made him confident enough to attack the Soviet Union a year later. It also brought his popularity to very high levels again, approximately where it had been after the Munich Conference. True, he had gone to war. But if this war could be fought with comparatively small German losses and with little interference with everyday life, as it was in 1939–40, then this could be forgiven.

Hitler did not have an exit strategy for the war he had started, however. Britain remained at war after the fall of France. In a few years, the United States might be able and willing to help Britain more actively. Italy, Hitler's much-acclaimed ally, proved to be poorly prepared for war and suffered one defeat after the other against the British in Africa and later against the Greek army in the Balkans. Meanwhile, Hitler remained largely dependent on the very country that it had been his declared intention to destroy: the Soviet Union. Hitler first tried to induce the British to recognize his conquests in continental Europe. When that failed, he decided to attack Britain. Preparations for an invasion were half hearted, however. The German army did concentrate forces in the area closest to the English coast, but the precondition for an invasion was winning aerial superiority and, at least for a limited time, naval superiority in the invasion area. To achieve the first and most important precondition, the German air force stepped up its bombing campaign against Britain in July 1940. It attacked at first only strategic installations: air fields, radar stations, and factories. Some historians believe that this strategy would have been successful had it been pursued longer. But in August 1940, German public opinion expressed increasing outrage over the (possibly accidental) British bombing of civilian areas in Germany and demanded revenge. In reaction, the German air force began to shift its priorities from targeted attacks to city bombing. This allowed the Royal Air Force to recover and ultimately to fight back with success. The air battle over Britain raged for several months. German bombing raids on London, Coventry, and the industrial cities of northern England did much damage, but the concentrated bomber fleets were easy targets for fighter planes and suffered heavy losses. German fighters sent to protect the bombers had the disadvantage of fighting far from their bases. Every damaged plane making an emergency landing was lost – and so was the pilot. In October 1940, the invasion plans were postponed indefinitely even though the bombing campaign continued well into 1941 and was resumed at various intervals later on. But it was clear enough that the German air force would not be able to establish air superiority in the short run. This conclusion left Hitler worried about the potential of Britain to become the base for an invasion of the continent with American help. Hitler also believed that Britain held out because it was considering the Soviet Union as a potential ally. In October 1940, Hitler therefore decided to attack the Soviet Union in the spring of 1941. Some historians see this step as a sign that Hitler was sacrificing pragmatic for ideological priorities. Other historians, without denying that the attack on the Soviet Union fit Hitler's ideological predilection, stress the immediate need Hitler saw to fortify the Nazi empire against an Anglo-American invasion. A quick defeat of the Soviet Union might induce Britain to conclude peace with Germany rather than waiting for American help and, if worst came to worst, give Germany a continental colonial empire that would make it impervious to blockade and very hard to defeat even by a united Anglo-American effort. To his circle of confidants, Hitler often spoke of the territory of the Soviet Union as "his" India or "his" American West. He would ruthlessly dominate and exploit that territory, whose population he considered to be "uncivilized" colonial subjects who could be decimated and put into reservations like Native Americans.

Stalin had no interest in an armed conflict with Nazi Germany for the time being. The pact with Hitler, and the defeat of the Allies, had allowed him to bring about a much-desired correction of the western boundary of the Soviet Union at the expense of Finland, the Baltic states, Poland, and Romania. He was expecting more: further expansion in the Balkans and in Finland. To this end, Stalin was even willing to enter the Tripartite Pact of Germany, Italy, and Japan – ironically the alliance that had been concluded as a pact against the Soviet Union! Some historians say that Hitler gambled away a strong position by needlessly attacking the Soviet Union and that this was the decisive mistake that led to his defeat. However, there were profound differences of interest between Nazi Germany and the Soviet Union. Germany could hardly tolerate a Soviet absorption of Finland, and the Soviet desire to expand on the Balkans and toward the old target of tsarist Russia, the Dardanelles, alarmed both Hitler and Mussolini. More importantly, the position of Nazi Germany remained vulnerable as long as it was economically so dependent upon the Soviet Union. The Achilles Heel of the Axis war effort always was oil. Nazi Germany had access to the oil fields of Romania (after all the Balkan states had concluded more or less willing alliances with Germany and Italy), but these oil fields produced far too little to satisfy the demand for oil in Germany and the occupied countries. Moreover, the Romanian oil fields were close to the Soviet border, and they would be within the range of British bombers, should the British land in Greece, as they had done in the First World War. Other historians therefore argue that Hitler's position was not as strong as it seemed. His fatal mistake according to this interpretation was to start a war in 1939 that he could not possibly win and for which he had no exit strategy.

Except for the air battle over Britain, however, the twelve months following the signing of the armistice with France were relatively peaceful. German troops kept the north of France and its Atlantic coast occupied, while Pétain established a collaborationist government in the spa town Vichy, just a few kilometers south of the demarcation line between occupied and unoccupied zones. A French general evacuated to Britain, Charles de Gaulle, declared himself head of an independent French government committed to keep fighting. De Gaulle rallied French Central Africa to his government but, with British help, failed to take French West Africa by force. Meanwhile, the Germans separated Alsace and Lorraine from France and consolidated some of the northern French regions with Belgium under a military administration. They agreed to leave the French colonies and the French fleet alone. This did not reassure the British government, however, which feared that the Germans sooner or later might seize the French fleet. The British air force therefore bombed the French fleet off the coast of French Algeria on 3 July 1940, killing over a thousand French sailors and prompting the Vichy government to sever diplomatic relations with Britain. In the East, the brutal German occupation policies continued. Nazi officials tried to carry out a huge resettlement project, moving Poles and Jews out of the annexed parts of Poland into the central area around Warsaw and bringing ethnic Germans from Soviet-occupied Lithuania into the areas where the Poles had lived. In the course of 1940, most Polish Jews in the German-occupied lands were forced into overcrowded ghettos – enclosed areas in the center of cities where disease and starvation became rampant.

The German army was preparing for the attack on the Soviet Union, but it first had to deal with other theaters of war that became critical through the bungled efforts of Mussolini. The Italian defeats in Africa continued, and the British were advancing into Libya, an Italian colony. Hitler decided to assist the Italian defense efforts by sending a German unit, the Afrikakorps under Rommel, to Libya in February 1941. The Afrikakorps and the Italian forces in North Africa were able to counterattack in April. The balance then tipped back and forth many times as Rommel advanced too far for his sparse supplies to reach him, and the British suffered the same fate when they beat the Axis forces back too far. More threatening was another Italian initiative: on 28 October 1940, Italy invaded Greece from Albania, which Italy had annexed already in April 1939 in imitation of the German invasion of Czechoslovakia. The Greek army repelled the Italians, however, and the British began landing troops in Greece in support. This prompted Hitler into action. A British presence in Greece was a threat to the Romanian oil fields and to the German southern flank in the planned attack on the Soviet Union. In April 1941, the German army, having stationed major forces in Romania and Bulgaria in the preceding months, attacked Greece. The Germans, with Italian and Bulgarian help, also attacked Yugoslavia, where a British-inspired coup against the pro-Axis government had just succeeded. Yugoslav resistance quickly broke down, and the Greek army also had to capitulate after a few weeks. The British evacuated their forces, and German paratroopers conquered the Greek island of Crete, where the British had hoped to establish a lasting base. It has often been argued that the Balkans campaign fatally delayed the German offensive against the Soviet Union, implying that this offensive would have succeeded had the German army had a few more weeks before the onset of the winter. This is a rather hypothetical argument, however. Perhaps the German army was weakened by the Balkans campaign; although it suffered only minor tank losses, many tanks had to be overhauled and were not immediately ready for the attack on the Soviet Union. But it is doubtful whether the attack on the Soviet Union could have started much earlier due to the spring rain season; even if it had occurred earlier and with slightly larger forces, it is uncertain whether this would have been decisive.

In the morning hours of 22 June 1941, Germany attacked the Soviet Union. The attack was a disaster for the Soviet army. Stalin had stubbornly ignored the stream of information predicting the attack – from his own intelligence sources, from the British secret service, and from German deserters. The Soviet forces therefore were completely surprised and quickly overwhelmed. They had not had time to build defensive fortifications on the border because this new border had just been established twelve to eighteen months before. In the light of the doubtful loyalty to the Soviet Union of some of the newly incorporated populations, moreover, the Red Army had focused on offensive dispositions, not on defense. The result was a defeat of unique historical proportions. Much of the Soviet air force was destroyed on the ground by German bombings. In huge encirclement battles, the Germans destroyed entire Soviet armies and captured over three million Soviet soldiers in 1941. By the end of November 1941, German spearheads were in front of Moscow, Leningrad, and deep in eastern Ukraine. Finland, understandably unhappy about the territorial losses imposed on it by the Soviet Union in March 1940, participated in the German attack, as did troops from Spain, Italy, and a variety of German-occupied countries. Although German losses had been much higher than in the earlier campaigns and although fierce Soviet resistance continued, it looked as if Germany had won yet again. In December, however, the Soviet Union counter-attacked in front of Moscow and later on the entire length of the front. Stalin had preserved much of the country's enormous industrial potential by transporting entire factories from the western republics to the regions behind the Urals, where they were safe from German conquest and bombings. Thanks to a German spy in Tokyo, moreover, Stalin knew that Japan had decided to attack the United States, and this allowed him to withdraw the sizeable Soviet forces in East Asia and deploy them in front of Moscow. Finally, the Soviet army was much better prepared for winter warfare than the Germans. Hitler had expected that the Soviet Union would crumble after the first shock and that the campaign would be over well before winter. When the frost set in, German troops, without winter uniforms, froze in their foxholes; hundreds of thousands suffered from frostbite. Hitler ordered the troops not to withdraw under any circumstances.

On 7 December, Japan launched a surprise attack on the American fleet at Pearl Harbor. Typical for Axis practice, the Japanese had not informed the German and Italian governments – just as Hitler had not informed his allies before his pact with Stalin and his attack on the Soviet Union, and just as Mussolini had left the others in the dark about his attack on Greece. Since Japan had not been attacked by the United States, Germany and Italy were under no obligation to enter the war against the United States. The United States had repeatedly acted in provocative fashion by attacking German U-boats in neutral waters, for example, and it had already committed itself heavily to supporting the British and to some extent even the Soviet war effort, but Hitler had so far always refused to let himself be provoked because he wanted to keep the United States out of the war as long as possible. With the Japanese attack, however, he changed his assessment. Japan would keep the United States focused on the Pacific Ocean long enough for Germany to finish the campaign against the Soviet Union (he assumed that the setback in front of Moscow was only a temporary reversal and that the German army would win in the following summer). On 11 December 1941, Hitler therefore declared war on the United States. He did not consult with anybody in his government. After the bad news from the eastern front, he was thursting for a propaganda coup, and he believed that the entry of the United States into the war was inevitable in the long run.

The war that had initially been meant to destroy Poland and ultimately the Soviet Union without any western involvement now was truly a world war. In retrospect, it is clear that the German failure to complete the war against the Soviet Union was decisive. Despite unimaginable defeats and gigantic losses, the Soviet Union had preserved its huge industrial potential and was fanatically committed to fighting on. Nazi policies toward Soviet citizens left the Soviet Union little choice, as we will see. Hitler's generals after the war argued that the German failure resulted from poor strategic choices made by Hitler. In particular, the German army should have concentrated on the conquest of Moscow in September and October instead of going for Ukraine, which was Hitler's directive. In the end, the German army succeeded in taking much of Ukraine, including Kiev, but the attack on Moscow started too late to be successful. This argument does not seem entirely plausible, however. Going straight for Moscow would have had advantages, given that Moscow was a crucial transportation center. But we have to consider that the actual German attack into Ukraine destroyed enormous Soviet forces; had the German army prioritized Moscow in September it would have left huge Soviet forces in Ukraine unharmed and able to attack northward into the flank of the German thrust toward Moscow. The fact was that both, Ukraine and Moscow, represented important targets but that the German army could only deal with one and not the other. Hitler is also blamed for having maximized German losses during the Soviet counter-attack by issuing an inflexible no-withdrawal order. Most military experts agree, however, that the order was not wrong in principle; it just should have been applied with more flexibility. Still, nothing changes the fact that Germany, Italy, and Japan now faced a vastly superior enemy coalition. Hitler stubbornly ignored the numbers because he argued that Germany had prevailed for a long time against vastly superior enemies in the First World War. But Churchill had it right when he remarked right after Pearl Harbor that the Allies had now won the war. Granted, it would take time until the enormous American potential would be fully mobilized; Japan would meanwhile launch its own wildly successful attack against American, British, Dutch, and Australian forces in Southeast Asia and in the Pacific, and the German army would hold tight throughout the winter and still be able to advance in the summer of 1942. But the combined resources of the United States, the Soviet Union, and the British empire were vastly superior. The Allies were already much stronger than the Axis in December 1941, and their superiority would increase every month. To contemporary observers this was not yet obvious, but unlike the First World War, which was decided only in the late spring or early summer of 1918 following the failure of the last German western offensive, the Second World War was decided a long time before it ended. The road to final Axis defeat was extremely long and arduous, however.

With Germany and the Soviet Union fighting a most brutal and unforgiving war, it is time to look at developments in the Nazi-occupied area. The heavy emphasis on war preparation after 1936 had come at a cost to German consumers. It was therefore no accident that German soldiers invading France in 1940 in every free minute crowded the appealing cafés, bakeries, and butcher stores of France. Real coffee, taken for granted in France, had been expensive and rare in Germany, as had been many other basic food and consumer items. The economy and industry of Nazi Germany were already in high gear at the outbreak of the war. In a pathbreaking article, Richard Overy has debunked the still widespread notion that Germany only fully mobilized for war after the setback in front of Moscow (or even later). A look at labor statistics, industrial output, and investment shows that the German economy continued to be geared toward intensive war right through the period 1939–41. What really changed in 1942 – coinciding with the appointment of the very capable architect Albert Speer as armaments minister – was a boost in efficiency, leading to a great increase of production culminating in the summer of 1944 despite very heavy bombings throughout 1943 and 1944.[2] The German war machine had a huge demand for labor and raw materials, and meanwhile the German population had to be fed adequately in order to prevent disorder similar to the First World War. With the army demanding huge numbers of men to replace the very heavy losses it sustained even during the overall successful advance into the Soviet Union in 1941, labor was a neuralgic point in German war industry. Hitler, as we have seen, refused to introduce a labor draft for German women, and it is doubtful that this would have made much of a difference; Overy shows that a high proportion of German women were already working. Other sources of labor were the prisoners of war and foreign labor – both voluntary and forced. The Germans kept over one million French POWs after the armistice and used them in their war industry – in many cases even in the armaments sector, which was against the Geneva Convention on the Treatment of Prisoners of War (1929). Voluntary laborers from the occupied regions were hard to draft, and forced labor programs, although yielding high numbers, brought poorly motivated workers to Germany. Concentration camp inmates, of course, were also a labor force, but their treatment by the SS made them sick, weak, and underfed. The largest potential labor force was the Soviet prisoners of war. Germany captured over three million of them in 1941 during the huge encirclement battles behind the border and in Ukraine. This is a point, however, where Nazi racial policies revealed some of their most criminal sides and worked against the interests of the German war effort. The treatment of the Soviet POWs, particularly in the first year, was absolutely atrocious. Hitler planned to make eastern Europe into a German colonial space, reckoning with the decimation and enslavement of the local population. There were therefore no preparations for large numbers of Soviet prisoners even though the German war plan made the capture of many Soviet soldiers very likely. The prisoners were left largely unsupplied, had to sleep in the open, and received no medical attention. The result was an atrociously high mortality rate. Disease was rampant, and thousands of prisoners, having tried to dig earth huts with their bare hands, froze to death in the late fall and winter. German soldiers who took pity on them – and there were many such soldiers – were reprimanded and ultimately forbidden to slip food, cigarettes, and blankets to them. The German Army Command had, at the behest of Hitler and the SS, issued gruesome orders for Soviet prisoners of war. It was argued that the Soviet Union had not signed the Geneva Convention and therefore could not claim its protection for its soldiers, but this was a hollow claim because the Soviet Union and Germany were both bound to more general international law, which also outlawed the inhumane treatment of POWs. Every political commissar of the Red Army, basically party officials watching over the party loyalty of the commanders and soldiers, had to be shot by special SS units. Increasingly, the SS widened this order to shoot Jews, Communist party members, and many more people who fell into its hands – both as POWs and as civilians. Generals close to Nazi ideology never tired of pointing out that the German war against the Soviet Union was no normal war but rather a war of annihilation. Pity, chivalry, and decency toward enemy soldiers and civilians were not only misplaced but a crime against the German people. The enemy had to be rooted out. Other generals, however, ignored the orders on the treatment of Soviet POWs or applied them only if they had a watchful SS unit behind them.

The Second World War allowed the Nazi regime to carry out much of its huge criminal genetic engineering project, leading to the decimation of many peoples and leading, most of all, to the extermination of most of the Jewish people in Europe. All of these aspects were connected to the war, although usually not in a rational sense. The Nazi leadership was obsessed with the idea that Jews always undermine the states in which they live. Jews were considered to be particularly dangerous during times of war because they allegedly tended to wreck a country's war effort through defeatist rumors, sabotage, and revolutionary conspiracies and uprisings. The Nazi leaders carried with them the extremely distorted view that Germany had lost the First World War because democrats and socialists, led by Jews, had stabbed the victorious army in the back. They were dead serious about not letting this happen again in the Second World War. Propaganda Minister Joseph Goebbels, for example, sincerely believed that a ruthless "removal" of the Jews from the German sphere of domination was necessary for victory, and many highly educated men in the leadership of the SS shared this opinion. The deep racism of the Nazi regime, spread tirelessly through the well-organized channels of state propaganda, affected the war from the start. German troops in Poland committed atrocities against Polish civilians and soldiers, including Polish Jews. In the wake of the army, SS units carried out atrocities on a much larger scale. Interestingly, some German generals objected to these practices and complained to the High Command and to Hitler about them. German officers sometimes protected Poles and Jews and punished the perpetrators. In one case, as reported by historian Alexander Rossino, a general disarmed and sent home an entire police unit under SS command after Polish Jews had complained to him about their behavior.[3] Hitler, however, issued a general amnesty right after the Polish campaign. He set a clear sign that transgressions against civilians and enemy soldiers considered to be of lower racial value were not only tolerated but desired. In the West, in 1940, the army was under strict orders to respect civilians (of course, western Europeans were considered of higher racial stock than eastern Europeans) and it by and large complied – at least during the campaign. The army also had orders to respect the Geneva Convention in the war against the western powers. With some exceptions, the treatment of white prisoners was indeed legal but, as shown in my book *Hitler's African Victims*, German officers ordered the execution of thousands of captured Black soldiers from the French army on the basis of allegations that these soldiers were animals who mutilated German prisoners and fought with unfair, beastly methods. A propaganda campaign in the German press had induced German officers and soldiers to perceive the feared Black Africans in this light and made them believe that, even in the absence of a specific order on the treatment of Black prisoners, the executions were sanctioned. Again, it has to be stressed that many officers and soldiers did not fall for this distortion and insisted on applying the Geneva Convention to all prisoners regardless of skin color. Some German soldiers even helped French officers and doctors to prevent a massacre of Black soldiers.[4]

After the victory in the West, the question as to what should be done with the Jews became increasingly pressing for the Nazi regime. It is important to remember that this "Jewish Problem" was something the Nazis imposed on themselves through their hallucinatory hatred of Jews. Objectively, there was no Jewish problem in Europe. Jews were a peaceful and law-abiding part of the German and non-German population. They represented no threat. In eastern Europe, they were an important asset to the local economies and – not a negligible aspect in light of the drastic labor

Figure 8.1 Execution of hostages in Pancevo (Serbia), 22 April 1941. Photo by Gerhard Gronefeld. (Geisel-Hinrichtung in Pancevo, Inv.-Nr.: GG 388/16, © G. Gronefeld/DHM, Berlin)

While Nazi propaganda still presented the war as a series of glorious victories, this photo exemplifies the violence and fierce repression that German occupation brought particularly to the populations of eastern Europe and the Balkans. The murders of Jews and non-Jewish civilians (as in this picture) often were personal and face to face. Hitler declared a general amnesty for all crimes against civilians already after the defeat of Poland in 1939, and he kept encouraging utmost brutality of German army soldiers and SS men throughout the war.

shortage of Nazi Germany – an important labor force. However, Nazi ideology stated that the Jews had to be "removed." What exactly "removal" meant was not clear. Before the war, it had meant pushing the Jews out of leading positions in the public and later the private sector and establishing a segregation system. It had also meant, with increasing emphasis, pushing Jews to emigrate. Although violence against Jews was no anathema, as Crystal Night and the following repression prove, orderly and "legal" procedures to get the Jews out of Germany seemed preferable. With the conquest of Poland, the Jewish question assumed a new dimension for the Nazi leadership. The number of Polish Jews was far larger than the number of Jews in Germany and Austria, and many Polish Jews were still Orthodox and not assimilated into mainstream Polish society. These Jews became easily identifiable targets of aggression. As Nazi Germany annexed large parts of Poland, it pushed Jews out of these territories into the *Generalgouvernement* around Warsaw and forced Polish Jews into ghettos in the cities with important railroad connections. The Nazis also began sending Jews from Germany to the Polish ghettos. In some ways, the ghettoization of the Jews already constituted the beginning of genocide. Forcing large numbers of people to live closely together without adequate nutrition and sanitary conditions had to provoke epidemics and famine and to drastically increase mortality, and this is exactly what happened. Extermination was not yet the official policy, however. Hitler and the SS leadership contemplated for a while to expel all European Jews to Madagascar, a large island off the coast of East Africa. Madagascar was a French colony, and the defeat of France seemed to make it possible for Nazi Germany to impose this policy on France. The fact that Britain stayed in the war foiled this plan, however. It was inconceivable to transport millions of Jews to this far-away island as long as Britain was at war and in control of the seas. The Madagascar Plan should not be considered a more humane alternative to open mass murder, however. Sending millions of Europeans into a poor tropical island without any infrastructure to accommodate them was not very different from mass murder. Alternative SS plans proposed to expel the European Jews further east, to areas in Soviet-controlled Poland or deep in the Soviet Union. This was still the official plan in 1941, but military developments thwarted these plans, too. A huge resettlement could only be carried out after the Soviet Union was defeated, not while heavy fighting was still going on.

How and when the transition to mass murder happened is a hotly debated subject. Some historians have stressed that Hitler always wanted the destruction of the Jews and that it was only a question of time until he would be capable to carry out his highest ideological priority. The approach of these historians has been called "intentionalist" because it sees the Holocaust as an outcome of an overriding intention coming from the top of the Nazi hierarchy. Other historians have stressed that this "intention" was not so clear from the start (Hitler suggested and pursued various ways of solving the "Jewish Question") and that grass-roots initiative has to be foremost considered. These historians, whose approach has been called "functionalist," explain the Holocaust as an outcome of pressures and problems faced by the people on the ground, mostly the SS and police units guarding the overcrowded ghettos and in charge of the huge and chaotic resettlement programs in the east.[5] In recent years, most historians have no longer taken a clear intentionalist or functionalist position because they have recognized a great deal of give and take between people at the bottom and the highest leaders.[6] Hitler did not leave a written order, probably as a consequence of his bad experience with the euthanasia program, where he had signed an order to kill handicapped children and later adults that had provoked much unrest among the relatives of murdered patients and from the churches. It is beyond doubt, however, that Hitler was not only informed but, together with the SS leaders Heinrich Himmler and Reinhard Heydrich, one of the driving forces behind the mass murder of the Jews. On the other side, it is impossible to deny that officials at the bottom also played an important role as they were searching for solutions to the problems they faced by an often-impossible situation created by earlier Nazi policies. What appears decisive is that whenever officials at the bottom suggested a range of options to their superiors about what to do with the Jews, the superiors consistently encouraged the most murderous option. Some questions remain debated, however. Some historians argue that Hitler decided on extermination in the euphoria of an expected imminent victory against the Soviet Union, which would make it possible for him to realize his most radical racial plans. Other historians date the decision later – after the setback in front of Moscow and after Pearl Harbor, although the reasoning for Hitler's thinking in this case is not entirely clear. Some historians argue that it was looming defeat that induced Hitler at least to win his "war" against the Jews, but Hitler may not have fully appreciated that defeat was looming. The two interpretations have in common that they focus on a decision at the top of the Nazi hierarchy. Whether Hitler decided for all-out genocide in the late summer or only in December, one thing is clear: the mass murder of Jews was already happening. The special SS units charged with dealing with political commissars and restive civilians, the *Einsatzgruppen*, shot large numbers of male Jews (POWs and civilians) from the start of the campaign. During the summer months, they also began shooting women, and by late summer they shot every Jew they encountered. These relatively small units (each of the four *Einsatzgruppen* had about one thousand men) alone killed several hundred thousand Jews. Meanwhile, the situation in the *Generalgouvernement* and in many of the occupied Soviet territories was so critical that thousands of Jews were dying of starvation and disease. Their intolerable situation – ghettoization or forced resettlement – was no accident; it had been imposed on them by previous Nazi policies.

Extermination had not been foreign to Nazi practice before 1941, and sections of the SS had already gained experience in murdering large numbers of people. Already in October 1939, Hitler had given an order to kill the mentally and physically handicapped in the hospitals. He had justified this euthanasia program by pragmatic considerations – to provide hospital space for the wounded soldiers of the army and to ease the expected food shortage during the war – and ideological arguments (those incapable of a useful life for the people's community should be sterilized or given a "mercy death"). Over almost two years, doctors killed over 70,000 patients through lethal injections, deliberate starvation, and poison gas. Gas vans pumping the exhaust fumes or carbon monoxide into the hermetically sealed loading area filled with patients were also developed. Although the program was secret, rumors began spreading. Relatives of the murdered patients and residents near the clinics used as killing centers spread the word of what was happening. The churches protested. Facing growing popular opposition, the SS decided to cancel the program officially in August 1941. Secretly, however, it was pursued until the end of the war, killing thousands more (close to 150,000 overall).

The expertise gained by the euthanasia doctors was an asset to the SS as it began organizing the mass murder of Jews. The *Einsatzgruppen* alone could hardly carry it out alone, even though they were reinforced by auxiliary SS and police units, received help from army units, and were given gas vans. The SS was observing, moreover, that the daily massacres of people, including women and children, took a high toll on the murderers. The killing units received lavish amounts of alcohol to numb their senses and to forget, but many SS and policemen became so drunk that they could hardly function. SS leaders drafted auxiliary units among the local people in the Soviet Union and Poland, but they were also looking for a more cost-effective way of killing Jews. Gradually, the plan emerged to send all the Jews of Europe to special killing centers where the Jews and other racially "undesirables" would be gassed. A gas chamber was constructed in Auschwitz, a large concentration and labor camp in the south of Poland, and tested in December 1941 with several thousand Soviet POWs. The gas chambers were camouflaged as mass shower rooms – also an idea carried over from the euthanasia program. Soon, new death camps were built in Poland designed exclusively for mass murder; others, like Auschwitz, were attached to existing concentration and forced labor camps. In January 1942, Heydrich met with state officials in a villa in the Wannsee district of Berlin, where he proposed a huge plan for transporting all Jews from Nazi-occupied Europe to camps in Poland. The protocol of the Wannsee Conference does not mention that the "Final Solution of the Jewish Question" would mean mass murder, but some participants of the conference later admitted that this was clearly understood. The Wannsee Conference is often misrepresented as the meeting that "decided" on the Holocaust, but the decision to murder all Jews in the Nazi empire had been taken before, and the Wannsee Conference mostly dealt with the organizational details.

Over the following years, Nazi officials carried out the "Final Solution" with relentless determination. Often with the help of the local police or collaborators, the Gestapo and SS rounded up the Jews all over Nazi-occupied Europe. Jews from the ghettos in Poland and in the occupied Soviet Union were also sent to these camps, many of which were located close to large Jewish ghettos. The trip was already extremely cruel and often deadly, given that the Jews were cramped into cattle cars sometimes for several days and nights without food and sanitation. In those places where a labor camp existed alongside the death camp, a Nazi doctor would select the arriving prisoners and send the more able bodied people to the labor camp and the weaker people to the gas chambers. Units of prisoners under SS guards would operate the gas chambers, clear them after use, and burn the bodies in the crematoria. Those Jews selected for labor were hired out to local industry by the SS (for a rather high price), but most of them died of exhaustion, disease, or starvation within a few months. The prisoners were subjected to all imaginable forms of torture and terror; some Nazi doctors conducted cruel experiments with them. The camps operated until the Soviet armies appeared in late 1944 or early 1945, but the surviving inmates had to line up for so-called "death marches" during which the guards often randomly shot prisoners and ruthlessly executed everybody who could not keep up. Estimates on how many Jews were murdered vary between 4.8 and 5.8 million victims (this includes people killed in the ghettos, those shot by special units, and those gassed or worked to death in the camps). Many other people were also murdered in the camps or by the *Einsatzgruppen* and their auxiliaries, including thousands of gypsies, resisters, criminals, some homosexuals, communists, and many more. In order to hide the evidence, the SS destroyed much of the documentation toward the end of the war.

The Holocaust has inspired moral and historical questions that reach far beyond the scope of a concise history of Germany. Some of the most frequent questions are: how much did contemporaries know about the Holocaust? How responsible were ordinary Germans? Why did people participate in the Holocaust (not only Germans) and why did so few try to stop it? Information about aspects of the Holocaust was widespread. Although the mass killing program was kept secret in Germany, it was obvious for many Germans that Jews were being deported. What happened at the end of deportation was less obvious, however. The Nazis painted a rosy image of cities given to the Jews by Hitler, where they would live a comfortable life according to their desires and secluded from surrounding society – as they had been in Germany in the late 1930s. True, there were rumors of mass murder. True, many soldiers wrote letters from Russia and mentioned mass executions of Jews. But these rumors and bits of information did not add up to a complete image. Maybe there had been a shipment of criminals who were executed? Maybe the execution in Russia had affected partisans? The segregation of Jews from German society before 1939 had cut most ties between Jewish and non-Jewish Germans. The latter sadly did not care much about the former, particularly as the war grew increasingly worrying and painful after the ultimate failure of the 1941 offensive in the Soviet Union. Even to those people who had reliable knowledge, it was difficult to believe what actually happened. Why would a regime fighting a ferocious war commission hundreds of trains and thousands of men to assemble, transport, and kill millions of innocent people who did not represent any threat at all? For those Germans who suspected that terrible things were happening to the deported Jews, the "Hitler

Myth" often served to exculpate the dictator; they believed that Hitler could not possibly have allowed such atrocious things to happen and that the Holocaust must be a special policy of Himmler or others in opposition to Hitler. Finally, there were undoubtedly many Germans who, after years of Nazi propaganda, believed that Jews were the poisoners of peoples and approved of the most severe measures against them. This is not to say that the Holocaust reflected a widely shared desire for mass murder of the Jews and that the Germans were "willing executioners" of Hitler's genocidal directives. But we have to consider that there were millions of avid Nazis in Germany; many undoubtedly believed that the new regime was endowed with unlimited potential, and they embraced its values – fully conscious that Nazi values fundamentally contradicted traditional European norms and moral guidelines. Still, there is no reason to believe that a vast majority of Germans actively condoned the Holocaust and the regime's racist agenda. The regime tried to propagate this agenda but kept the atrocities secret for fear of raising opposition. Occasional resistance and small-scale help for Jews (such as assistance with hiding) existed in Germany as in all other countries occupied by the Germans. Memoirs of Jews from Nazi Germany usually draw a complex picture: some non-Jews gave little signs of solidarity and support, others showed hatred, still others (the majority) did not want to look. Outside Germany, knowledge of the Holocaust also spread. Whoever analyzes the wartime editions of the *New York Times* or *The Times* of London will find many articles about mass murders of Jews, but usually these articles were hidden between other news and not placed on the front pages. There was some disbelief because of the First World War atrocity stories, which had been exaggerated. Intelligence files opened in the 1990s show that the western governments had complete knowledge of what was happening through the British decodes of German army and *Einsatzgruppen* wireless communications as early as the summer of 1941. The British shared their insight with the United States government but not with Stalin, who very probably had complete knowledge from his own sources. The disbelief that many Germans may have felt when confronted with the possibility of the mass murder was also typical for the reaction of many people in the Allied countries – government officials as well as civilians. The mentality that there is an international responsibility to prevent and stop genocide is very much a product of the Holocaust, but it was not widespread in the early 1940s.

Who participated in the Holocaust and why so? The Holocaust was a complex undertaking involving thousands of men and women who shared different degrees of responsibility and participated for different reasons. The train engineer or switchboard operator in a random small town was involved just as was the *Einsatzgruppen* member, the camp guard, the person denouncing hidden Jews anywhere in Europe, the industrialist using forced labor from the camps, the SS commander, or the doctor conducting human experiments. No single explanation can account for the variety of situations and motives of those involved in the killings, although some interpretations carry further than others. The political philosopher Hannah Arendt pointed out that the Holocaust was implemented in a bureaucratic fashion and that the executors showed a technocratic mentality. Arendt claimed that the mass murderers were frighteningly "normal," that the administrators of death in many ways looked like "normal" administrators. They believed to be doing something necessary and correct and tried to do it as they were told.[7] Although it is probably safe to say that people who worked in the death machine had on average a stronger commitment to Nazi ideology than most others, they rarely had a totally different morality and system of beliefs. This observation was shared by the first incisive scholarly study of the Holocaust (by Raul Hilberg) and by the findings of American prison psychiatrists who analyzed captured Nazi leaders in 1945–6. Careerism often seems to have been a decisive motivation as well. Service in the SS became a fast route to higher status and income for soldiers, policemen, administrators, physicians, and experts in different professions. Young physicians could advance quickly if they signed up for human experiments in a death camp. They equated eugenic policies with scientific modernity and progress. The regime, moreover, tried to imbue the participants with the spirit of being an elite at the very top of scientific and political-social progress. On a more opportunistic note, service in the extermination machinery was infinitely less risky for able-bodied men than service in the army on the eastern front. The division of labor and the hierarchy of orders may have made it easier for people to carry out mass killings. One person could feel as only one wheel in a big machine: one was rounding up Jews without asking what would happen to them, another would run the deportation train, somebody else would open the doors of arriving trains, his (or her) comrade would lead the prisoners to the gas chamber after a physician had "examined" them, somebody else would close the doors of the gas chamber, another person would open the gas valves, and so on. Every single person could claim to have done only small things in the whole process. The decisive fact is that all of these people overrode whatever misgivings they may have had toward what they were doing. Not all people who carried out the Holocaust were radical anti-Semites, Jew-haters, or convinced pseudo-Darwinists. Some did what they were asked to do with the detachment of bureaucrats. Emotional detachment was considered a strength, as becomes clear in Himmler's famous speech to SS comrades in October 1943: "Most of you know what it means to see a hundred corpses lie side by side, or five hundred, or a thousand. To have stuck this out and – excepting cases of human weakness – to have remained decent persons [sic!], that is what has made us hard. In our history, this is an unwritten and never-to-be written page of glory." The Nazi stigmatization of Jews as enemies, drawing from a long history of European anti-Semitism, made the killings more plausible to the considerable number of men and women who were involved in the mechanics of genocide. Most perpetrators after the war claimed that they had acted on orders. This is almost never a valid excuse, however, and it often masks the fact that many participated with enthusiasm and conviction. But it is perhaps also a reflection of the way Himmler wanted the SS to work. On several occasions, Himmler told SS officers who felt haunted by what they were doing that they should take reassurance from the fact that he and Hitler had wisely decided what had to be done and bore the ultimate responsibility for it.

The "bureaucratic" view, argued by Arendt and others with persuasive originality, has found many followers. It elucidates important aspects of the Holocaust but is weak on others. The terror of the *Einsatzgruppen* and the killing of Jews on death marches in late 1944 and early 1945, for instance, were not bureaucratic but blatantly bloody and brutal. It is not always true that these people had to follow orders, since there often was a possibility, at least for a limited number of individuals, to refuse to kill without being punished. As long as a person refused to kill Jews because of what was perceived to be a personal weakness in Nazi parlance (inability to see suffering or revulsion to killing due to a Christian conscience, for example) no sanctions followed. It was taboo, however, to refuse to kill while saying that it was wrong, and it was also taboo to talk to colleagues and induce others to refuse to kill. People who did one of the latter were shot. It has to be considered, moreover, that the opportunity to recuse oneself from murder was only available to a few individuals. If too many people in a unit refused to kill, making the task impossible to accomplish, it would have constituted a mutiny – with brutal consequences.

There is no question that anti-Semitism had a very long tradition in Germany. But the same was true in other European countries. Anti-Semitism was hardly stronger or more vicious in Germany before 1914 than it was in Austria-Hungary, Russia, or France. It intensified during the First World War and the Weimar Republic, but it is notable that the Nazis did not win their big electoral victories through emphasizing anti-Semitism. Most historians see Germans after 1933 increasingly drawn to anti-Semitism because of the success of the Nazi regime and because of its propaganda, but they do not see anti-Semitism as the key factor in the stabilization of the regime. Interpretations focusing on the Holocaust as a specific product of German history tend to downplay or ignore European anti-Semitism. Even though Germans (including Austrians) were undoubtedly the "movers" and organizers of genocide in the Second World War, the participants in the Holocaust were not only Germans. Without cooperation of many people in the German-occupied territories the Holocaust would not have been possible on the same scale. Outside Germany, local citizens and officials helped to round up Jews for transportation to the death camps. The camps employed many local people, and the order police shooting commandos often included large non-German units. In Latvia, a volunteer corps of Latvians did most of the killing. There was an endemic shortage of German personnel in eastern Europe, so that many camps in the occupied Soviet Union were staffed by a majority of local people. In one camp, only the commander was German. If passive compliance or a conspiracy of silence apply to the Germans, they also mattered in the attitude of many French, Belgians, Croats, Slovenes, Poles, Ukrainians, and others. Significant resistance to the Nazi Jewish policies existed only in Denmark, Bulgaria, and – with less success – in the Netherlands. Moreover, it is important not to see the Holocaust as an isolated aspect of Nazi Germany. The four hundred thousand forced sterilizations (mostly non-Jewish Germans – men and women in about equal numbers), the elimination of the Polish elites, discriminatory marriage laws, policies to increase the German birth rate, and the mass murder of Jews and Soviet prisoners of war all belong to the most radical and brutal case of implemented racism that has ever occurred. The ultimate aim was to breed a new race of healthy and strong Aryan "supermen" and "superwomen" and to provide a vast living space for this new "master race," derived from the actual Germans of 1933–45 in central and eastern Europe.

Back to the war: Germany was fighting an increasingly frustrating battle on vastly overextended fronts from late 1941 on. Temporary successes were still possible, but defeats multiplied, and the Allied bombing campaign increasingly brought the horrors of war directly to German civilians. In June 1942, Hitler launched a second major offensive against the Soviet Union. The goal was to conquer the oil-producing regions in the South of the Soviet Union. Again, the German advance was successful at first, even though Soviet losses were not as high as the previous year because the Red Army became better at avoiding encirclement. Stalin, in yet another major and costly blunder, had insisted that the expected German offensive would be directed at Moscow, and the southern sector was therefore not well prepared. By September 1942, German armies had reached the Caucasus Mountains and began fighting their way into the city of Stalingrad on the Volga River. The conquest of Stalingrad, which never succeeded completely, proved to be a costly mistake – and this time it was entirely Hitler's responsibility. The Red Army concentrated large reserves and cut off the German Sixth Army in the city. A relief effort came within fifty kilometers of the city, but Hitler did not allow the Sixth Army to attempt a breakout, which was the only feasible way of saving it. Göring, as air marshal, made his usual hollow promises that the German air force would be able to fly enough supplies into the city to allow the Sixth Army to hold out through the winter. In early February 1943, however, the last German defenders of Stalingrad surrendered – against Hitler's explicit orders. Only 95,000 starving and exhausted soldiers of an army once over 200,000 strong remained. Of these, just over 5,000 survived the Soviet POW camps. The defeat in Stalingrad forced the German armies in the entire Caucasus region to withdraw to positions not far from where they had left in June 1942. Stalin pushed for another success in eastern Ukraine in early 1943, but the German army recovered and inflicted heavy losses on the Red Army. The next major attempt to turn the tide in the East was a strong German attack on the region of Kursk on the central section of the front in July 1943. This time, Stalin listened to his generals, and the German attack found a very well prepared defender. Both sides fought extremely hard and suffered heavy losses of men and tanks. The Germans, however, were much less capable of replacing these losses. After Kursk, the Red Army launched massive offensives in the fall of 1943 and again in June 1944, liberating Ukraine and, by July 1944, most of the prewar Soviet territory. In August 1944, the Red Army conquered Romania and cut off the last oil supply to Nazi Germany.

Defeat came in other theaters of the war as well. The German submarines, after having inflicted much damage on Allied shipping in the North Atlantic, were finally defeated in the period March to May 1943. That the British had deciphered the German naval code, discovering in the process that the Germans had broken the Allied convoy codes, proved very helpful. The Germans developed new types of submarines that were able to remain submerged much longer, but these ships arrived too late (April 1945) to make a difference. In North Africa, Rommel and his Italian allies were beaten in September 1942 at El Alamein, not far from Cairo. Rommel, who was notoriously undersupplied, had to withdraw into Libya. In November, the United States and Britain landed troops in Morocco and Algeria. The Germans and Italians made a last stand in Tunisia, but they had to surrender in May 1943. The Allies followed up on their victory in North Africa by landing in Sicily and then on the Italian mainland, prompting the fall of Mussolini and a request for an armistice from Italy. German troops then occupied the northern two-thirds of Italy and disarmed the Italian occupation troops in Yugoslavia, Albania, and Greece. On some occasions, the German army murdered disarmed Italian officers and soldiers. Most men from the old Italian army were brought to forced labor camps in Germany. Their treatment was extremely harsh, causing a high mortality rate. Few men chose to join the government of Mussolini, whom the Germans had liberated and installed as leader of an "Italian Social Republic." The Allied advance in Italy proved to be frustratingly slow, however. The territory favored the defending side, and the Germans held the front with relatively small forces. More promising was the Allied landing in Normandy on 6 June 1944. Although the Germans managed to contain the Allied bridgeheads for eight weeks, they were not strong enough to force the Allies back and lost most of their western reserves in the attempt. At the end of July, the Allies broke out of the Normandy pocket, and the Germans had to evacuate most of France within a few months. Allied armies came to the German border in the fall of 1944 but were hamstrung by supply problems for the time being. The war in the Pacific did not promise much relief for Nazi Germany, given that Japan also fought mostly a defensive war after decisive reversals in July 1942. The road to the Japanese defeat proved to be as hard and arduous as the road to the defeat of Nazi Germany, but there was no question in the second half of 1942 that the tide had turned.

On the defensive against on overwhelmingly superior coalition, the Nazi regime revealed again its most brutal and repressive side. The exploitation of all occupied countries proceeded with extreme rigor, causing huge famines in the occupied Soviet Union and in Greece. Millions of foreign workers were forced to work for the German war industry. Mounting resistance efforts were crushed and avenged with utmost brutality, be it in France, Yugoslavia, Greece, Poland, Slovakia or the Soviet Union. Only in Yugoslavia and some parts of the Soviet Union did the resistance establish some liberated areas. In Germany itself, the regime also became harsher and more repressive. Fixated on the fear of a new "stab in the back," the Nazi justice system prosecuted every sign of wavering determination with ruthlessness. Listening to foreign radio news or expressing doubt about a final Nazi victory brought death sentences for thousands of Germans. In the army, military judges passed around 25,000 death sentences for soldiers who had criticized the Nazi regime, doubted the final victory, or withdrawn in hopeless positions. The vast majority of these death sentences were carried out (18,000–22,000). By comparison, only 393 death sentences had been carried out in Germany in the entire period 1907–32 (which includes the First World War!). The statistics of Germany's military judges under the Nazis also dwarf the numbers for the American and British armed forces, which carried out 146 and 40 death sentences respectively during the entire Second World War. German propaganda suggested that the reversals were not decisive and that Germany was developing new "revenge weapons" that would turn the tide of the war again. Hitler personally believed that the enemy coalition was unstable and would fall apart if he could deal one of the two sides a major blow. He was correct in analyzing the profound differences between the Soviet Union and the democratic powers, but he did not acknowledge that it was he himself who kept this coalition together. It would not fall apart until Nazi Germany had surrendered unconditionally and Hitler was dead. Japan encouraged Hitler to seek an understanding with the Soviet Union in order to concentrate all resources on fighting the democratic powers, but Hitler's ideological fanaticism by now had completely superseded his pragmatic skills. He might have agreed to a peace with the United States and Britain, but a truce with the Soviet Union, which he had stigmatized as a sub-human, deadly enemy, would have contradicted what he saw as the central mission of his life and of the German people. Stalin – despite the bitterness of the war – seems to have been inclined to consider some deal with Germany, but it would have been very difficult for him to make plausible to his country a truce with an enemy who had brought devastation and mass murder upon Russia. With over twenty million war dead (including the civilian population) the Soviet Union eventually suffered the heaviest losses in the war. A compromise peace was shunned by the Allies at a conference in Casablanca in January 1943, where they committed themselves to fighting until Germany surrendered unconditionally.

The terror machine of the Gestapo as well as the regime's still considerable reserves of popularity (particularly Hitler's own popularity) left little latitude for opposition. To many people, there appeared to be no alternative to the Nazi regime except foreign domination by the Soviet Union, which was seen by most as the worst possible fate. Resistance in the Third Reich nevertheless existed at all times. It assumed different shapes and often mixed with partial or temporary cooperation. There was a gliding scale from cooperation and consent to indifference, disagreement, and active, determined opposition. Resistance during the war carried the connotation of betrayal (the person who resisted allegedly stabbed the German army in the back and opened the gates for murderous Bolshevists); unlike in the German-occupied countries, resisters in Germany could not claim to fight a war of liberation from foreign oppression, and they could not offer a governmental alternative with broad popular support. Nevertheless, the total coherence of the *Volksgemeinschaft* that the regime claimed was fiction. Although Hitler personally was very popular, attitudes of Germans toward the system and its policies covered a wide range. Many people did not hate the regime enough to be willing to risk their lives (and usually the lives of their family members) in fighting it. But keeping one's children out of the Hitler Youth or its equivalent for girls was an act of resistance in a state that demanded, and claimed to possess, total loyalty. Thousands of Germans lost their lives by opposing the regime. Communist underground resistance operated under terribly difficult conditions; its repression by the Gestapo led to 20,000 deaths; thousands of other Germans were also killed or put into concentration camps for acts of defiance such as hiding a Jew, listening to a foreign radio station, doubting that Germany would win the war, cracking a joke on the regime, or writing an anti-Nazi phrase on the wall of a public restroom. Some individuals also took more spectacular action: Georg Elser, a south German artisan, nearly killed Hitler in Munich in November 1939 with a self-made bomb; the Catholic priest Bernhard Lichtenberg prayed for the Jews in his church in Berlin until he was deported to a death camp; the general Henning von Treskow placed a bomb in Hitler's plane when the dictator flew back to Berlin after a visit to the eastern front in March 1943 (the bomb did not explode); Hans and Sophie Scholl, with fellow students and one professor, formed a resistance group at the University of Munich, the White Rose, and distributed anti-Nazi leaflets. The group was caught in February 1943, and its members were executed by guillotine. Several conspiratorial circles were formed in the army and within the churches. The oppositional army circles were the most powerful centers of resistance since they had weapons and direct access to Hitler. Some resistance circles included such diverse groups as military officers, conservative politicians, Social Democrats, and clergy. Some planned to remove Hitler and the Nazis from power already before the war, but they postponed their plans when Hitler became extremely popular after the victory over France and when the war assumed existential proportions, in which every form of resistance would have been considered as betrayal by most Germans. When some officers and civilians nevertheless took decisive action in July 1944, they hoped at least to state a heroic example documenting "another" Germany than the one claimed by the Nazis. After several failed attempts, Count Claus Schenk Graf von Stauffenberg, a high officer with direct access to Hitler, managed to place a bomb next to the dictator on 20 July 1944. But due to an unfortunate series of circumstances Hitler survived with only minor injuries. The putsch plan that the resisters had prepared failed quickly when the survival of the dictator, to whom the whole army had sworn an oath of allegiance, became known. Stauffenberg and his fellow conspirators were executed in the evening of the same day, and a special court run by the Gestapo condemned to death 5,000 people who had been involved in the plot. Some resisters committed suicide, such as Field Marshal Rommel. The revenge of the Nazi regime lasted until its final days: some of the executions were carried out as late as April 1945, days before the ultimate breakdown of the Third

Reich. Unfortunately, many Germans did not understand what had happened on 20 July. Nazi propaganda depicted the plot as a conspiracy of ambitious and selfish aristocratic officers, and many Germans believed this, particularly since Hitler was still rather popular personally. It is true that the resistance had many faces, not all of them democratic. Some resisters were Stalinists. Some resisters, particularly in the army, were not interested in democracy and hoped above all to avert the total defeat toward which Hitler was steering the country. Others, however, were motivated by the outrage over the racial crimes of the regime. Whatever their motivation, all resisters deserve recognition. They all shared the correct assessment that the regime they were fighting represented unprecedented evil.

The Nazi regime remained in total control until almost the end. Hitler himself had been extremely successful at eroding all established structures of government, making himself the supreme arbiter of German politics and warfare. The cabinet existed only pro forma. Hitler had rarely consulted it before the war, and it never met with him during the war. Underneath Hitler, whose personal secretary, Martin Bormann, wielded much power, a fierce rivalry of government and party agencies took place that led to much overlap and waste of resources. Hitler, in his crude Darwinist mindset, welcomed this scenario. He benefited from the competitive dynamics beneath him because he became the supreme arbiter, while competing agencies and officials were working hard to read his will and gain his favor (including the funding and power that came as a reward). The most successful of all competing groups was the SS under Himmler. It consistently proved most successful at reading Hitler's will and consequently became the most powerful organization in Germany. Already in the 1930s, the SS had taken over the complete police apparatus of Nazi Germany. During the Second World War, it became a huge economic empire as well through seizing foreign and Jewish-owned enterprises and by exploiting the millions of forced laborers under its control (these laborers were "rented out" to industry by the SS for high rates, which the SS pocketed and did not use to improve the living conditions of the workers). The SS even had its own army, the Waffen-SS. Part elite unit, part ideologically most dedicated corps, the Waffen-SS got the best materiel and was sent to many critical places. The Waffen-SS also committed some of the most heinous war crimes, such as the mass murder of the citizens of Oradour, a French village near which a resistance group had launched an assault. The army itself was initially an independent institution in Nazi Germany, but it was increasingly controlled by people devoted personally to Hitler and by Hitler himself who, despite having no training and being essentially an amateur strategist, took an ever larger role in directing military affairs. The Nazi Party itself for many years did not play a foremost role, particularly after its organizational head, Rudolf Hess, flew to Britain in May 1941 in order to convince Britain to support Germany in its crusade against communism. Toward the end of the war, however, the party expanded its role, particularly as relief efforts for displaced Germans after bombings and after the Soviet invasion of East Germany provided an important field for social aid.

The last two years of the war brought a rapidly unfolding inferno to Germany. Already in 1943, the Allied bombing campaign had devastated some German cities, such as Hamburg and Cologne. The power of the bombs often was so overwhelming that firestorms developed, sucking all air from people's lungs and often sucking people into the flames. The German air force was unable to halt the bombing offensive, although it was temporarily able to inflict high losses on Allied fleets. The targeting of civilians was not accidental but the essence of the campaign. British air force leaders hoped that massive nighttime attacks on residential areas would "dehouse" the German working class and lead to an uprising. This idea was based on a belief that German civilians had weaker moral fiber than British civilians and would not be able to stand a bombing campaign, and it reflected the memory of the German revolution of 1918, which also haunted the Nazi leaders. The American air force believed that targeted attacks against bottlenecks of German war production were more effective, but such attacks had to be flown during daylight and were more costly to the bombing fleet than indiscriminate night-time bombing. By 1944, however, the distinction between both air forces had blurred, and German resistance had largely been broken. Defense against the bombings was not a high priority on Hitler's list in any case. He insisted that the world's first jet fighter, developed by the Messerschmitt works (the ME 262), be used as a light bomber rather than as a fighter plane, in which role it would have given the German air force a better chance at defense. Moreover, Hitler invested much in the development of "revenge weapons," mostly missiles. These weapons were deployed after long delays caused in part by targeted bombing in the middle of 1944, and they caused damage particularly to London and Antwerp, but they were not able to change the tide of war.

In 1944–5 the Allied bombing campaign against German cities reached its climax. In 1944, 650,000 tons of explosives fell on Germany (up from 120,000 in the previous year) and in the few months of fighting in 1945 the bombing still reached 500,000 tons (more than twice the intensity of 1944). The most famous bombing attack happened in Dresden in February 1945. It is still unclear how many people were killed in that one night because the city was filled with thousands of refugees from the east of Germany. The lowest figures estimate approximately 20,000 dead. By the end of the war, Berlin was a field of ruins, as were nearly all other large and mid-sized cities. Over 600,000 German civilians perished due to the bombings, mostly women, children, and the elderly. Some POWs and concentration camp inmates were killed as well. A crucial military impact was not made by the bombing of cities but rather by a targeted and sustained bombing campaign against the German synthetic fuel industry in the summer of 1944. This series of attacks dealt a blow to a crucial sector of the German war industry from which it could not recover. That the attacks on cities such as Dresden and Freiburg in late 1944 and early 1945 still had a plausible strategic sense is questionable. In Britain, some clergymen and politicians criticized the bombing campaign on moral grounds. True, Nazi Germany had bombed British cities, although doing much less damage, and

Hitler would have relished it had his air force achieved the destructive impact of the Allied bomber fleets, which was around ten times higher than German bombing at its most intense. But the Allied bombing campaign killed Germans and non-Germans indiscriminately; it did not distinguish between Nazis and resisters, victims, or innocent civilians.

The other major threat to German civilians came from the east. The Russians took their bloody revenge for German war crimes when they occupied German territories in late 1944 and in 1945. Huge numbers of civilians were killed, and rape by Russian soldiers became a common experience of many German women. The fear of the Russians triggered a wave of German refugees from the east – millions of desperate people crowding the destroyed cities and falling prey to bombings, as in Dresden, or being attacked by the many low-flying American and British fighter planes, which shot at civilians on the roads and fields. The evacuation of civilians from the east was haphazard because the Nazi officials refused to take adequate preparations (which would have been tantamount to admitting defeat – a crime in Nazi Germany). The worst shipping catastrophe of all time occurred when the passenger ship *Wilhelm Gustloff,* overloaded with refugees, mostly women and children, was torpedoed by a Soviet submarine on 30 January 1945. Approximately 8,000 people perished in the icy Baltic Sea that night.

Hitler pursued the war with ruthless determination, drafting older and very young Germans into the army (he even agreed to the creation of a women's army, which never became operative, however). In December 1944, he ordered an offensive in the West, the Ardennes Offensive (called the Battle of the Bulge). The Germans broke through in the same area in which the Manstein Plan had been successful four years and seven months earlier, but after a few days the inevitable happened: the German tanks ran out of fuel. Instead of driving the Allies back into the sea, as Hitler had hoped, the offensive wasted some of Germany's last resources. American, British, and Free French troops were able to counter-attack in early 1945 and to penetrate the outnumbered German border defenses. Meanwhile, the Russians had started their last giant offensive in the East. They swept through most of Hungary and eastern Germany and threatened Vienna and Berlin. In March of 1945, Hitler gave orders for a destruction of all that was left of Germany (the so-called "Nero order"). He wanted his people either to win or, as looked increasingly likely, to vanish with him, after it had failed to live up to his once-in-a-millennium mission. During the agony of Nazi Germany, open uprisings and mutinies happened rarely, but many Germans hindered the execution of Hitler's orders. Towns and villages in the West and South surrendered peacefully to the Allies – against orders. There were instances of passive resistance both among troops and civilians, but there were also dedicated Nazis fighting to the last and draconically punishing everybody who did not. In April, the Soviets were closing in on Berlin. Hitler Youth, essentially schoolboys, were trained for last-ditch resistance and for an underground struggle in areas of Germany occupied by the Allies. But Hitler at this time was commanding armies that existed only on paper. Given his propensity to erupt into violent fits of rage following bad news and to dismiss even his best generals if they told him the truth, his entourage had carefully sealed him off from reality. Nevertheless, the Soviet shells falling on his chancellery above his bunker could not be ignored. After his last hope for a break in the enemy coalition had evaporated with President Roosevelt's death (completely distant from reality, Hitler imagined that the United States would now switch sides and help Germany defeat the Soviet Union), he took his life in the bunker on 30 April 1945. His successor, Grand Admiral Karl Dönitz, agreed to unconditional surrender on 8 May. American and Soviet troops had already met in central Germany by that time. The Germans lived in a field of ruins, threatened by starvation, loaded with an atrocious collective guilt, and totally uncertain about the future. For many Germans soldiers, the war was not yet over. In the days following the surrender, the Allied troops took hundreds of thousands of German soldiers as prisoners of war. The Soviets deported them to forced labor camps, and the US army let them starve for a while on huge fields along the Rhine River. Czechoslovak, Polish, and Yugoslav civilians took a bloody revenge on ethnic Germans in the east. Millions of displaced persons – liberated POWs, voluntary laborers, forced laborers, concentration camp inmates – crowded the streets of war torn Germany, sometimes taking revenge on guards, but mostly in desperate search of food and shelter. They were joined by a stream of German refugees from eastern Europe that continued until 1948, as Poland, Czechoslovakia, and Yugoslavia expelled millions of Germans. There was no German state and no German government. Bismarck's state, founded in the wake of military victory, had been buried in the ruins of a total defeat following a total and unprecedentedly ruthless war.

Epilogue

Germans had a difficult way to recovery after 1945. The first experiences on this path were nearly total destruction, starvation, a depressing uncertainty, and a nightmare of guilt for the crimes of the Nazi era. The Nazi regime, obsessed with the trauma of November 1918, had made sure that Germans did not suffer famines during the war – at the expense of exploiting all other peoples in Nazi-occupied Europe. But the supply network broke down once the victors arrived, and the first three years following the war brought widespread famines. Many people were living in the cellars of destroyed houses. Over one-quarter of all houses were destroyed, in most cities over half of them. The centers of most towns were almost totally burned. Millions of Germans had become refugees. Most people were hungry and inadequately dressed. Diseases and epidemics were rampant. Poverty was grim for several years (and much longer for Germans in the Soviet sector). For a few potatoes or cigarettes one could get a grand piano or whatever family treasure had survived the war. Observers found that dogs and cats had almost completely vanished from the ghost cities; either starving people had eaten them or there had been no food left to feed them. The hardships of everyday life were compounded by insecurity over missing relatives or grief over their death. Germany lost over seven million people in the war (including civilians). Millions of German soldiers remained in foreign prisoner of war camps, and many died in Siberia long after the war. The breakdown of communications in Germany in 1945 and the reluctance of the Soviet Union to hand out information about the prisoners in their camps created enormous insecurity. Women often waited for their missing husbands for many years, never knowing whether they had been widows all the time or whether the husband would show up one day. Some returning soldiers found their wives married to someone else because they had been believed dead. Industrial production was down to one fifth of the prewar level. Germans were hated everywhere and treated as pariahs once the Nazi atrocities finally occupied center stage in newspaper reporting in the spring and summer of 1945. Citizens of towns near concentration camps were forced by the victor armies to visit the camps full of corpses. Many broke out in tears when they saw the traces of the atrocious crimes that had happened not far from their homes. (These were not the worst camps, of course; the death camps had all been in Poland.) In the east of Germany and the Sudetenland, German citizens now experienced ethnic resettlement policies themselves as they were expelled, often with the use of vengeful violence. The northern half of East Prussia was annexed by the Soviet Union, whereas the southern part as well as all German areas east of the Oder and Neisse rivers (a line about 50 miles east of Berlin) became Polish. In a vast "ethnic cleansing" program, ten to twelve million Germans were expelled from these territories. The rest of Germany was divided into four occupation zones, a French one in the Southwest, a British one in the North, and an American one in the West and Southeast. The Soviet Union occupied the centerpiece of former Germany (Saxony, Thuringia, Mecklenburg, western Pomerania, and the lands around Berlin). Berlin and Vienna were divided into four zones; the Soviets granted the western powers passage rights to Berlin (which they tried to revoke during the Blockade in 1948–49). Austria was divided as well, but the occupation was terminated in 1955 in exchange for a guarantee of Austrian neutrality. Unlike in 1918, the German defeat in 1945 was total. There was no German state or government left. Only gradually did some local self-administration emerge. The defeat of National Socialism was also total. Already in the last months of the war, popular belief in the ultimate victory and loyalty to the system had quickly and almost totally waned. There was no major Nazi insurgency.

Map 4 Germany in 1945.

Apart from dividing Germany into zones of interest, the victors did not have long-term plans for Germany and agreed only on a few things. The Soviets envisioned some form of communist state and hoped to include all of Germany in it. The western allies soon felt threatened by the Soviet Union, which repressed all democratic movements and established communist governments in all countries occupied by its troops. For Poland, whose eastern territories the Soviet Union annexed (giving Poland large German lands as a 'reimbursement'), Soviet repression often followed right after German repression had ended. The western powers gradually reconciled themselves to building up a capitalist German state out of the three western zones, which conveniently included the Ruhr district, Germany's former industrial power-house. All victor powers agreed, however, that foreign occupation of Germany should be temporary. They also did not initially intend to split the country and tried to administer what was left of Germany together. They formed the Allied Control Council in June 1945 as the supreme political authority for all of Germany (except the eastern parts of Germany, which were already annexed by Poland and the Soviet Union). But this Council did not make much headway because every member had a veto right, which the French and Russians used frequently (of the western victors the French were by far the most resentful against Germans in the first postwar years).

In July 1945 the leaders of the victor powers met for the Potsdam Conference. They could not agree on final boundaries for Germany and decided that a peace treaty sometime in the future would have to resolve this issue. The victors decided to demilitarize Germany, to introduce democratic self-government, to decentralize the country (which did not mean to divide it, however), to punish former Nazis, and to dissolve the big industrial cartels. (These decisions were called the five Ds: demilitarization, democratization, decentralization, denazification, and decart-elization). They also agreed that the Germans' living standard should remain lower than that of their neighbors. The victors further granted each other the right to take reparations in form of machines and industrial equipment. While the West – after an initial phase of taking away or blowing up industrial installations – tried to help its 'own' part of Germany, the Russians seized almost all of the industry and railroads left in the eastern sector. East Germany, as the Soviet occupation zone came to be called later, therefore had a much more painful and difficult start into the postwar period than did the West; the brutality of the Red Army during the invasion of Germany and the Soviet exploitation following the war naturally made it extremely difficult for the German Communist leaders installed by Stalin to gain popularity. This, along with the repression soon prevalent in the Soviet-occupied sector, explains the stream of refugees from the East to the West, which did not end before East Germany built a deadly wall along its border with West Germany and finally closed the last loophole, Berlin, in 1961. The planned peace conference of the victors never met (only the talks of the two German governments with the four victor powers in 1989–90 finally led to a definitive border agreement) because tensions became too strong soon after

Potsdam. The Soviets began restricting mobility between the two parts of Berlin and between East and West Germany (it remained possible to flee, however, until 1961) and made sure that Communists got elected to the local self-administration offices in their sector. Electoral fraud and intimidation started immediately.

Denazification led to a series of war crimes trials in Nürnberg in 1946–8, in the course of which Göring and a few other surviving Nazi leaders received death sentences. Rudolf Hess, Hitler's proxy until 1941, and Albert Speer, the armaments minister, received long prison sentences. But the prosecution of other former Nazis in many cases did not make much headway. Hoping to tie many former Nazi elites to a democratic West German state, the Allies and later the German justice apparatus failed to prosecute and punish many of the less famous war criminals (for example the members of the *Einsatzgruppen*, the lawyers who had sent many people to their death because of their listening to foreign radio stations or mentioning their doubts about final victory, the death camp guards, and many, many more). The problem was that in Germany whole professional groups that were needed after 1945 were infested with Nazi guilt, such as the lawyers, policemen, doctors, businessmen, and administrators. They just continued their former professions and had little interest in shaking up the depressing past. The Soviet Union may have applied the strictest regime against ex-Nazis at first, but soon it allowed former Nazis to change their identities if they became eager Communists. In the West, many trials of severe Nazi criminals led to acquittal because the witness evidence was not considered reliable enough or because the accused claimed to have followed orders or existing Nazi law. To challenge these people – outside the courtroom – became the task of a new generation of Germans, of those who were born in the war or shortly thereafter.

For the first few years after 1945, the occupying powers often determined the policies in their own sectors without too much consideration for what the others did. France wanted Germany weakened as much as possible and hoped to separate the Ruhr and Saar districts from Germany. The French, as in 1919, received extra powers in the Saar district with its coalmines, but their more expansive aims failed, partly because France, as a country first defeated by Germany and then liberated by the western allies, had a weaker position now than in 1918. The Soviet Union was frustrated by having received the predominantly agrarian parts of Germany in the East. Most of the heaviest fighting had occurred on Soviet territory, and the retreating Soviet and later German forces had both pursued a scorched earth policy. The Soviet Union therefore had a keen interest in reparations drawn from all sectors of occupied Germany (mostly from the still potentially powerful Ruhr district). Having received the less industrialized part of Germany, the Soviets were least interested in partition. They hoped to hold on to their parts of Germany and exploit the others as much as possible.

Britain and the United States faced a particular dilemma: their sectors were relatively industrialized but therefore heavily dependent upon food imports. These sectors were also becoming vastly overpopulated because the millions of Germans driven away from their homes in the East and in the Sudetenland rarely liked to stay under Soviet rule. The food shortage in the western sectors became dramatic, and the British and Americans brought in as much food for the Germans under their occupation as they could. This helped to relieve the famines, though not the shortages, but it was questionable whether American and British taxpayers would agree to feed the Germans for an extended period. The Americans and the British therefore abandoned their policy of demolishing the remainders of German factories. Instead they decided to let German industry rebuild on the spot so that it could produce enough to fund the much needed food imports. This led them to coordinate their policies between their zones; after a year the French decided to join this policy. The Marshal Plan, an American reconstruction program, helped to rebuild the economies of Germany's three western sectors and the other countries of Western Europe after 1948. With the currency reform in the western sectors in 1948, life became better. West Germany was constituted as a state in 1949 (the Federal Republic of Germany), and the Soviets immediately followed by proclaiming their own sector a new German state too (the German Democratic Republic). The economic miracle of the early 1950s created unprecedented wealth in the West, since October 1949 under the direction of a democratic government in Bonn. Recovery in the East occurred at a slower pace and always remained on a much lower level.

The Germans' attitude toward their past has been ambivalent, particularly during the first twenty years after the end of the Third Reich, when the sparkling facade of the economic miracle helped to cover the depressing past in West Germany. On the one hand, there could be no doubt that Nazism was thoroughly discredited. Hardly anybody stood up for Nazi ideology or Hitler any more. Neo-Nazis have existed all along since 1945, but they never formed more than a loud and violent minority at the lunatic fringe of West German politics. On the other hand, the first generation of Germans often felt very defensive toward their role in the Nazi past. Not that most people would have defended Hitler and the NSDAP, but they generally tried to dissociate themselves from the regime and resented conjuring up a dark, guilt-ridden past. Almost everybody claimed either not to have played a significant role in the Third Reich or not to have had a choice. This gave rise to various seduction theories, which put most of the blame on the top representatives of the Nazi regime. The common (and usually hollow) excuse for the perpetrators was: "I had to follow orders." This does not mean, however, that West Germans repressed their past. The first West German government under Chancellor Konrad Adenauer (a former Center Party member and major of Cologne), acknowledged German responsibility for the racial crimes of the Third Reich. The West German government paid indemnifications to the survivors of the Holocaust (but almost exclusively to Jewish survivors; the Gypsies never got anything). An institute for contemporary history (Institut für Zeitgeschichte) was founded by the West German government in Munich, and access to documents from the recent past became almost free, which was a novelty as most official documents become available only after thirty to fifty years. The historical research conducted by the Munich institute and by German universities produced much critical insight and debate, but for the population at large the guilt feeling about the Third Reich in the 1950s often expressed itself in a denial of guilt (not usually in a denial of the basic facts, however: Holocaust deniers have always been rather rare). Only a new generation, the young people of the 1960s, aggressively challenged the comfortable myths of many members of the older generation. A new, more public, critical, and thorough exploration of the past started around 1960. One reason the older generation may have been defensive about the past was that they felt punished. Unlike most of the young of the 1960s, they had experienced the war, the bombings, the violence of the invading Russians, the misery of the postwar years, and – not least of all – the defeat of their country, which led to a loss of territory and status that makes the Treaty of Versailles look extremely generous. Many Germans of the generations who experienced the horrors of the last war years and the misery of the postwar period (which for most people did not end before 1948 or 1949) felt that they had suffered retribution for many crimes committed in their name and by their people. Initially, surviving the depressing postwar present became the highest priority. Few people wanted to "work through" the past as long as the present required all of their energy. Later, they felt pride in having rebuilt their country (or their countries, since this feeling was shared in the East and West) and preferred to look to the future rather than to the past. In East Germany, the communist regime soon established a comfortable solution to the guilt problem by stressing that Communists had been victims of Nazism, too. Although this was undeniable, this explanation exculpated many Germans who had become Communists only after 1945, and it gave the East German government a way out of confronting the *German* responsibility for Nazism. To the East German Communists, Nazism was the most radical form of capitalism. Capitalism persisted in West Germany, and therefore West Germany should shoulder the burden of Nazism alone.

After reunification in 1990, attacks by right-wing groups on foreigners, desecration of Jewish cemeteries, and neo-Nazi meetings have been alarming phenomena (though not confined to Germany), but it would be wrong to conjure up the specter of the last Weimar years. Anti-democrats both on the left and right form small minorities, and the democratic government is securely entrenched in the consciousness of by far the largest number of Germans. High unemployment and social insecurity are serious problems today, but they hit a wealthy welfare state with an almost unparalleled social security net that has its origins in the agitation of the SPD and in Bismarck's social security laws more than a century ago. Reunited Germany is continuing the tradition of the stable democracy that formerly ruled West Germany alone. The Russian, British, French, and American occupation troops left in peace and friendship during the 1990s.

Today, the condemnation of the Nazi period and the admission of some form of collective responsibility (however defined) are widely accepted in Germany. Germans have made a clear break with the times before 1945, and the hesitance of the older generation to confront the Nazi past has been overcome by their children. There is nowadays a very strong willingness to accept the most criminal sides of the Nazi past across all generations. When I tried to visit an exhibit on the crimes of the German army in Bielefeld in 2002, I was unable to get in because the line was so long that it would have taken over an hour to get a ticket. When I published an article in the German weekly newspaper *Die Zeit* on my research on German crimes against Black French soldiers in January 2006, other German newspapers reported about my findings in a strong self-accusatory mode, often throwing out the nuances I had made in the original article, which put the behavior of German soldiers in a less grim light. Members of the radical right, however, took offense; bloggers on neo-Nazi websites with names such as 'Blond Poison' and a radical right-wing newspaper claimed that I was paid by the CIA and had made up everything. Recently, German scholars and writers have taken a greater interest in the suffering of German civilians in the last years of the war. This is a touchy issue because it cannot be addressed without acknowledging the vast German crimes that preceded this suffering and continued up to the end of the war. It is a challenge for future historians to address both, German crimes and German suffering, in a balanced way, and it is a challenge for today's Germans to find a nuanced German identity that fully acknowledges the Nazi past but does not let the twelve worst years of German history completely overshadow the other thousand years of German history.

Notes

1 Introduction: A Plea for Understanding History in its Openness

1. This is the argument of Eugen Weber, *Peasants into Frenchmen: The Modernization of Rural France, 1870–1914*. Stanford: Stanford University Press, 1976.
2. For the articulation of Wehler's argument, see Hans Ulrich Wehler, *The German Empire, 1871–1918*. Translated by Kim Traynor. Leamington Spa: Berg Publishers, 1985.
3. See Manfred Rauh, *Die Parlamentarisierung des Deutschen Reiches*. Düsseldorf: Droste, 1977. Also Geoff Eley and David Blackbourn, *The Peculiarities of German History*. Oxford: Oxford University Press, 1984.
4. Arno J. Mayer, *The Persistence of the Old Regime: Europe to the Great War*. New York: Pantheon, 1981.
5. Friedrich Meinecke, "The Old and the New Germany," in Anton Kaes, Martin Jay, and Edward Dimendberg (eds), *The Weimar Republic Sourcebook*. Berkeley: University of California Press, 1994, p. 88.

2 German Unification

1. Robert Darnton, *The Great Cat Massacre and Other Episodes in French Cultural History*. New York: Basic Books, 1984.
2. For a powerful account of this campaign by one of the few survivors, see Jakob Walter, *The Diary of A Napoleonic Footsoldier*. New York: Penguin, 1991.

3 Germany under Bismarck

1. Hans-Ulrich Wehler, *Deutsche Gesellschaftsgeschichte*. Vol. 3. Munich: C. H. Beck, 1995, pp. 849–54.
2. The standard works on this issue are Celia Applegate, *A Nation of Provincials: The German Idea of Heimat*. Berkeley: Stanford University Press, 1990, and Alon Confino, *The Nation as A Local Metaphor: Württemberg, Imperial Germany, and National Memory, 1871–1918*. Chapel Hill and London: University of North Carolina Press, 1997.
3. Joachim Remak, "The Healthy Invalid: How Doomed the Habsburg Empire?" *The Journal of Modern History* 41 (2) (1969): 127–43.

4. Gale Stokes, *Three Eras of Political Change in Eastern Europe*. New York and Oxford: Oxford University Press, 1997.
5. Wehler, *Deutsche Gesellschaftsgeschichte*. Vol. 3, pp. 901–2.
6. Wehler, *Deutsche Gesellschaftsgeschichte*. Vol. 3, pp. 904–5.
7. See www.ssa.gov/history/ottob.html. Accessed 15 May 2008.
8. Edgar Feuchtwanger, *Bismarck*. London and New York: Routledge, 2002, pp. 193–4.
9. David G. Williamson, *Germany Since 1815: A Nation Forged and Renewed*. Houndmills and New York: Palgrave Macmillan, 2005, pp. 135–6.

4 Wilhelmine Germany

1. Jonathan Sperber, *The Kaiser's Voters: Electors and Elections in Imperial Germany*. Cambridge: Cambridge University Press, 1997.
2. Thomas Nipperdey, *Deutsche Geschichte 1866–1918*. Vol. 2. Munich: C. H. Beck, 1992, p. 569.
3. Wehler, *Deutsche Gesellschaftsgeschichte*. Vol. 3, p. 835.
4. Alfred Kelly, *The Descent of Darwin: The Popularization of Darwinism in Germany, 1860–1914*. Chapel Hill: University of North Carolina Press, 1981.
5. For a summary of Berghahn's theses in English, see Volker R. Berghahn, *Germany and the Approach of War in 1914*. Second edition. New York: St Martin's Press, 1993, chapters 2 and 3.
6. Jonathan Steinberg, "The Copenhagen Complex." *Journal of Contemporary History* 1 (1966): 23–46.
7. Christopher Clark, *Kaiser Wilhelm II, Profiles in Power*. Harlow: Longman, 2000, p. 133.
8. Clark, *Wilhelm II*, pp. 73–6 and 106–7.
9. Robert Aldrich, *Greater France: A History of French Overseas Expansion*. New York: St Martin's Press, 1996, p. 34.
10. Fritz Fischer, *War of Illusions: German Policies from 1911 to 1914*. Translated by Marian Jackson. New York: Norton, 1975.
11. Nipperdey, *Deutsche Geschichte*. Volume 2, p. 696; Margaret Lavinia Anderson, *Practicing Democracy: Elections and Political Culture in Imperial Germany*. Princeton: Princeton University Press, 2000.

5 The First World War

1. Ernst Jünger. *The Storm of Steel: From the Diary of a German Storm-Troop Officer on the Western Front*. New York: Howard Fertig, 1996. Reprint of 1929 edition, pp. 109–10. This book is interesting to read in conjunction with Erich

Maria Remarque's better known pacifist novel *All Quiet on the Western Front* because it reaches different conclusions on the basis of similar experiences.

2. Gerald D. Feldman, *Army, Industry, and Labour in Germany, 1914–1918*. Second edition, *The Legacy of the Great War*. Providence and Oxford: Berg Publishers, 1992.

3. Alfred von Tirpitz, *Erinnerungen*. Leipzig: Koehler, 1919, pp. 404–5.

4. Martin Kitchen, *The Silent Dictatorship: The Politics of the German High Command Under Hindenburg and Ludendorff, 1916–1918*. New York: Holmes & Meier, 1976.

5. Quoted after Raffael Scheck, *Alfred von Tirpitz and German Right-Wing Politics, 1914–1930*. Leiden: Brill, 1998, p. 76.

6. Erich Maria Remarque. *The Road Back*. Translated by A. W. Wheen. New York: Fawcett Columbine, 1931, pp. 28–33.

6 Germany's First Democracy

1. Sally Marks, *The Illusion of Peace: International Relations in Europe 1918–1933, The Making of the Twentieth Century*. New York: St Martin's Press, 1976.

2. Wehler, *Deutsche Gesellschaftsgeschichte*. Vol. 4, p. 318.

3. Hans Fallada, *Little Man, What Now?* Translated by Eric Sutton. Chicago: Academy Chicago Publishers, 1983, pp. 17–20.

4. Benjamin Lapp, *Revolution from the Right: Politics, Class, and the Rise of Nazism in Saxony, 1919–1933*. Atlantic Highlands, New Jersey: Humanities Press, 1997, pp. 204–6.

5. Peter Fritzsche, *Germans into Nazis*. Cambridge, Massachusetts, and London: Harvard University Press, 1998.

6. Henry Ashby Turner, *Hitler's Thirty Days to Power: January 1933*. Reading: Addison-Wesley, 1996, particularly pp. 172–3.

7. Richard Bessel. "Why did the Weimar Republic Collapse?" In *Weimar: Why Did German Democracy Fail?* Edited by Ian Kershaw. New York, St Martin's Press, 1990, pp. 120–52.

8 Germany in the Second World War

1. Ian Kershaw, *Hitler 1936–1945: Nemesis*. New York: Norton, 2000, p. 171.

2. Richard Overy, "Mobilization for Total War in Germany 1939–1941." *English Historical Review* 103 (1988): 613–39.

3. Alexander Rossino, *Hitler Strikes Poland: Blitzkrieg, Ideology, and Atrocity*. Lawrence: University of Kansas Press, 2003, pp. 103–9.

4. Raffael Scheck. *Hitler's African Victims: The German Army Massacres of Black French Soldiers in 1940*. New York: Cambridge University Press, 2006.

5. Among the material available in English, I would stress the books of Eberhard Jäckel and Lucy Dawidowicz as examples of the intentionalist approach and Raul Hilberg and Karl Schleunes as examples of functionalist historians: Eberhard Jäckel, *Hitler's Weltanschauung: A Blueprint for Power*. Translated by Herbert Arnold. Middletown CT: Wesleyan University Press, 1972; Lucy S. Davidowicz, *The War Against the Jews, 1933–1945*. New York: Holt, Rinehart & Winston, 1975; Raul Hilberg, *The Destruction of the European Jews*. Third edition. New Haven: Yale University Press, 2003; Karl A. Schleunes, *The Twisted Road to Auschwitz: Nazi Policy Toward German Jews, 1933–1939*. Urbana: University of Illinois Press, 1970.

6. See, for example, Christopher R. Browning, *Nazi Policy, Jewish Workers, German Killers*. Cambridge: Cambridge University Press, 2000, pp. 26–57.

7. Hannah Arendt, *Eichmann in Jerusalem*. New York: Viking Press, 1963.

Suggestions for Further Reading

The following section means to give advice for background reading on many of the subjects mentioned in this book. It lists only works in English (including translations) and privileges books that belong to many library collections and are easily understandable. I am aware that the section omits innumerable good, important, and accessible works, but I hope that it will open new horizons to readers and consequently lead them into the spheres of so many other great works that space limitations forbid me to mention.

For the period leading up to German unification, three major works offer detailed information and place German history into its European context: James J. Sheehan, *German History 1770–1866* (Oxford and New York: Oxford University Press, 1989); Thomas Nipperdey, *Germany from Napoleon to Bismarck, 1800–1866* (translated from German by Daniel Nolan) (Princeton: Princeton University Press, 1996); David Blackbourn, *History of Germany 1770–1918: The Long Nineteenth Century* (Malden: Blackwell, 2003). A good and concise summary of the Bismarckian and Wilhelmine periods is Lynn Abrams, *Bismarck and the German Empire, 1871–1918* (London: Routledge, 2006). For an excellent survey of the wars of unification by a leading military historian, see Dennis Showalter, *The Wars of German Unification* (London: Arnold, 2004). A large number of biographies of Bismarck exist, and many are good. For a detailed look, consider the three-volume biography by Otto Pflanze, *Bismarck and the Development of Germany* (second edition, three volumes) (Princeton: Princeton University Press, 1990). Of the many shorter biographies, I find the following the most readable: Edgar Feuchtwanger, *Bismarck* (London: Routledge, 2002); Katharine Lerman, *Bismarck* (Harlow: Longman, 2004), is more up to date, but my students have found it harder to read. A landmark work on the Bismarckian and Wilhelmine period is Hans-Ulrich Wehler, *The German Empire, 1871–1918* (translated from German by Kim Traynor) (Leamington Spa: Berg, 1985), although its theses no longer find widespread acceptance and were toned down in Wehler's more recent *Deutsche Gesellschaftsgeschichte Band 3 (1849–1914)* (Munich: Beck, 1995), which has not yet been translated into English. For critical essays on the approach represented by Wehler, see Geoff Eley and David Blackbourn, *The Peculiarities of German History: Bourgeois Society and Politics in Nineteenth-century Germany* (New York: Oxford University Press, 1984). A good summary of the Bismarckian and Wilhelmine period (up to the First World War) is Volker R. Berghahn's *Imperial Germany, 1871–1914* (Providence: Berghahn Books, 1994). David P. Calleo's interpretation in *The German Problem Reconsidered:*

Germany and the World Order, 1870 to the Present (Cambridge and New York: Cambridge University Press, 1978) remains an interesting approach by a historian with a greater strategic and international lens. To gain a better feel for German society and culture under Bismarck, I recommend the novels of Theodor Fontane, many of which are available in translation, for example *Effi Briest* (translated from German by Edward Parmee) (New York: Penguin, 1967).

For the Wilhelmine period, I highly recommend Christopher Clark's *Kaiser Wilhelm II* (Harlow and New York: Longman, 2000). This short book is thought provoking, refreshing, and well considered throughout. Clark presents some surprising but compelling arguments. He shows, for example, that Prince Eulenburg, an unofficial advisor of the Kaiser who became the subject of a huge homosexuality scandal in 1906, had exercised a moderating influence on the Kaiser before the scandal severed their friendship. Clark also does much to distinguish between Wilhelm's pompous public persona and his limited real influence. For much more detailed information, readers should consult John Röhl's multi-volume biography, of which only the first two volumes are available at this time: *Young Wilhelm: The Kaiser's Early Life, 1859–1888* (translated from German by Jeremy Gaines and Rebecca Wallach) (Cambridge and New York: Cambridge University Press, 1998) and *Wilhelm II: The Kaiser's Personal Monarchy, 1888–1900* (translated from German by Sheila de Bellaigue) (Cambridge and New York: Cambridge University Press, 2004). I also find many of the articles in Röhl's *The Kaiser and His Court* (translated by Terence F. Cole) (Cambridge and New York: Cambridge University Press, 1994) quite useful. Thomas Kohut's *Wilhelm II and the Germans: A Study in Political Leadership* (Oxford and New York: Oxford University Press, 1991) presents an interesting psychological approach centered on the idea that Wilhelm II, an insecure emperor, and Germany, an insecure nation, mirrored each other. Katharine Anne Lerman's *The Chancellor as Courtier: Bernhard von Bülow and the Governance of Germany, 1900–1909* (Cambridge and New York: Cambridge University Press, 1990) is a crucial work on a decisive period of Wilhelm's reign. On Tirpitz and fleet building, see the clear and concise book by Jonathan Steinberg: *Yesterday's Deterrent Tirpitz and the Birth of the German Battle Fleet* (New York: Macmillan, 1966). Good is also Holger Herwig, *"Luxury" Fleet: The Imperial German Navy, 1888–1918* (London and Atlantic Highlands: Ashfield Press, 1987). A magisterial analysis of Anglo-German relations before the First World War is Paul M. Kennedy, *The Rise of the Anglo-German Antagonism, 1860–1914* (London and Boston: Allen & Unwin, 1980). Good work exists on the German parties and on elections, much of it including both the Bismarckian and Wilhelmine period. James Retallack is a specialist on the right-wing parties who examines the long-term trends and problems of right-wing organizations: *The German Right, 1860–1920: Political Limits of the Authoritarian Imagination* (Toronto: University of Toronto Press, 2006). Vernon Lidtke offers a look at the culture of social democracy, especially at the broad range of support and leisure organizations associated with the SPD: *The*

Alternative Culture: Socialist Labor in Imperial Germany (Oxford and New York: Oxford University Press, 1985). Ellen Lovell Evans has provided a history of the Center Party up to its dissolution in 1933: *The German Center Party, 1870–1933: A Study in Political Catholicism* (Carbondale: Southern Illinois University Press, 1981). Margaret Lavinia Anderson offers an important interpretation of elections and electoral politics in *Practicing Democracy: Elections and Political Culture in Imperial Germany* (Princeton: Princeton University Press, 2000), arguing that universal manhood suffrage, although introduced from above, offered a stage for practicing democracy even in an undemocratic state. Jonathan Sperber, *The Kaiser's Voters: Electors and Elections in Wilhelmine Germany* (Cambridge and New York: Cambridge University Press, 1997) provides a good analysis of elections and the profile of voters behind the parties. An insightful analysis of some Reichstag elections offers Brett Fairbairn in *Democracy in the Undemocratic State: The German Reichstag Elections of 1898 and 1903* (Toronto and Buffalo: University of Toronto Press, 1997). On the issue of church-state relations, see Helmut Walser Smith, *German Nationalism and Religious Conflict: Culture, Ideology, Politics, 1870–1914* (Princeton: Princeton University Press, 1995). An influential contribution on an astute observer, participant, and great scholar is Wolfgang J. Mommsen, *Max Weber and German Politics, 1890–1920* (translated from German by Michael S. Steinberg) (Chicago: University of Chicago Press, 1984). For the German colonies, see Woodruff D. Smith, *The German Colonial Empire* (Chapel Hill: University of North Carolina Press, 1978). The mass killing of Herero and Nama peoples in German Southwest Africa has recently become a subject of intense discussion, as it is now increasingly seen as a precursor not only to the Holocaust but also to the rigid and brutal practices of the German army in both world wars. See Isabel V. Hull, *Absolute Destruction: Military Culture and the Practices of War in Imperial Germany* (Ithaca: Cornell University Press, 2005). A good summary of the events is Jon Bridgman, *The Revolt of the Hereros* (Berkeley: University of California Press, 1981). Generally, the impact of colonialism on German nationalism has become a new focus of analysis. See, for example, Russell Berman, *Enlightenment or Empire? Colonial Discourse in German Culture* (Lincoln: University of Nebraska Press, 1998). At the same time, much research is now devoted to local identity and stresses that most Germans envisioned and lived the nation across local identifications, which changed at a slower pace than the political landscape and the economic world. See Alon Confino, *The Nation as a Local Metaphor: Württemberg, Imperial Germany, and National Memory, 1871–1918* (Chapel Hill: University of North Carolina Press, 1997). A comparative analysis of working-class life in the age of industrialization is Mary Jo Maynes, *Taking the Hard Road: Life Course in French and German Workers' Autobiographies in the Era of Industrialization* (Chapel Hill: University of North Carolina Press, 1995). For a survey of German women's history not limited to the Wilhelmine period but very resourceful on it, see Ute Frevert, *Women in German History: From Bourgeois Emancipation to Sexual Liberation* (translated from German by Stuart McKinnon-Evans in association with Terry Bond and Barbara Norden) (New York: Berg and St Martin's Press, 1993). Among the literary works of the period that serve most to illustrate the historical-cultural context, I recommend in particular Thomas Mann's *Buddenbrooks* (translated by John E. Woods) (New York: Vintage International, 1994) and Heinrich Mann's *Man of Straw* (New York: Penguin, 1984). The latter gained notorious fame as a depiction of the spineless, blindly obedient, and opportunistic German bourgeois, but one should read this novel with a critical eye (while still enjoying its scathing satirical humour). A powerful short story that can be read as a cultural analysis of the mood among many European intellectuals before the First World War is Thomas Mann's *Death in Venice* (translated by Kenneth Burke) (New York: Knopf, 1925).

Good surveys of the First World War are easy to find. I recommend in particular Hew Strachan's *The First World War* (New York: Penguin, 2005). The best book dealing specifically with Germany is Roger Chickering, *Imperial Germany and the Great War, 1914–1918* (Cambridge and New York: Cambridge University Press, 1998). The question of war guilt has filled entire bookshelves in many libraries. For a fine summary, see James Joll, *The Origins of the First World War* (third edition, Harlow and New York: Pearson Longman, 2007), or Mark Hewitson, *Germany and the Causes of the First World War* (Oxford: Berg, 2004). A good analysis of the home front and of women's role in it is Belinda Davis, *Home Fires Burning: Food, Politics, and Everyday Life in World War I Berlin* (Chapel Hill: University of North Carolina Press, 2000). For the economic side of the war, see Gerald Feldman's classic *Army, Industry, and Labor in Germany, 1914–1918* (Princeton: Princeton University Press, 1966, reprinted by Berg Publishers in 1992). This book is a great case study on the enormous complexity of maximizing industrial production in modern societies at war. Jeffrey Verhey's *The Spirit of 1914* (Cambridge and New York: Cambridge University Press, 2000) is very good on the myth of national unity and the nostalgia with which many Germans later looked back to the allegedly unifying experience of 1914. Verhey traces the disturbing abuses of this nostalgia by parties and nationalist mass movements. A specialized study focusing on the German massacres of Belgian and northern French civilians in the first weeks of the war is John Horne and Alan Kramer, *German Atrocities, 1914: A History of Denial* (New Haven: Yale University Press, 2001). Martin Kitchen's *The Silent Dictatorship: The Politics of the German High Command under Hindenburg and Ludendorff, 1916–1918* (London: Croom Helm, 1976) is an important analysis of the domestic political scene in the last war years, although I tend to see German politics in these years more as a contested ground between the military command, big business, the trade unions, and the Reichstag rather than as an informal dictatorship of the military command. A fascinating look into Germany's food problems is Avner Offer, *The First World War: An Agrarian Interpretation* (New York: Oxford University Press, 1989). Offer discusses German planning for the food supply and presents an economically informed defense of the rationale behind German fleet building. Dealing with the difficulties of memory and grief is George Mosse's *Fallen Soldiers: Reshaping the Memory of the World Wars* (Oxford and New York: Oxford University Press, 1990). Among literary sources, Erich Maria Remarque's *All Quiet on the Western Front* (translated by Brian Murdoch) (London: Jonathan Cape, 1994) is still an excellent read. I also recommend Ernst Jünger's *Storm of Steel* (translated by Basil Creighton) (Garden City, NY: Doubleday, Doran & Company, 1929; reprinted: New York: Howard Fertig, 1975), which describes some of the same battle experiences as *All Quiet on the Western Front* but comes to radically different conclusions. Unlike Remarque, who reflects on the war as a pacifist, Jünger heroizes the war as a modern form of personal sacrifice.

The Weimar Republic is richly documented in English. For the initial period, I recommend Richard Bessel, *Germany After the First World War* (Oxford: Clarendon Press, 1995), because it gives a good picture of the enormous difficulties of restoring a peacetime economy. A difficult but worthwhile read on the international context is Klaus Schwabe, *Woodrow Wilson, Revolutionary Germany, and Peacemaking, 1918–1919: Missionary Diplomacy and the Realities of Power* (translated from German by Rita and Robert Kimber) (Chapel Hill: University of North Carolina Press, 1985). For a good description of the Versailles peace conference, see Margaret O. Macmillan, *Paris 1919: Six Months That Changed the World* (New York: Random House, 2002). Many outstanding surveys of Weimar history exist. A new book that is rich on the cultural and artistic aspects of the period is Eric Weitz, *Weimar Germany: Promise and Tragedy* (Princeton: Princeton University Press, 2007). Very good is also Hans Mommsen, *The Rise and Fall of Weimar Democracy* (translated from German by Elborg Forster and Larry Eugene Jones) (Chapel Hill, University of North Carolina Press, 1996). An interpretation that places Weimar Germany into a larger context of modernity in crisis is Detlev Peukert, *The Weimar Republic* (translated from German by Richard Deveson) (New York: Hill & Wang, 1993). Very useful and well written is the long-term analysis of Peter Fritzsche, *Germans Into Nazis* (Cambridge: Harvard University Press, 1998). Organized along specific mass rallies, this book documents the mobilization of a radical popular right-wing nationalism from the war enthusiasm of 1914 to the Nazi takeover of the trade unions in May 1933. Weimar culture has also generated a wealth of literature. Peter Gay's classic *Weimar Culture: The Outsider as Insider* (New York: Harper & Row, 1970) is very accessible and still worth reading. I personally like Otto Friedrich's portrait of Weimar culture in *Before the Deluge: A Portrait of Berlin in the 1920s* (New York: Harper & Row, 1972). Although Friedrich errs on some political details, his book presents an authentic look at the feverishly creative atmosphere of Weimar-era Berlin based on interviews with artists in the 1960s. For a segment of Weimar popular culture that touches on the ideological ground of Nazism, see Jost Hermand, *Old Dreams of a New Reich: Völkisch Utopias and National Socialism* (Bloomington: Indiana University Press, 1992). This book traces German hopes for a miraculous weapon and a charismatic leader able to undo the defeat of the First

World War in pulp fiction. The voting patterns during the Weimar Republic, based on detailed statistics from the period, are well explored in Thomas Childers, *The Nazi Voter* (Chapel Hill: University of North Carolina Press, 1983), and Richard Hamilton, *Who Voted for Hitler?* (Princeton: Princeton University Press, 1982). For an excellent description of the rise of the Nazi party, see Richard J. Evans, *The Coming of the Third Reich* (New York: Penguin, 2004). A detailed study that traces the decline of the German Democratic Party and the German People's Party is Larry E. Jones, *German Liberalism and the Dissolution of the Weimar Party System, 1918–1933* (Chapel Hill: University of North Carolina Press, 1988). Jones points out how the frustrations associated with inflation and the inadequate schemes for revaluation of lost assets fragmented and ultimately dissolved the electorate of two important Weimar parties, which in the long run benefited the Nazi rise to power. Donna Harsch, *German Social Democracy and the Rise of Nazism* (Chapel Hill: University of North Carolina Press, 1993) offers a survey of the SPD, the largest Weimar party until 1930. On the inflation, Gerald Feldman presents a long-term analysis in *The Great Disorder: Politics, Economics, and Society in the German Inflation, 1914–1924* (New York: Oxford University Press, 1993). In one thousand pages, this book reveals what a stunningly complicated economic, political, and social process the inflation was, tracing it back to German war spending in the First World War. Michael Hughes, in *Paying for the German Inflation* (Chapel Hill: University of North Carolina Press, 1988), offers more analysis on the fallout from this catastrophic event. For the German right in the Weimar period, I recommend Geoff Eley's *Reshaping the German Right* (New Haven: Yale University Press, 1980), which reaches back into the Wilhelmine Empire. For women in right-wing parties, see Raffael Scheck, *Mothers of the Nation: Right-Wing Women in Weimar Germany* (Oxford and New York: Berg, 2004). A great study of propaganda toward women in this period is Julia Sneeringer, *Winning Women's Votes: Propaganda and Politics in Weimar Germany* (Chapel Hill: University of North Carolina Press, 2002). Many literary works from this extremely productive and innovative period are classics and accessible in English. The most famous plays by Bertolt Brecht are translated, and every student of German history should read at least one of them. A masterwork of literature that also sheds much light on the Berlin underworld of the 1920s is Alfred Döblin's *Alexanderplatz, Berlin: The Story of Franz Bieberkopf* (translated from German by Eugene Jolas) (New York: Ungar, 1976). Less ambitious on literary terms but very worthwhile as a historical document is Hans Fallada's *Little Man What Now?* (translated by Eric Sutton) (Chicago: Academy Chicago Publishers, 1983). In an uncomplicated and touching style, this novel conveys the desperation and existential anxiety of many small employees during the Great Depression. In a similar vein, I also recommend Erich Maria Remarque, *The Road Back* (translated from German by A. W. Wheen) (New York: Grosset & Dunlap, 1931), and *Three Comrades: A Novel* (translated from German by A. W. Wheen) (New York: Popular Library, 1953). These two books form part of the trilogy whose first volume is *All Quiet on the Western Front*, although the two later volumes are much less well known than the first. *The Road Back* deals with the reintegration of traumatized veterans into a society in turmoil, and *Three Comrades* addresses the suffering of many in the Great Depression. We are fortunate to have a treasure trove on many aspects of Weimar culture, thought, and politics in Anton Kaes, Martin Jay, and Edward Dimendberg (eds.), *The Weimar Republic Sourcebook* (Berkeley: University of California Press, 1994).

As one enters the Nazi period, the amount of available literature becomes completely overwhelming. Much of what is published on Hitler himself is speculative and sensationalist (beware in particular of books and documentaries that spell Hitler's first name with "ph" instead of "f"), but the popular demand for publications in this field is huge. I once had to evaluate a proposed book manuscript on Hitler for a reputable university press, found the manuscript severely flawed, and advised against publication. A year later, I received a beautifully bound copy of the book with minor revisions only! Still, the Nazi period has also inspired much excellent work. A great, although time-consuming, entryway is Ian Kershaw's *Hitler 1889–1936: Hubris* (New York: Norton, 1999) and *Hitler 1936–1945: Nemesis* (New York: Norton, 2000). These two volumes are extremely readable and well informed. Although Kershaw did write a biography, he started out as an expert on public opinion in the Third Reich, and this shows throughout the book. Given the centrality of Hitler to the Third Reich, Kershaw's book is a crucial work for the entire period. Sadly, however, I cannot recommend a single short Hitler biography in English. Many short Hitler biographies are out of date or of dubious value. Kershaw published a condensed version of his later biography in the series "Profiles in Power," but this is more a history of Nazi Germany than a biography of Hitler. Eberhard Jäckel, *Hitler's World View: A Blueprint for Power* (translated from German by Herbert Arnold) (Cambridge: Harvard University Press, 1982), is a good and concise resource, and his *Hitler in History* (Hanover and London: Brandeis University Press, 1984) is an inspiring short think piece, but neither aims to offer a biography of Hitler. The other Nazi leaders have, like Hitler, drawn the attention of scores of sensationalist biographers who have advanced countless poorly supported arguments. There are a few very good works, however. Richard Breitman, *The Architect of Genocide: Himmler and the Final Solution* (New York: Knopf, 1991) stands out. I also recommend the collection of good short biographies of leading Nazis is the two-volume work edited by Ronald Smelser and Rainer Zitelmann, *The Nazi Elite* (translated from German by Mary Fischer) (New York: New York University Press, 1993). For the history of Nazi Germany in general, Richard Evans' *The Third Reich in Power* (New York: Penguin, 2005) is a very good resource. It is the second volume of a planned trilogy (the first is *The Coming of the Third Reich*). An unorthodox look at Nazi society is Detlev Peukert's *Inside Nazi Germany: Conformity, Opposition, and Racism in Everyday Life* (translated from German by Richard Deveson) (New Haven: Yale University Press, 1987). Peukert addresses topics such as the private sphere, dreams, and jokes. Given the centrality of propaganda for the Third Reich, David Welch's book *The Third Reich: Politics and Propaganda* (London and New York: Routledge, 1993) is essential reading. In the context of propaganda, one should also consult Robert Gellately's works on the secret police, *Backing Hitler: Consent and Coercion in Nazi Germany* (Oxford and New York: Oxford University Press, 2001), and *The Gestapo and German Society: Enforcing Racial Policy, 1933–1945* (Oxford and New York: Oxford University Press, 1990). Gellately makes a good point when he argues that the German secret police was so horribly effective because Hitler and his regime enjoyed so much support from the German populace, but he has also been criticized for not appreciating the weight of Nazi terror enough. A crucial topic is, of course, the racist agenda of the Nazi regime. An introduction provides Michael Burleigh and Wolfgang Wippermann, *The Racial State: Germany 1933–1945* (Cambridge and New York: Cambridge University Press, 1991), although its introductory chapter is outdated. A very good more recent analysis is Claudia Koonz, *The Nazi Conscience* (Cambridge: Belknap Press, 2003), which takes the Nazi claim to establish a new ethical system seriously and traces the efforts of propaganda and state policy to disseminate and enforce a grisly new ethical belief system based on a quasi-scientific racism. One of the most enlightening passages of the book is the section on the Nürnberg Laws, showing how Nazi administrators tried desperately to produce a scientific definition of a Jew and how hopelessly inadequate their efforts were. Good work exists on women in the Third Reich. My favorite is Jill Stephenson, *Women in Nazi Germany* (Harlow and New York: Longman, 2001). A very good summary provides Matthew Stibbe in *Women in the Third Reich* (London and New York: Oxford University Press, 2003). For Nazi education, see Gilmer W. Blackburn, *Education in the Third Reich: A Study of Race and History in Nazi Textbooks* (Albany: State University of New York Press, 1985). Two very good collections of translated primary sources exist: Jeremy Noakes and Geoffrey Pridham (eds.), *Nazism 1919–1945* (4 vols) (Exeter: Exeter University Publications, 1983), and the more concise but very helpful volume edited by Benjamin C. Sax and Dieter Kuntz: *Inside Hitler's Germany: A Documentary History of Life in the Third Reich* (Lexington: D. C. Heath, 1992). Of interest are also the interviews in the collection of Johannes Steinhoff, Peter Pechel, and Dennis Showalter (eds.), *Voices from the Third Reich* (Washington DC: Regnery Gateway, 1989). Of course, these interviews tell us more about memory than about the reality of the Nazi past, but, if read critically, they offer interesting insights.

The literature on Nazi Germany in the Second World War and the Holocaust is also enormous. On all aspects of the war, I highly recommend the decades-long opus of the German Military Research Institute (Militärgeschichtliches Forschungsamt). It is now completed in German, but the last volumes are still being translated into English: *Germany and the Second World War* (Oxford and New York, Oxford University Press, 1990–). Whoever wants a shorter summary of the war has a rich choice. I like John Keegan's *The Second World War* (second edition) (New York:

Penguin, 2005), but Gerhard Weinberg's *A World at Arms: A Global History of World War II* (second edition) (Cambridge and New York: Cambridge University Press, 2005) is also excellent. Specifically for Germany, I recommend Martin Kitchen's *Nazi Germany at War* (London and New York: Longman, 1995), which takes a close look at society and daily life. Good, too, is Earl R. Beck, *Under the Bombs: The German Home Front 1942–1945* (Lexington: University Press of Kentucky, 1994), which focuses on the effects of the bombings on German society. For German soldiers, I recommend Stephen Fritz, *Frontsoldaten: The German Soldier in World War II* (Lexington: University Press of Kentucky, 1995), which is based on memoirs and diaries of German soldiers. With a broader focus on the German army and its historiography, Wolfram Wette provides a balanced summary of controversies in *The Wehrmacht: History, Myth, Reality* (translated from German by Deborah Lucas Schneider) (Cambridge: Harvard University Press, 2006). I also shamelessly recommend my own *Hitler's African Victims: The German Army Massacres of Black French Soldiers in 1940* (Cambridge and New York: Cambridge University Press, 2006; paperback 2008), which is now available in French and soon also in German translation. There is unfortunately no good overarching work dealing generally with the Nazi occupation of Europe, and this would be a very difficult task given the complexity and diversity of situations. Still, some books on single countries are very good and insightful. See Mark Mazower, *Inside Hitler's Greece* (New Haven: Yale University Press, 1993), Wendy Lower's *Nazi Empire-Building and the Holocaust in Ukraine* (Chapel Hill: University of North Carolina Press, 2005), and Julian Jackson's *France: The Dark Years, 1940–1944* (Oxford: Oxford University Press, 2001). Texts on the German resistance have proliferated in recent years, as the reunification of Germany led to a fundamental re-evaluation of the resistance (East Germany and West Germany had very different views on what constituted resistance, and reunification has provided a chance to negotiate a more inclusive memory). The classic from before German unification is Peter Hoffmann's *German Resistance to Hitler* (Cambridge: Harvard University Press, 1988). Theodore S. Hamerow's *On the Road to the Wolf's Lair: German Resistance to Hitler* (Cambridge and London: Belknap Press of Harvard University Press, 1997) does an excellent job at situating emerging opposition and resistance in the context of the evolving political and military situation. A fresh look provides Hans Mommsen in *Alternatives to Hitler: German Resistance under the Third Reich* (translated from German by Angus McGeoch. Princeton: Princeton University Press, 2003), whereas Klemens von Klemperer deals with the quest of the German resistance for Allied support: *German Resistance Against Hitler: The Search for Allies Abroad, 1938–1945* (Oxford and New York: Oxford University Press, 1993). The literature on the Holocaust includes many comprehensive and very good textbooks that are widely available. Just to mention a few: Doris Bergen, *War & Genocide: A Concise History of the Holocaust* (Lanham: Rowman & Littlefield, 2003), Leni Yahil, *The Holocaust: The Fate of European Jewry, 1932–1945* (translated from Hebrew by Ina Friedman and Haya

Galai) (New York: Oxford University Press, 1990), and Saul Friedlander's two-volume study *The Years of Persecution: Nazi Germany and the Jews, 1933–1939*, and *The Years of Extermination: Nazi Germany and the Jews, 1939–1945* (New York: HarperCollins, 1997 and 2007). The classic is, of course, Raul Hilberg, *The Destruction of the European Jews* (New York: Harper, Row & Collins, 1961 and many later editions). The leading authority on the origins of the Holocaust is Christopher Browning, all of whose works I recommend. His case study of a group of "ordinary" men who became callous killers, *Ordinary Men: Reserve Police Battalion 101 and the Final Solution in Poland* (second edition) (New York: Harper Perennial, 1998), has become a classic in the burgeoning literature on mass killings. His more recent *The Origins of the Final Solution: The Evolution of Nazi Jewish Policy, September 1939–March 1942* (Lincoln: University of Nebraska Press, 2004) is a detailed and incisive work. I also appreciate very much Henry Friedlander's *The Origins of Nazi Genocide: From Euthanasia to the Final Solution* (Chapel Hill and London: University of North Carolina Press, 1995) because it outlines so well the ideological and institutional connections from murderous (pseudo-) science to the euthanasia killings and the Holocaust. Memoirs from the Nazi period and particularly of Holocaust survivors run in the thousands. One of them has achieved iconic status and is always worth a close look: Victor Klemperer, *I Will Bear Witness* (two volumes, translated from German by Martin Chalmers) (New York: Random House, 1998). The memory of the Nazi past and the German efforts to cope with this past are the subject of Jeffrey Herf's *Divided Memory: The Nazi Past in the Two Germanys* (Cambridge: Harvard University Press, 1997) and William [Bill] Niven's *Facing the Nazi Past: United Germany and the Legacy of the Third Reich* (London and New York: Routledge, 2002). A brief and fascinating account by a journalist touches on many of the big themes in easily understandable fashion: Timothy Ryback, *The Last Survivor: Legacies of Dachau* (New York: Vintage, 2000). I have assigned Ryback's book many times, and it has always sparked good discussions.

Index

purge of leadership, 164–5, 166
rivalry with army, 163–5
role during Crystal Night, 181–2
role in consolidation of power, 159, 161,
164
Saar district, 121, 174, 220
San Stefano, Treaty of, 45–6
Saxony, 15, 19–20, 57, 130–1, 134, 144,
218
Schacht, Hjalmar, 166
Scheidemann, Philipp, 108, 116
Schiller, Friedrich von, 11, 116
Schindler, Oskar, 122
Schleicher, Kurt von, 149–50, 154, 155,
159, 165, 174
Schleswig, *see* Schleswig-Holstein
Schleswig-Holstein, 17–19, 31, 33, 121,
140
Schlieffen, Alfred von, 78
see also Schlieffen Plan
Schlieffen Plan, 78, 82, 87, 88, 89, 189
Scholl, Hans, 212
Scholl, Sophie, 212
Schopenhauer, Arthur, 11
Schubert, Franz, 11
Schurz, Carl, 14
Sedan, Battle of, 22
Seeckt, Hans von, 131, 132, 133
Seisser, Hans von, 132
September Program, 98–9
Serbia, 44–6, 49, 73–4, 79, 201
in Balkan Wars, 77
in World War I, 89, 91, 97, 102
role in outbreak of World War I, 81–3
Siegfried Line (also called Hindenburg
Line), 95–6, 97
Silesia, 6, 11, 30, 35, 121
Social Democratic Party of Germany, *see*
SPD
Socialist Workers' Party (SAP), *see* SPD
Somme, Battle of the, 92
South Tyrol, 34, 48, 121
Soviet Union, 12, 95, 102, 142, 171–80
passim, 202–11, 213, 215
after World War II, 217–21 passim

excluded from Munich Conference, 179
German attack against, 192–9
invasion of Germany, 215–16, 219
KPD and, 128, 142
Soviet POWs in German hands, 199, 209
war against Finland, 189, 193
war against Poland, 188
see also Hitler-Stalin Pact, Stalin
Spain, 9, 10, 50, 71, 111, 140, 142, 196
and causation of Franco-German War,
21, 27
Civil War, 175–6
Spartakist uprising, 115, 125, 128
SPD, 40–2, 68, 111–13, 116, 123, 126, 130,
136, 140, 142, 143, 145, 151–2, 156,
222
aims and programs, 31–2, 58–60, 80
commitment to democracy in Weimar
Republic, 113, 118, 152
dissolution of, 161
during Great Depression, 144, 145, 146,
148, 149–50, 152, 154
efforts to contain, 60–1, 64, 65, 75, 79
elections of 1890, 52
elections of 1907, 71–2, 75
elections of 1912, 75, 79
elections of 1919, 115
elections of 1920, 126–7
elections of 1928, 138–9
exile organization, 167
foundation of, 31
growth in 1890–1912, 57–60, 62, 75
Nazi terror against, 159–61
opposition to Enabling Act, 161
opposition to fleet building, 67
outbreak of World War I, 84–5
participation in Grand Coalition, 139–40,
152
resistance against Nazi regime, 212
revolution of 1918–19, 114–15, 125
role in World War I, 99, 101–2, 103–4,
106, 107, 108
toleration of Brüning cabinet, 148, 154
see also anti-socialist laws
Speer, Albert, 198, 220